C000292961

# THE
# BATTLEFIELD
# MEDICAL
# MANUAL
## 1944

# THE
# BATTLEFIELD
# MEDICAL
# MANUAL
## 1944

## THE US WAR DEPARTMENT

AMBERLEY

First published in 1944
This edition published 2014

Amberley Publishing
The Hill, Stroud
Gloucestershire, GL5 4EP

www.amberley-books.com

Copyright © Amberley Publishing, 2014

The right of Amberley Publishing to be identified as the Author
of this work has been asserted in accordance with the
Copyrights, Designs and Patents Act 1988.

All rights reserved. No part of this book may be reprinted
or reproduced or utilised in any form or by any electronic,
mechanical or other means, now known or hereafter invented,
including photocopying and recording, or in any information
storage or retrieval system, without the permission in writing
from the Publishers.

British Library Cataloguing in Publication Data.
A catalogue record for this book is available from the British Library.

ISBN 978 1 4456 4312 0 (print)
ISBN 978 1 4456 4328 1 (ebook)

Typesetting and Origination by Amberley Publishing.
Printed in the UK.

# Contents

# Introduction

Over the last 100 years, the Medical Department of the United States Army has manifested considerable knowledge in its realisation that its efficiency has and will always depend to a considerable degree upon the instruction and training of its listed personnel. In no place is medicine more valued than the battlefield.

In 1862, Surgeon General Hammons, realising a long-felt deficiency in the training of the hospital stewards, wardmasters and attendants, commissioned Assistant

29. La Grande Guerre 1914-18
LILLE. — Aspect de la rue Faidherbe après le bombardement

Surgeon J. J. Woodward to prepare a manual to be known as the *Hospital Stewards' Manual*, which was subsequently adopted for the training of this personnel, and as an authority in all military hospitals in the United States.

Soon after Congress authorized the organisation of the Hospital Corps for the Army in 1888, Assistant Surgeon General Smart wrote and published a handbook for the Corps, which was successfully used for a number of years. The adoption of a regular scheme of instruction for the Hospital Corps necessitated a handbook that would include in concise form and in one volume all the various subjects to be taught. To supply this need Major Surgeon Mason edited and published, in 1906, a comprehensive handbook for the Hospital Corps of all armed forces of the United States.

Specialisation necessitated a new handbook in order to present up-to-date instructions, and in 1927 Colonel

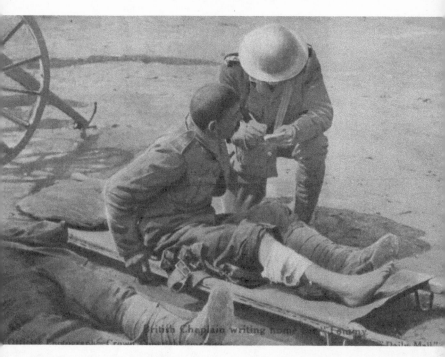

British Chaplain writing home for Tommy

Tuttle edited and published his handbook for the Medical Department soldier.

Since the formation of the Medical Corps over 100 years ago, under the authorship of Smart, Mason and Tuttle, a handbook has been in use without interruption throughout the entire period, and has served as a most valuable training tool. It has provided an inherited culture and an enduring inspiration for the medical soldier. With the decision of the War Department to take over the publication of this work, its title and much of its material were borrowed. This material represents the understanding, experience and knowledge of the several

authors and as a sound practical training tool has stood the test of time.

In 1944, the US War Department published this handbook in preparation for the horrors of the Second World War. Giving an intriguing insight into not only field medicine but also living conditions and army training at the time, *The Battlefield Medical Manual* is a book that has, no doubt, saved millions of lives. Topics covered range from everyday illnesses to battlefield triage, how soldiers could aid nurses and fellow combatants, and what to do in the event of chemical attacks. Illustrated throughout with diagrams and notes, this would have been an essential manual for the average soldier as well as the specialist.

M. M.
Br.

6. ZEEBRUGGE. — Le Cimetière. — Tombe de 14 marins et chauffeurs du «VENDICTIVE».
The Cemetery. — Graves of 14 sailors & stokers of the «VENDICTIVE».

# Rules of Land Warfare

## SECTION I

## LAWS OF WAR IN GENERAL

**1. General.**—The laws of war are the well-established and generally recognized rules that regulate the conduct of war both on land and on sea. In this chapter, only such laws as apply to land warfare will be considered.

**2. Laws of war.**—These include—

*a.* Unwritten rules not formally agreed upon, although generally observed. Such rules change with the times, as public opinion changes and new means of waging war are devised.

*b.* Rules agreed upon in international conference binding only those that agree to the rules in writing.

## SECTION II

## THE HAGUE CONVENTIONS

**3. General.**—The Hague Convention and several international conferences have been held to consider, among other things, the treatment of prisoners of war and of inhabitants of occupied territory, and the general conduct of hostilities. The last Hague Convention was held in 1907.

**4. Declaration of war.**—No nation may commence hostilities against another without first making a formal declaration of war.

This law of war is frequently violated today; yet, curiously enough, it was the one rule that the framers of The Hague Conventions agreed upon unanimously. Neutral powers are supposed to be notified of the state of war.

**5. Belligerents and nonbelligerents.**—The laws of war separate the population of a nation at war into two classes—belligerents (those belonging to recognized military forces) and nonbelligerents (the civil population).

*a.* Belligerents may engage in any of the acts of war recognized as legal by the laws of war without forfeiting protection guaranteed to prisoners of war in case they are captured by the enemy.

*b.* Nonbelligerents are prohibited from engaging in combat and in other forms of direct action against the enemy except in self-defense. If they violate this law of war and are captured by the enemy, they are not entitled to the protection guaranteed prisoners of war and may be punished.

**6. Prisoners of war.**—Prisoners of war must be treated humanely. They are permitted to keep their personal property, but all military equipment and papers are taken from them. Except commissioned officers, they may be required to work, provided the labor is not excessive and has no connection with military operations. Work connected with the care of the sick and injured has been considered proper, and prisoners of war have been required to assist in medical service. Every prisoner of war is required, when asked, to give his true name and grade, and he may be punished for refusing so to do. *He is not required to name his organization.*

### Section III

### GENEVA CONVENTION

**7. General.**—The laws of war applying to every aspect of warfare, other than the problems associated with sick and wounded, are included in The Hague Conventions (see sec. II); but The Hague Conventions merely approve the rules established in the Geneva Convention in these words: "The obligations of belligerents in respect to the sick and wounded are regulated by the Geneva Convention."

**8. Care of sick and wounded.**—Officers, soldiers, and other persons officially attached to armies, who are sick or wounded, will be respected and cared for, *without distinction of nationality*, by the belligerent in whose power they are.

**9. Abandonment of sick and wounded.**—Whenever it becomes necessary to abandon sick and wounded to the enemy, if military conditions permit, a detachment of medical troops with essential equipment and supplies must be left with the sick and wounded to care for them until the enemy has taken them over.

**10. Duties of belligerent after engagement.**—After every engagement, the belligerent who remains in possession of the field of battle will take measures to search for the wounded, and to protect the wounded and dead from robbery and ill treatment. He will see that a careful examination is made of the bodies of the dead prior to burial or cremation, and will make every effort to record the identity of dead enemies as well as of his own men.

**11. Protection of medical troops and property.**—Medical troops, installations, and equipment are to be protected *so long as they are not used to commit acts injurious to the enemy*. This protection is extended to the dental, *but not to the veterinary service*.

**12. Medical service emblem.**—The distinctive emblem of medical service (the Red, or Geneva, Cross) must be displayed on all flags and brassards, as well as on all equipment, used by the medical service. This emblem cannot be used by any other branch of the military service.

## Section IV

## VOLUNTARY AID SOCIETIES

**13. General.**—Voluntary aid societies who provided a great part of care and treatment of the sick and wounded prior to the development of the medical service of the Army, have no responsibility to the Government for such care and they are now restricted for the most part to providing comforts and luxuries not obtainable officially. Their personnel and equipment while so engaged are protected by the Geneva Convention in the same manner, and are subject to the same provisions, as those of the Medical Department. The Medical Department cannot share its responsibility for care or treatment of sick and wounded soldiers with any agency.

**14. American National Red Cross.**—See AR 850–75.

# Basic Anatomy and Physiology

## SECTION I

## MEDICAL

**15. General structure.**—The human body consists of a bony or skeletal framework which supports the soft parts or tissues. As a preliminary to the description of the gross appearance of the separate parts of the body it is appropriate that consideration be given to the finer structure of the tissues.

**16. Minute anatomy.**—*a.* The structural unit of every part of the human body is the microscopic animal cell, and the various activities of the body result from the activities of the cells which compose it.

*b.* These body cells vary in size and shape, but all are very minute, the largest rarely exceeding one-fifth of a millimeter in diameter. In some parts of the body they lie side by side; in other parts they may be separated from one another to a varying degree by an intercellular substance. They differ greatly in structure and function. muscle cells are long fibers having the power to contract; bone cells form the hardest and most enduring tissue in the body; nerve cells possess elongated processes whose special function is conductivity; the cells of the skin are very flat, especially those comprising the outermost layers, and their function is principally a protective one.

*c.* A cell may be defined as living matter called *protoplasm*, surrounded by a membrane and containing a smaller, denser inner body called the nucleus or kernel. The protoplasm is a colorless, semitransparent, gelatinous, mobile, and irritable substance which is the "physical basis of life." One of the principal constituent parts of the protoplasm of the nucleus is *chromatin*, which carries all of the hereditary potentialities of the individual and is directly concerned in the reproduction, or division, of the cell.

*d.* When cells with similar structure and function are grouped together there is formed what is known as *tissue*. Between these cells there are always small spaces even in the most compact tissue. There are points of union between cell and cell, but the intercellular spaces are necessary in order that each cell may be in contact with the fluids of the body in which nourishment is carried to the cell and waste products are removed. This interchange takes place through the cell membrane.

*e.* In considering the properties of protoplasm we find that it is a mixture of complex organic and simpler inorganic substances. The organic substances comprise principally proteins, fats, lipoids, and carbohydrates, while the inorganic substances are water and many chemical elements.

*f.* Protoplasm has the power to absorb oxygen and oxidize, or burn, some of its substance, thus producing heat energy. It is able to take up certain chemical compounds, or non-living materials, as food and convert them into its own substance, causing repair and growth. This power of nutrition is known as metabolism. Protoplasm is irritable and responds to stimulation. It has the capacity for motion.

**17. Development of body.**—The human body is developed from a single cell called the *ovum*. The ovum divides and subdivides, and the daughter cells thus formed arrange themselves as a membrane comprising three layers of cells. The outer layer is the *ectoderm*, the middle layer the *mesoderm*, and the inner layer, the *entoderm*. These three layers of cells later in the process of development assume different sizes and shapes forming the various types of cells found in the body; for example, from the ectoderm come the skin and nerve cells; the muscle cells derive from the mesoderm; the entoderm provides the lining cells of the intestines. As stated above, collections of cells of like structure and function form tissues. Combinations of tissues form body organs or structures. The characteristics of tissue depend upon the type of cells and the intercellular substance composing it, and the structure of any organ depends upon the properties of the tissue of which it is composed.

**18. Varieties of tissues.**—Some tissues perform but one physiologic function, others perform several. It is therefore difficult to classify tissues in this way except by the most important of their physiological functions. The following arrangement has been suggested by several authorities:

*a. Undifferentiated tissues.*—Composed of cells which have developed along no special line but retain the properties of the cells forming the very young body before cell differentiation takes place. Lymph and white blood corpuscles are examples of this tissue.

*b. Supporting tissues.*—This type of tissue is used to support and protect more delicate tissue and to resist strain or pressure.

*c. Nutritive tissues.*—These form a large group and include assimilative, eliminative, and respiratory tissue.

*d. Storage tissues.*—These tissues are composed of storage cells of which fat cells and liver cells are examples. These cells store reserve supplies of food which they supply when needed.

*e. Excitable or irritable tissues.*—Tissues which are especially susceptible to changes in their surroundings and are therefore useful in giving to the body information as to what is going on around it. Any change in the environment which serves to arouse response in an excitable tissue is called a *stimulus.*

*f. Conductive tissues.*—Serve to bring into communication the various parts of the body. This is exhibited to a very high degree by nervous tissue.

*g. Motor tissues.*—The two best examples of this type of tissue are muscular tissue and the ciliated cells which line certain organs of the body. These cells have fine thread-like appendages which are kept in constant motion. These appendages are called *cilia.* The constant motion of the cilia causes material on the surface to be moved along in one direction or another.

*h. Protective tissues.*—As the name indicates these tissues line or protect certain parts of the body, as the enamel of the teeth, the epithelium covering the body, etc.

*i. Reproductive tissues.*—These tissues are concerned in the production of new individuals. The different sexes have different types which conjoin for the origination of offspring. Various types of these tissues are combined to form the different parts of the body.

**19. Skeletal system.**—*a.* The skeletal or bony structure of the body is made up of over 200 bones. It has a threefold function: To support the body; to afford protection to certain organs of the body which might easily be injured; and to furnish a system of levers which when acted upon by the muscles causes the body to move.

*b.* The skeleton may be divided for descriptive purposes into the *axial* skeleton, which includes the skull, the spine, the breastbone, and the ribs, and the *appendicular* skeleton, which is composed of the bones of the arms and the legs and the bones by means of which these appendages are attached to the axial skeleton.

*c.* The *skull* is made up of 22 bones, 8 of which form the cranium, and 14 the face. Of the cranial bones, the one forming the forehead is the *frontal* bone. The top of the skull is formed by the two *parietal* bones. In the back is the *occipital* bone, and at either side is the *temporal* bone, the upper part of which corresponds to the temple, the lower part including the ear. In addition to these there are the *sphenoidal* bone, which forms a part of the floor of the cranium, and the *ethmoid*, which lies in front and forms the roof of the nasal cavity. The more important bones of the face are the *nasal* bones, which form the bridge of the nose; the two *malar*, or cheek, bones; the two upper and one lower jaw bones. These bones of the skull, with the exception of the lower jaw bone are, in the adult, immovably joined together. At the back part of the base of the skull is the large opening through which the spinal cord passes from the spinal column on its way to the brain.

*d.* The *spine* or vertebral column consists of 26 irregularly shaped bones, all possessing a general sameness in outline except for modifications in the several parts of the column. Each has a flattened body at the back of which appears the arch which serves to enclose and protect the spinal cord. Spinous processes project posteriorly and lateral processes from the sides of the vertebral arches, their principal purpose being to limit the movement of the intervertebral joint.

*e.* The *thoracic wall* consists of the *sternum*, or breastbone, 12 ribs on either side, and the vertebral column at the back. While all of the ribs articulate with the vertebral column, only the upper seven pairs are connected directly, by means of cartilage, with the sternum. These are called true ribs. The next lowermost three pairs of ribs have their cartilages attached to the rib above. The remaining two pairs have no anterior cartilaginous attachments. These five pairs of ribs are spoken of as false ribs.

*f.* The shoulder girdle consists of the *scapula* or shoulder blade, and the *clavicle* or collar bone. The scapula lies embedded in the muscles on the outside of the ribs and at the sides of the vertebral column and to it is articulated the arm bone. The clavicle serves to keep the scapula in place.

*g.* The pelvic girdle consists of the hip bone on either side and the wedge-shaped base of the spinal column, the *sacrum*, at the back. Each hip bone possesses a deep socket into which the head of the thigh bone articulates.

*h.* The upper and lower limbs may be considered at one and the same time, for each contains 30 bones, the arrangement of which in each is very similar. The differences in structure have resulted from changes in function resulting from adaptation of the upper limb to prehensile purposes and the lower to weight bearing and locomotion. The socket of the scapula into which the round head of the humerus fits is shallow and this fact together with the relative looseness of

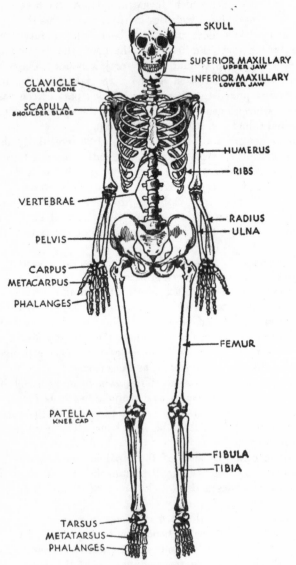

FIGURE 1.—Bony skeleton.

attachment of the shoulder girdle permits a wide range of motion at the shoulder. The articulation of the arm and forearm at the elbow permits not only flexion and extension, but also pronation and permits not only flexion and extension, but also pronation and radius over the ulna. The eight small wrist bones are loosely connected together by ligaments, allowing great freedom of movement. Then, too, the elongated digits, more especially the thumb which is opposable to any of the other fingers, permit the hand to grasp and manipulate objects readily. The lower limb would serve no good purpose were its flexibility as great as that of the upper limb. Since it must bear the weight of the body, its bones must be sturdier, therefore heavier, than the corresponding bones of the upper extremity. The hip girdle, unlike the shoulder girdle, is firmly fixed; the socket of the hip bone, into which the femur fits, is much deeper than the socket of the scapula; consequently, while there is a limitation of flexibility at the hip joint there is also considerably less of a liability to dislocation than there is at the shoulder. In the knee there is very little more than a forward motion, and because the fibula, the more slender of the two leg bones, is attached firmly to the upper end of the tibia, pronation and supination are lacking in the leg. The bones of the foot which correspond to the bones of the wrist are larger, and being closely bound together by ligaments do not possess a similar degree of freedom of motion. But because there must be elasticity to permit springiness in the step so as to avoid jarring, the bones of the foot are arranged in arch formation. The bones of the toes are much shorter than those of the fingers, consequently, they are less flexible, and because the great toe cannot be opposed to any of the other toes the foot lacks prehensile qualities.

20. **Development of bone.**—*a.* When a child is born the bones of the body, although formed, are not continuous masses of bony tissue. Each is partly composed of cartilage. The process of bone formation is very complicated and in these areas of cartilage starts from small points or centers of ossification. These centers finally enlarge and when adult life is reached have replaced all of the cartilaginous tissue.

*b.* In the large bone of the arm in a child both ends are separated from the shaft by cartilage and it is in these areas that the bone grows in length by new cartilage appearing and later being replaced by bone. The bone grows in thickness by new bony tissue being formed beneath the covering membrane or *periosteum*.

*c*. The bones of children are quite flexible but as old age comes on this flexibility is slowly lost and they become very brittle.

**21.   Joints.**—Where two bones of the skeleton come into apposition they form a *joint* or *articulation*.   Some joints permit of no motion while others permit motion in many directions.   The principal kinds of joints are the following:

*a.   Fixed joints.*—Best illustrated by the union between certain bones of the skull which permit no motion and are called *sutures*.

*b.   Ball-and-socket joints.*—As the name implies, in a joint of this type the rounded end of one bone fits into a hollowed surface of the other and its characteristic is that it permits a greater degree of motion than do other joints.   The shoulder and hip joints are examples.   At the hip joint the thigh may be flexed, that is, moved upward and forward, or extended, that is, moved backward.   It may be moved toward or away from the other thigh, and it may be made to produce a cone-like motion, the apex of the cone being at the joint, which is in reality a combination of the other possible motions.

*c.   Hinge joints.*—A joint of this type permits of a movement in one plane as in a hinge.   The knee joint is one of the best examples of this kind of joint.

*d.   Pivot joints.*—The best example of this type is between the first and second bones of the spine.   One bone rotates around another which remains stationary.

*e.   Gliding joints.*—In the closely packed bones of the wrist, for example, little motion is permitted except that provided by one of the bones sliding a short distance over the surface of the other.

**22.   Muscular system.**—The muscles make up the main motor organs of the body.   There are three types of muscle tissue:

*a.   Voluntary muscles*, which are under our control and may be moved at will.   These make up the mass of skeletal muscles and on account of their appearance under the microscope are sometimes called *striped* muscles.

*b.   Involuntary muscles* are not fixed to the skeleton, but largely surround cavities or tubes in the body.   These muscles act without our will and from their microscopic appearance are called *smooth* muscles.   The muscles surrounding the stomach are examples of this type.

*c.   Heart muscle* is involuntary muscle but differs somewhat from other involuntary muscle tissue when examined under the microscope.   In fact, it more closely resembles voluntary muscle.

**23. Relationship of bones and attached muscles.**—*a.* Muscles are attached by means of *tendons* to the bones of the body and by their contractions cause parts of the body to move. The point where one tendon is attached is called the *origin* of the muscle and where the other end is attached is called the *insertion.* The origin is usually in that part of the skeleton which is less freely movable than the part to which the insertion is attached. Muscles are of various sizes and shapes and may have a tendon only at one end or along one side, depending on the function of the muscle.

*b.* When the muscles serve to move bones they act as levers. The most common muscular movements used are levers of the third order, where the power is between the weight and the fulcrum. An example of this may be seen in bending the forearm. The fulcrum here is the elbow joint and the power is applied by muscles having their insertion in the bones of the forearm and the weight being the weight of the hand itself. Some other motions of the body illustrate levers of the first and second order; for example, the nodding movement of the head illustrates a lever of the first order and the act of standing on the toes illustrates one of the second order.

**24. Activity of voluntary and involuntary muscles.**—When we send a nervous impulse to a voluntary muscle, the muscle moves either rapidly or slowly, as we will it to do. On the other hand, involuntary muscle acts without any direction sent to it by our will and may contract at varying intervals like the muscles of the stomach and intestines or may stay in an almost permanent state of contraction.

**25. Posture.**—The posture of the body is applied to those positions of equilibrium of the body, such as standing, sitting, or lying, which can be maintained for some time. When the body is held in any one of these positions there is always a slight, sustained contracture of the muscles to prevent the joints from bending. This is called *tonus.* If the position is held for any considerable length of time a certain amount of fatigue is produced, and should the muscles not be in a healthy condition this fatigue is produced earlier than if they were healthy. The result of this fatigue causes relaxation of the muscles and improper posture. When a person not well developed stands erect for a long period the muscular relaxation or lack of tone causes him to slump.

**26. Effect of exercise on muscle.**—*a.* Good food, pure air, and a proper functioning of the body are necessary for the healthy working of the body. In addition to these, the muscles must be exercised. In fact, a muscle must be exercised in order to get the proper nourishment, as each muscle acts as a sort of chemical engine and the contraction and relaxation are required to throw off waste products and take in new fuel from the surrounding body fluids.

*b.* When a muscle is not used at all it becomes much smaller and wastes away. This is called *atrophy* of the muscle. On the other hand, when any muscle or group of muscles is used over and over again in excess of normal the muscles become larger or undergo *hypertrophy.* The calf muscles of runners are examples of this. In hypertrophy the muscle cells become larger but do not increase in number.

**27. Heart and circulation.**—The heart, together with the blood vessels, form what is known as the *cardio-vascular system.* This system consists of a series of closed tubes of various sizes (arteries, veins, and capillaries) through which the blood circulates, being propelled by a muscular pump, the heart. This system of vessels leads to and from all the tissues of the body.

**28. Blood vessels.**—The tubes or blood vessels which carry the blood away from the heart are called *arteries,* while the vessels returning the blood to the heart are called *veins.* Connecting the arteries and veins in the various tissues are minute hair-sized vessels known as *capillaries.* These have very thin walls and form dense networks throughout the body, and it is through these networks that the blood comes in close contact with the tissues of the body in order to give up food and oxygen and take away the various waste products.

**29. Heart.**—*a.* The heart is a large hollow, cone-shaped organ of muscular tissue about the size of a fist. It is enclosed in a tough fibrous sac, the *pericardium.* The heart is situated between the lungs near the front part of the chest where it is well protected by the bony skeleton.

*b.* The heart is divided vertically into two lateral halves which do not have any opening between so that we really have two hearts, a right and a left. Each side of the heart is made up of two cavities, an *auricle* and a *ventricle,* the auricles being smaller, thinner walled, and situated above the ventricles.

*c.* The right side of the heart is called the venous side, as it receives into its auricle the impure blood collected by the veins. From the right auricle the blood passes to the right ventricle and then to the lungs to be purified. When purified it is returned to the left auricle and from there to the left ventricle, which by its powerful contractions forces the blood out through the arteries to the various parts of the body.

*d.* It will be seen from *c* above that there are really two circulatory systems connected with the heart. The one going through the lungs

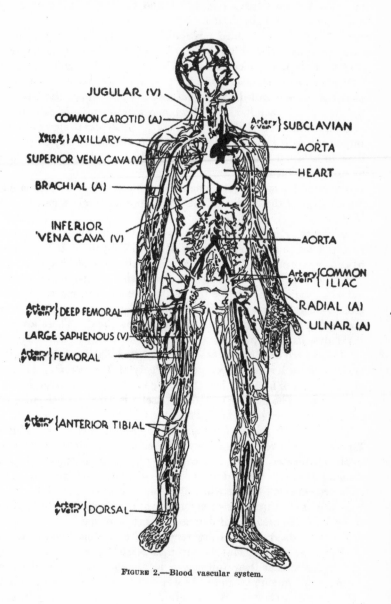

JUGULAR (V)

COMMON CAROTID (A)

X...& } AXILLARY

SUPERIOR VENA CAVA (V)

BRACHIAL (A)

INFERIOR VENA CAVA (V)

Artery & Vein } SUBCLAVIAN

AORTA

HEART

AORTA

Artery & Vein } COMMON ILIAC

RADIAL (A)

ULNAR (A)

Artery & Vein } DEEP FEMORAL

LARGE SAPHENOUS (V)

Artery & Vein } FEMORAL

Artery & Vein } ANTERIOR TIBIAL

Artery & Vein } DORSAL

FIGURE 2.—Blood vascular system.

is called the *pulmonary* circulation and the one going through the body, the *systemic* circulation.

*e.* There is still a third circulatory system although this is not directly connected with the heart. This is the *portal* system. When that portion of the blood leaving the heart in the systemic circulation goes to the stomach, intestines, spleen, and pancreas, it is collected in a vein called the *portal vein*, which enters the liver and breaks up into capillaries. The blood subsequently is collected by ordinary veins for return to the heart. This portal system is very important, as it brings food material from the alimentary tract to the liver to be acted upon by that organ and either placed in circulation or stored for future use.

**30. Blood.**—*a.* The total quantity of blood is usually estimated at one-twelfth of the weight of the body, approximately a gallon and a half for an average adult.

*b.* The color of the blood, due to variation in its oxygen content, is bright red in the arteries and dark red in the veins. It is composed of cells or corpuscles floating in a liquid called the *plasma.*

*o.* The plasma is composed of *fibrin* and a true liquid element called *serum.* The fibrin is the active agent in causing the blood to clot or coagulate when bleeding occurs. The serum, which is plasma less fibrin, contains the food elements of the blood. There are three types of cells or corpuscles:

(1) The red cells or *erythrocytes* are round, flattened discs, slightly concave on each side and composed largely of *hemoglobin.* This substance contains iron and has the capacity of carrying large amounts of oxygen. The number of red corpuscles is 5,000,000 per cubic millimeter in the male and 4,500,000 in the female.

(2) The white cells or *leucocytes* are spherical in shape and slightly larger than the red cells. They number between 5,000 and 7,000 per cubic millimeter. They are capable of changing their form and passing through the unbroken walls of the blood vessels. These cells are capable of destroying disease-producing organisms. In the presence of most infections the number of these cells greatly increases. They form the first line of defense against infection.

(3) The blood *platelets* are very small and almost colorless cells. The average number may be given as 300,000 per cubic millimeter. It is believed that their function is to aid clotting of the blood and to maintain immunity against certain diseases. In addition to the cells described above there are several other cells occurring in small numbers of which very little is known.

**31. Lymphatic system.**—*a.* The lymphatic system is much like the blood circulatory system except that the fluid is clear and there is a heart to propel the blood.

*b.* The lymph is a clear fluid of essentially the same composition as blood plasma. This lymph circulates between the cells of the body and the capillaries of the blood vascular system.

*c.* The lymph vessels begin in the small spaces between the individual cells, unite to form larger channels, and finally empty into the venous blood system by way of a large lymph vessel called the *thoracic duct*.

*d.* The lymph nodes are lenticular-shaped bodies occurring along the course of the larger lymph vessels. Where these nodes are present the lymph passes through the substance of the node and is filtered and purified. In case of infection these nodes usually become inflamed. They are of great aid in localizing and overcoming infections.

**32. Respiratory system.**—The term *respiration*, as commonly used, means the function of gaseous interchange between the blood and air taken into the lungs. This is really only a part of respiration and is *external respiration* as there is an exchange going on all the time between the tissues of the body and the minute blood vessels, which is called *internal respiration*.

**33. Air passages.**—Air reaches the lungs through the *nose*, *pharynx*, *larynx*, and *trachea*.

**34. Nose.**—Air enters from outside the body through the nose under ordinary conditions, although it may be taken in through the mouth. The nose is divided inside into two *nasal* passages by a *septum* and nature has so shaped the nasal passages that the cooler outside air is slightly warmed and certain foreign material, such as dust particles, may be removed prior to the air reaching the lungs. Leading from the nasal passages are irregularly shaped recesses called the *sinuses*. The inner surfaces of the sinuses are lined by a moist membrane similar to that found in the nose. Inflammation of these recesses is called *sinusitis* and may arise from an extension of an ordinary cold in the nose.

**35. Pharynx.**—*a.* The pharynx is the large opening back of the cavity of the mouth. It is a common passageway for both food and air as it also communicates with the nasal passages. The pharynx continues downward as the larynx in front and a tube for food, the *esophagus*, in the rear.

*b.* At the root of the tongue there is a small triangular-shaped flap covering the opening into the larynx; when food is swallowed this

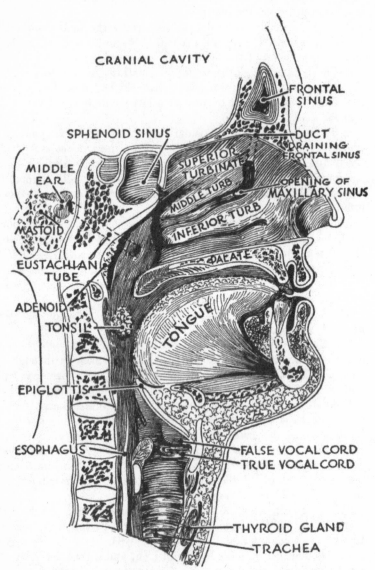

**FIGURE 3.**—Longitudinal section through nose, throat, and mouth.

flap closes and prevents food from entering the larynx. This flap is called the *epiglottis*.

**36. Larynx.**—The larynx or "voice box" is that portion of the respiratory tract connecting the pharynx and the trachea. It is composed of nine cartilages and muscular and connective tissues. This organ contains two bands of tissue called the *vocal cords*. When the vocal cords are placed in a certain position and air is driven past them they are set in vibration and emit a certain sound. The strength of the blast of air determines the loudness of the sound, the size of the larynx itself determining the pitch. In women and children the larynx is smaller than in men and the pitch is higher. The sounds made by the vocal cords are strengthened by the resonance of the air in the pharynx and mouth and are altered by the movements of the tongue, cheeks, throat, and lips into speech.

**37. Trachea.**—The trachea, or windpipe, is a tube extending from the lower part of the larynx to the lungs. It is about 4 inches long and at its lower end divides into two parts, the *bronchi*, one of which goes to each lung. The trachea is composed of irregular rings of cartilage connected by supporting tissue.

**38. Lungs.**—*a.* The lungs are two in number, a right and left. Each has a bronchus connecting it with the trachea. These bronchi continue into the lung dividing and redividing until they end in a minute dilation or sac. As the bronchial tubes divide and redivide they become smaller and their walls become thinner until the smallest one as well as the terminal sacs or *alveoli* consist of but a single layer of cells. This single layer of cells is all that separates the inspired air from the very thin-walled capillaries surrounding them so that the diffusion of gases may take place readily.

*b.* The lungs are covered by a thin membrane, the *pleura*, and are not connected with any other tissue except at the *hilum* or root. The arteries, veins, and bronchi enter at the roots of the lungs.

**39. Chest cavity.**—The chest cavity or thorax is a cone-shaped cavity with the narrow end upward. It is surrounded on the outside by the ribs, breastbone, and spinal column, the bottom being closed by the *diaphragm*. In addition to the lungs the thorax contains the heart, trachea, and esophagus. The chest cavity is lined by the same kind of membrane that covers each lung, the *pleura*. In fact, the membrane covering the lung folds back on itself to line the chest wall so that between the lung and the chest wall it forms a sac called the *pleural cavity*.

**40. Mechanism of respiration.**—*a.* The respiratory movements are to a certain extent under the control of the will in that we can breathe rapidly or slowly or take either deep or shallow breaths. But this is limited in extent, as our ordinary breathing goes on involuntarily. This ordinary type of breathing is controlled by certain centers in the brain which are excited by the type of blood flowing through them. That is, when venous blood flows through them the respirations are increased and the greater the demand of purification of the blood the greater the stimulation.

*b.* When a breath is taken in, the chest increases in size in all diameters. The diaphram, which at rest is dome-shaped, contracts and flattens the dome, which in turn increases the vertical diameter of the chest. By movement of the ribs on their articulations with the vertebrae the diameters from front to back and side to side are also increased. Inspiration, or the taking in of a breath, requires considerable muscular action. Expiration, on the other hand, requires very little, as the chest simply returns to a resting position.

*c.* The lungs contain a certain amount of air at all times, even after a forced expiration. The lung capacities of different individuals vary greatly but in an average size man, even after forced expiration, the lungs contain about 1,000 cubic centimeters of air, called the *residual* air. Under ordinary circumstances we do not make forced expirations so that in addition to this amount there are between 1,500 and 2,000 cubic centimeters left, known as the *supplemental* air. These two make up the *stationary* air. The air ordinarily taken in is known as the *tidal* air and in addition that taken in on forced inspiration is known as the *complemental* air.

**41. Digestive system.**—The digestive system is made up of the alimentary canal and various organs or glands attached to it. The function of this system is to prepare food so that it can be used by the various parts of the body.

**42. Foods.**—In order to provide energy for the body and to maintain and repair the tissues it is necessary to furnish material which can be made available for this purpose. Foodstuffs are usually classified as being *carbohydrate*, *fat*, or *protein*. In addition to these the body requires water, certain inorganic salts, and certain food constituents which are known as *vitamins*.

**43. Proteins.**—Proteins are required to replace worn-out tissue. They also furnish much of the fuel supply of the body. Meat, eggs, cheese, and beans are all rich in proteins.

**44. Carbohydrates.**—Carbohydrates are oxidized in the body to give it energy to carry on its work. They are mostly of vegetable origin. Flour, sugar, and rice are examples of food rich in carbohydrates.

**45. Fats.**—Fats may be of animal origin, as in butter, or may occur in vegetables, as in olives. They act very much like the carbohydrates in furnishing energy to the body machine.

**46. Composition of foods.**—Most foods contain more than one nutriment. Milk, for instance, contains two proteins, several fats, and a carbohydrate. In addition there are several salts and vitamins.

**47. Enzymes.**—Food to be used by the body must be reduced from a complex substance to more simple compounds. This reduction is carried on by means of substances called *enzymes*. There are enzymes for the various types of food; they split carbohydrates into simple sugars, fats into fatty acid, and glycerine and proteins into acids. These enzymes are present in the various secretions of the alimentary canal, each secretion having its specific enzyme. Some of the secretions contain more than one enzyme.

**48. Absorption.**—*a.* After the food has been acted upon by the digestive juices it must be taken to the various tissues of the body in order to supply them with nutritive material. The transfer of food from the alimentary canal to the circulatory system is called *absorption*. This takes place almost entirely in the small intestine.

*b.* The simple food compounds are taken up by the receptive cells of the small intestine and pass either directly into the blood stream, or into lymph vessels which later discharge them directly into the blood stream. As the blood itself comes in contact with very few tissue cells there has to be some way of getting food to these cells. This is done by a process called *diffusion* which goes on between the blood in the capillaries and lymph outside. This same interchange goes on between the tissue cells and the lymph. The interchange of fluid is governed by *osmotic pressure*.

**49. Metabolism.**—Metabolism is that process by means of which foods are broken down and rebuilt into living tissue.

*a.* The *mouth* is the first organ taking part in the preparation of food for absorption. The food after it is taken into the mouth is broken apart by the teeth in the act of chewing and is mixed with a substance called *saliva*. This is secreted by a group of glands located inside of the cheeks, under the tongue, and under the lower jaw. Saliva contains an enzyme (*ptyalin*) which acts on starches to reduce them to maltose. After the food becomes semi-liquid it is swallowed and passes down the *esophagus* or gullet to the stomach.

*b.* The *stomach* is a muscular, sac-like organ which lies just below the diaphragm and is lined with cells which secrete the *gastric juice*. This juice is an acid liquid which contains pepsin, an enzyme acting on the proteins to break them up into simpler compounds. At either

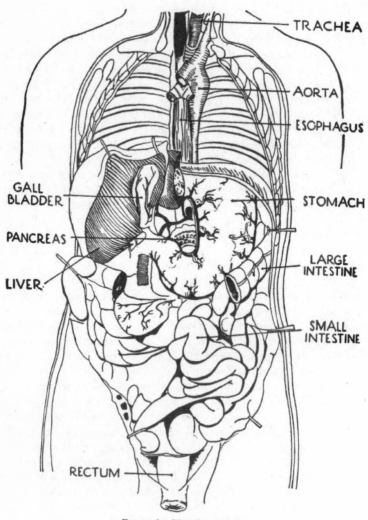

FIGURE 4.—Digestive system.

end of the stomach there are rings of muscular tissue which, when contracted, close the openings and keep the food in the organ until gastric digestion has been completed. When this has occurred the muscle fibers in the wall of the stomach contract and force the food into the small intestine.

*c.* The *small intestine* is a long tube (about 22 feet) which lies coiled up in the abdominal cavity. It is in this organ that digestion is completed and from which the food is absorbed.

(1) There is a small opening in the small intestine which receives juice from the *pancreas* and bile from the *liver.* These two organs are very important accessory glands of digestion.

(*a*) The pancreas, which secretes *pancreatic juice,* is a long, narrow gland located back of the stomach. This juice carries on the work of breaking down the proteins and starches already started in the stomach and in addition acts on the fats.

(*b*) The liver is the largest gland in the body and lies on the right side of the abdomen just beneath the diaphragm. *Bile* is formed by the liver cells and is collected in ducts which unite to form the one opening into the intestine. Some of the bile is by-passed up a small duct to a sac called the gall bladder. Here it is stored for future use. Bile does not contain any specific enzyme used in digestion, but it does aid the action of the pancreatic juice, especially in its action on fats.

(2) Certain cells of the small intestine secrete the last digestive juice to come into contact with the food. This *intestinal juice* completes the breaking down of the proteins and starches.

*d.* The *large intestine* or colon is between 3 and 4 feet long and is much larger in diameter than the small intestine. It starts in the right lower part of the abdomen where the small intestine empties into it, extends upward to the under-surface of the liver, then across the upper abdomen, and down the left side to end in the anus. Most of the nutritive matter from the food has been absorbed in the small intestine, but the contents discharged into the colon are very liquid and as these are churned around whatever remains of value is absorbed together with much of the water content. The material remaining consists of undigested substances, bacteria, and some waste products which collect in the lower part of the colon and are passed as fecal material.

**50. Excretory system.**—Waste material of the body is gotten rid of through the skin, lungs, and urinary system, as well as the large intestine. The liver also acts as an excretory organ as it separates waste material from the blood and also changes certain harmful excretory substances into harmless ones and returns them to the blood for excretion through the skin and in the urine.

**51. Skin.**—The skin, in addition to being a protective covering, acts as an excretory organ. Skin consists of two layers, the *cuticle* or *epidermis* and the *true skin*. Located in the true skin are many very small glands, the sweat glands. These glands secrete the sweat, which varies greatly in amount, depending upon the environmental temperature, activity of the individual, and certain other conditions. Sweat contains a certain amount of waste products similar to some contained in the *urine*.

**52. Urinary system.**—The urinary system consists of the kidneys, ureters, bladder, and urethra.

*a.* The *kidneys* are two in number each one lying on the side of the spinal column in the back of the abdomen. They are bean-shaped organs between 4 and 5 inches in length and on the concave side of each is a notch called the *hilum.* Here the large blood vessels enter and leave the organ and the tube (ureter) which takes away the urine has its origin. The blood enters the kidneys and when it has reached the fine capillaries the cells of the gland remove the impurities which pass into the ureters as urine.

*b.* The *ureters* are small tubes which carry the urine from the kidneys to the bladder. There is one ureter for each kidney.

*c.* The *bladder* is a hollow, muscular organ lying low in the body just behind the pelvic bone. A ureter enters each side of the organ and as the kidneys secrete the urine it passes on to the bladder, where it is stored, having to be emptied only at intervals.

*d.* The *urethra* is the tube through which the urine is discharged from the bladder.

**53. Nervous system.**—The nervous system is the most complex system of the body and may be thought of as two systems, as the functions of one differ from the other. The *cerebro-spinal system* is that part made up of the brain and spinal cord and the nerves given off by these organs, namely, 43 cranial and spinal nerves. The other system is called the *sympathetic nervous system* and consists of two rows of central ganglia (masses of nerve cells) lying along the front of the spinal column, the ganglia being united with each other by strands of nerve fibers and connected by means of sympathetic nerves with various parts of the body. The sympathetic system has largely to do with the movement of involuntary muscles and the activities of glands.

*a. Brain.*—The brain lies well protected in the skull. The organ consists of a large *cerebrum* and a much smaller *cerebellum.* The

cerebrum is the seat of the mind. When it is removed all pow
of moving voluntary muscles is gone. Without it all sensations
light, taste, smell, touch, and heat are lost. The cerebrum decid
what we shall do. It sends out the messages to the muscles wh

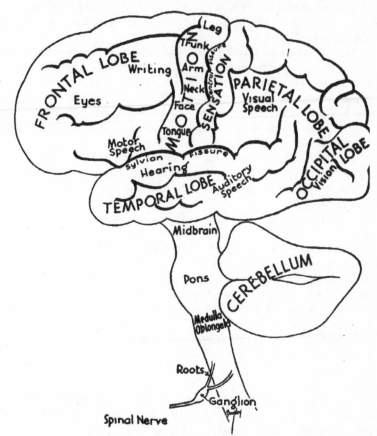

FIGURE 5.—Diagrammatic illustration of lateral aspect of the brain.

we wish to move and is that part of the brain that thinks and fe
Without a cerebrum an animal can live but all of its intelligence
gone. It still breathes but is only a machine.

*b. Cerebellum.*—The cerebellum causes all the muscles to ke
the proper amount of contraction (*tonus*) and it assists in governi
the muscles in standing and walking.

*c. Spinal cord.*—The spinal cord is a continuation of the nerv
tissue extending from the brain down through the spinal can

The spinal cord widens out on its upper end where it is attached to the brain to form the *medulla oblongata*. The medulla is a very important part of the brain as it contains the nerve centers governing the action of the heart and respiration. The spinal cord itself is a large bundle of nerve fibers which carry nervous impulses from the various parts of the body to the brain as well as impulses in the opposite direction.

54. **Glands and their products.**—The fact that certain groups of tissue cells supply certain secretions to the body has been pointed out under the description of the alimentary tract. Some of these same glands also secrete substances which are absorbed directly into the blood stream. The pancreas, for example, not only secretes pancreatic juice but it secretes a substance directly into the blood which has to do with carbohydrate metabolism.

*a.* The *endocrine* glands is a term applied to these glands and the active substances contained in their secretions are called *hormones*. These hormones influence such functions as growth, reproduction, and metabolism.

*b.* The *thyroid* gland, in the neck, one of the largest glands whose secretion is entirely an internal one, was one of the first to be studied from this view. Overactivity of this gland causes nervousness, loss of weight, rapid heart, and other symptoms, while an insufficient amount of secretion, in children, causes mental dullness, retardation of growth of the long bones, coarse hair, etc.

*c.* The following glands secrete one or more hormones: Adrenals, ovaries, glands in the lining of the stomach and duodenum, testicles, pancreas, thyroid, parathyroid, and pituitary. It is also believed that certain other glands secrete hormones but it has never been definitely proved.

55. **Special senses.**—The special senses are feeling, tasting, smelling, hearing, and seeing. These senses are due to the peculiar development of the ends of sensory nerves in various parts of the body. The sense of feeling is more or less generally distributed over the body surface. However, in some places as the finger tips, the nerve endings are very close together and feeling is more acute. The sensory nerves of taste are all located in the mouth and those of smell in the nose. The other two special senses have rather complicated end organs which aid in the reception of either light or sound waves.

56. **Eye.**—The eye may be likened to a small camera which is constantly photographing objects and sending the picture to the brain.

*a.* The eyes are well protected from injury by being placed in a hollow or socket in the front of the skull. On the exposed side they are protected by the eyelids, eyebrows, and eyelashes. The exposed surface of the eye and the inner surface of the lid are kept moist by the secretion of the tear glands.

*b.* The eyeball is generally spherical in shape being made up of two hollow segments of unequal size. The larger, posterior segment comprises about five-sixths of the eyeball and the anterior, one-sixth. These segments form two chambers, the larger containing a gelatinous material, the vitreous humor, and the smaller, the aqueous humor.

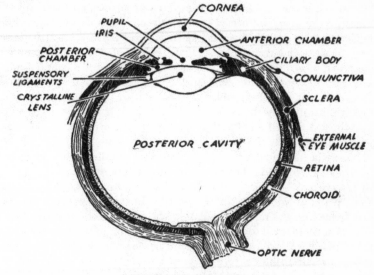

FIGURE 6.—Cross section of eye.

*c.* The eye has three coats, a thick outer protective one which is continuous with the clear *cornea* in front, but otherwise is thick and white; a middle coat which contains blood vessels, a small muscle, and in front the *iris;* and an inner coat which contains the end organs of sight of the optic nerve. This inner coat is called the *retina.*

*d.* The *lens* is placed right behind the pupil, being held in place by the *ciliary* muscle.

*e.* If the eye is compared with a camera it will be seen that rays of light, entering the front of the eye through the pupil, pass through the lens and are registered on the retina, which corresponds to the film. Now in taking pictures with a camera the operator has to regulate his light by means of a stop or diaphragm. This is done in the eye by the iris which produces a small aperture in bright light and a larger one in dull light. In a camera the lens is moved away from or toward the film in order that the light rays from the object to be photographed will fall on the film. This focus is changed depending upon the distance of the object from the camera. In the eye the focus is not changed by shortening or lengthening the box, but by contraction and relaxation of the ciliary muscle the lens is made thicker or thinner as required.

**57. Vision.**—*a.* The first phase in vision, insofar as the eye is concerned, is the formation on the retina of an image of a luminous object. The image is formed by the refractive actions of the cornea, aqueous humor, crystalline lens, and vitreous body. These structures are colorless and transparent. Their refractive indices are greater than that of air. The cornea and aqueous humor form a concavo-convex lens. The crystalline lens is bi-convex, the curvatures of its surfaces different and changeable. The amount of light admitted to the eye is controlled by the action of the lids and of the iris. The eyes are directed toward an object being viewed by movement of the head and of the eyeballs themselves. The extrinsic muscles of the eye act to keep the principal axes of the two eyes parallel, convergent, or divergent as required. The combined effect of the refractive structures of the eye may be considered as that of a bi-convex lens, the posterior focal plane of which lies in the retina. Images of external objects are formed on the retina stimulating the sensory cells thereof. The sensation is conveyed to the visual tracts of the brain where perception takes place. Although the image formed on the retina is inverted this gives rise to no confusion as we have learned by experience to make proper interpretation of the sensation.

*b.* The production of a clear, distinct image on the retina is dependent, in the normal eye, upon the distance of the object from the optical center of the refractive system. When this distance is greater than 20 feet all light rays from each of the innumerable luminous points of the object are practically parallel and will be focused properly. As the distance decreases the rays will be divergent hence will not be focused. This difficulty is overcome by a change in the focal distance of the refractive system, a change which is produced by alteration of the curvature of the surfaces of the crystalline lens. This power of accommodation, as it is designated, is greatest in early life and decreases steadily with age. At 10 years of age the normal eye can form a distinct image of an object 2¾ inches from the eye; by the fortieth year this distance has increased to about 8¾ inches and by the fiftieth year to 15¾ inches. Between the fortieth and fiftieth years, therefore, most people find it necessary to use convex lenses for near vision.

c. In the normal eye the optical center of the refractive system is 15.5 millimeters from the retina. In many individuals the distance is either greater or less than this. When such is the case a distinct image is not formed on the retina. In the myopic (short sighted) eye the antero-posterior diameter of the eyeball is greater than normal, or the curvature of the cornea, or lens, too great. Lengthening of the eyeball is the more common case. Rays of light are focused before reaching the retina and the retinal image is indistinct as a consequence. Myopia may be congenital or acquired; usually it is acquired. The defect may be produced by the increase in tension within the eyeball which results when the eyes are much converged, as for example, in reading with the book too near the eyes, a thing which is often done when the illumination is poor. If the fibrous coat of the eyeball be weak the increased tension tends to produce elongation of the antero-posterior diameter.

d. In the hypermetropic (far sighted) eye the focal point of the refractive system is beyond the retina and the retinal image is diffuse. The condition may be due to lessened curvature of the cornea or lens but is generally the result of a diminished antero-posterior diameter of the eye-ball. In most instances the defect is congenital.

e. Astigmatism is a common optical defect. In the so-called normal eye the refractive surfaces are sections of true spheres; all the meridians of the cornea are of equal curvature, the same being true of the anterior and posterior surfaces of the crystalline lens. In this event refraction is equal at all meridians. But if there is variation in the meridional curvature of any of the surfaces it can be seen refraction will be unequal, producing inequalities of the focal lengths in different planes. This is the case in astigmatism.

58. Ear.—The ear consists of an external, a middle, and an inner ear.

a. External ear.—The external ear is ovoid in shape, flattened, wider above than below, and presents several depressions and eminences. This organ collects the sound waves and directs them through the external auditory canal to the middle ear. The external auditory canal is a tube about an inch long, slightly curved and lined with skin containing a few hairs. In the skin of the canal are a few glands which secrete a waxy substance which, together with the hairs, serves to prevent the entrance of foreign particles. The canal ends with the *eardrum* which separates it from the middle ear.

*b. Middle ear.*—The middle ear is a small, irregular bony cavity in the temporal bone. The eardrum separates it from the external ear. A thin bony wall in which are located two small openings separates it from the inner ear. Stretched across the cavity of the middle ear from the eardrum to one of the small openings to the inner ear are three small movable bones called the *malleus* or hammer, the *incus* or anvil, and the *stapes* or stirrup. The Eustachian or auditory tube connects the cavity of the middle ear with the throat. Generally this tube is closed by the tissues of the throat. On swallowing it is opened, allowing air to enter the ear, thereby maintaining an equality of air pressure between the inside and outside of the ear.

*c. Internal ear.*—The internal ear consists of two complicated structures, the spiral-shaped organ of hearing called the cochlea and the semicircular canals.

**59. Mechanism of hearing.**—In hearing, the sound waves are collected by the external ear and passed through the ear canal to the eardrum. These impulses are transmitted across the middle ear by the three small bones to the inner ear. Impulses received by the inner ear set in motion a fluid material filling the hearing organ proper, the cochlea. The sensory nerve cells for hearing are located in the cochlea. These cells are stimulated by the vibration of the fluid, thus giving rise to sensations which are conducted to the brain by the auditory nerve. The semicircular canals are concerned with the sense of equilibrium.

**60. Male genital system.**—*a.* The *testicle* is the reproductive organ of the male; however, the vas deferens, seminal vesicles, prostate gland, and penis are considered as accessory organs of reproduction.

*b.* The testicles are two ovoid glands which lie in a pouch of skin called the *scrotum.* They are covered with a thin membrane which doubles back on itself to line the scrotum. Before birth the testicles develop in the abdominal cavity and descend into the scrotum, usually, just before birth. The passageway closes up in most cases but sometimes remains open or at least weak so that the intestine may descend along it causing a *hernia* or *rupture.*

*c.* The testicles have two important functions, the first being the formation of the male cells or *spermatozoa* and the secretion of a substance necessary for the development of sexual characteristics in the male.

*d.* When the spermatozoa are formed they pass into a long convoluted tubule on the back of the testicle called the *epididymis.* This tube measures about 20 feet in length but is coiled up so that it takes up but little space.    The tube of the epididymis is continued in a more or less direct manner as the *vas deferens* to a membranous pouch (one on each side) lying between the base of the bladder and the rectum.

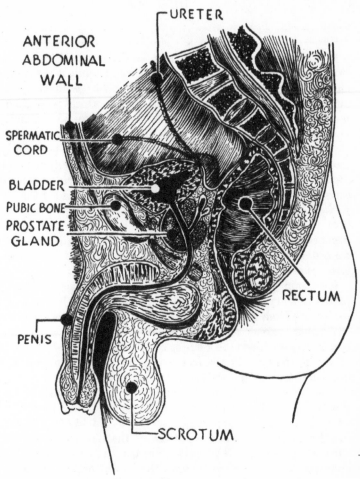

FIGURE 7.—Male genital system.

These are called the *seminal vesicles*.    The seminal vesicles act as a reservoir for the spermatozoa and discharge them through small ducts into the back part of the *urethra*.    At the same place where these ducts empty the *prostate gland* empties a secretion which is added to the spermatozoa. The prostate gland is shaped somewhat like a chestnut and surrounds the urethra just as it leaves the bladder.

## Section II

### DENTAL

|  | Paragraph |
|---|---|
| Mouth | 61 |
| Teeth | 62 |

**61. Mouth.**—*a.* The mouth may be defined as the cavity at the beginning of the digestive tract. With its contents, it is the organ of chewing, taste, and speech. The mouth cavity is lined by mucous membrane containing many mucous glands which pour their contents, saliva, into the mouth. It is divided into two portions—the *vestibule*, a narrow, slit-like space which lies between the lips and cheeks anteriorly and laterally, and the dental arch posteriorly and medially, and the *mouth cavity proper*, the space within the dental arches. The mouth cavity proper is open posteriorly and communicates with the pharnyx by a constricted aperture, called the *isthmus facium*. Its roof is formed by the hard and soft palates, while its floor is the mylohyoid and geniohyoid muscles covered by mucous membrane on which rests the tongue. The side walls and front are formed by the alveolar processes and the teeth of the upper and lower jaws.

*b.* Opening into the mouth cavity are the ducts of the three paired salivary glands discharging their secretion, the *saliva*. *Stenson's duct*, from the *parotid* gland, opens into the vestibule opposite the upper second molar tooth. *Wharton's duct*, from the *submaxillary* gland, and the *ducts of Rivinus*, from the *sublingual* gland, open into the floor of the mouth anteriorly in the sublingual space beneath the tip of the tongue.

*c.* The tongue is a highly muscular organ, covered by mucous membrane, resting on the floor of the mouth cavity proper, and to which it is attached on its under surface by a fold of this membrane called the *frenum*. On the surface of the tongue are seen several varieties of papillae, which give to the tongue its characteristic rough appearance. The tongue contains the special organs of taste, is an important organ of speech, and aids in the process of chewing and swallowing food.

**62. Teeth.**—*a.* The teeth of man make their appearance in two sets or series. The first, having only temporary usage (the last of them disappearing about the twelfth year), is known as the deciduous, temporary, or milk teeth; the second set, having to serve for the remaining life period, is known as the permanent teeth. The deciduous teeth number 20 in all, and the permanent teeth number 32 when complete. Both sets of teeth are similarly arranged, in the form of two arches, half of their number (10 for the deciduous, and 16 for the permanent) being arranged in an upper arch and the other half in an opposite lower arch.

*b.* The bones within which the teeth are set are known respectively as the superior maxilla, for the upper jawbone, and the inferior maxilla or mandible for the lower jawbone. An imaginary, vertical, central line dividing the body into right and left, known as the median line, divides the teeth into the same number and kind on both right and left sides. The permanent teeth are named as follows, starting from the median line:

| Tooth | Name | Tooth | Name |
|-------|------|-------|------|
| 1st_____ | Central incisor. | 5th_____ | Second bicuspid. |
| 2d_____ | Lateral incisor. | 6th_____ | First molar. |
| 3d_____ | Cuspid. | 7th_____ | Second molar. |
| 4th_____ | First bicuspid. | 8th_____ | Third molar. |

*c.* In the Army, for the purpose of convenience, uniformity, and briefness of records, the teeth are numbered from 1 to 16, right and left, beginning with the upper central incisors. Thus, the upper left central incisor would be designated as L1, the upper left third molar as L8, the lower left central incisor as L9, the lower left third molar as L16, and similarly for the right side. See figure 8.

*d.* Grouped collectively, the incisors and cuspids are referred to as the anterior teeth, and the bicuspids and molars as the posterior teeth. Certain other terms used in describing the teeth with which one should become familiar are—

(1) *Labial surface.*—That surface of the incisors and cuspids which lies next to the lips.

(2) *Buccal surface.*—That surface of the bicuspids and molars presenting toward the cheeks.

(3) *Facial surface.*—A term used to designate the side of a tooth next to the lips or cheeks and may be applied to either an anterior or a posterior tooth.

(4) *Lingual surface.*—That surface of a tooth toward the tongue.

(5) *Proximal surface.*—That surface which adjoins the next tooth.

(6) *Mesial surface.*—That proximal surface nearest the median line of the arch, that is, a line drawn between the central incisors.

(7) *Distal surface.*—That proximal surface that is farthest away from the median line.

(8) *Occlusal surface.*—That surface of a bicuspid or molar tooth that makes contact with a tooth of the opposite jaw when the mouth is closed.

(9) *Incisal surface.*—The cutting edge of the incisors and cuspids.

e. A tooth is divided into two main parts, the crown and root. The crown is that portion which projects above the gum and is the chewing part of a tooth. The remaining part, or root, is firmly embedded within the bony structure of the jawbone, and so designed as to withstand the stresses of chewing. (See figs. 9 and 10.) The end of the root is called the *apex* and through the opening in it the nerve and blood supply enter the tooth. The incisors, cuspids, and bicuspids (with the exception of the upper first bicuspid which may have two roots) have only one root, while the molar teeth have from two to three roots. At the junction of the crown and root of the tooth is found a constriction in greater or less degree, which is known as the *neck* or *cervix*. Occupying the central portion of the crown and root is the *pulp cavity*, containing the dental pulp. This cavity is divided into two parts—that in the crown, known as the *pulp chamber*, and that in the root, known as the *pulp canal*.

f. The *alveolar process* is that portion of the maxilla and mandible formed for the reception and support of the roots of the teeth. When a tooth is removed from its process an opening is left that resembles in outline the shape of the root. This cavity or socket is called an *alveolus*. The alveolar process is composed of an inner and an outer plate of compact bone. Between these two plates the bone is less compact, being of a spongy or cancellous nature. The inner plate of compact bone approximates the roots of the teeth and is called the *peridental lamella*. That portion of the alveolar process which lies in the bifurcation of the roots of multirooted teeth or between the roots of two adjacent teeth is called the *septum*. Surrounding the root and separating it from the bony wall of the socket is a layer of fibrous connective tissue known as the *peridental membrane*, which has the important function of binding the tooth to the surrounding bone. Covering the alveolar process and investing the necks of the teeth is a firm tissue called the *gingiva*, or gum. (See fig. 10.)

g. In structure, a tooth is composed of four tissues, the enamel, dentin, cementum, and the dental pulp.

(1) *Enamel.*—Enamel is the hard, calcified, glistening substance which covers the crown of a tooth. It is thickest at the biting surfaces of the teeth, where it is most required to resist the stress of mastication, and gradually thins out as it approaches the neck, where it is, in most instances, slightly overlapped by the cementum. The enamel is the hardest tissue of the body and is composed of a series of prismatic rods held together by a cementing substance which, like the rods, is composed chiefly of inorganic salts.

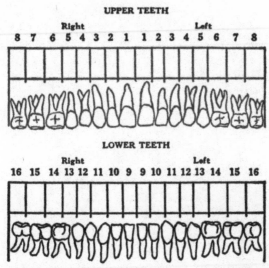

FIGURE 8.—Numerical designation of permanent teeth as used in the United States Army.

(2) *Dentin.*—Dentin is the hard, calcified, yellowish substance that makes up the mass of the tooth, giving to the tooth its general form. The dentin matrix is highly resilient and tough and gives strength to the tooth. Extending throughout the matrix and radiating from the pulp cavity are minute tubules, containing the *dentinal fibrils* which are protoplasmic extensions from the outermost layers of cells of the dental pulp. In the center of the dentin, extending the whole length of the root and into the crown of the tooth, is the pulp cavity.

(3) *Cementum.*—Cementum is the calcified tissue covering the root portion of the tooth, which closely resembles bone in structure. It is arranged in concentric layers around the tooth root varying in thickness according to the position on the root, being thinnest at the neck and thickest at the apex. The cementum gives attachment to the fibres of the peridental membrane holding the tooth firmly in its socket.

(4) *Dental pulp.*—The dental pulp, often called the nerve on account of its sensitiveness, occupies the central cavity or pulp chamber and canal of a tooth. It is composed of embryonic connective tissue,

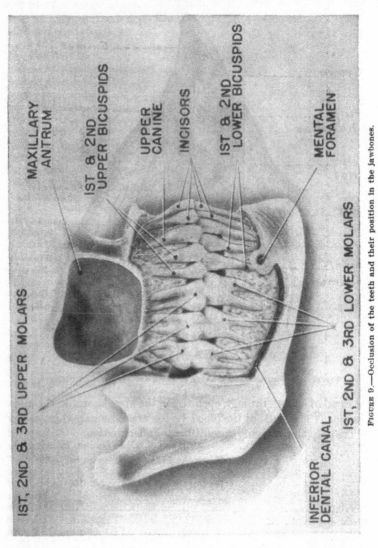

FIGURE 9.—Occlusion of the teeth and their position in the jawbones.

rich in blood vessels and nerves. Lying along the outer border of the pulp in contact with the dentin wall is a layer of specialized connective cells, the *odontoblasts*, which have the important function of forming dentin. Protoplasmic processes from these cells pass into the dentinal tubules and have the property of transferring sensations of pain to the nerve fibrils within the pulp. Blood vessels and nerves enter the

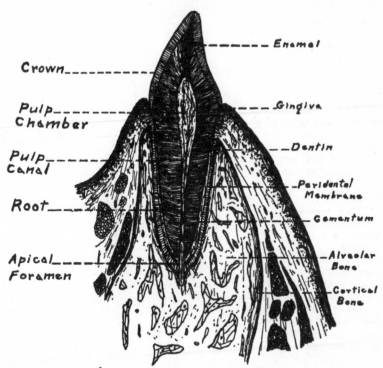

Crown

Pulp Chamber

Pulp Canal

Root

Apical Foramen

Enamel

Gingiva

Dentin

Peridental Membrane

Cementum

Alveolar Bone

Cortical Bone

FIGURE 10.—Diagrammatic drawing of tooth and supporting structures.

root canal of a tooth through openings in the apex known as the *apical foramina*. The walls of the blood vessels are extremely thin, rendering the pulp tissue highly susceptible to inflammation.

## SECTION III

## VETERINARY

**63. General.**—The intelligent operation and care of any mechanism is based on a good working knowledge of its general structure and normal functions. The animal body may be considered as a complex machine of many parts, with each of these various parts normally functioning in a more or less definite manner. The science which treats of the form and structure of the animal body is known as *anatomy*. The science which treats of the normal functioning of the animal body is known as *physiology*. It is quite essential that the study of animal management include a basic knowledge of the anatomy and physiology of the horse, in order that the student may more intelligently recognize the reasons upon which the fundamental principles of animal management are based. In this text the study of anatomy and physiology will be correlated as much as possible and limited to those parts of greatest essential interest. The body of the horse is in general structure quite like the body of man. Their chief differences are in the relative size and relationship of the various parts, and for these reasons the various structures of the horse will in many instances be compared with the similar parts of the human body. The body of the horse, like that of man, is made up of a skeletal system, a muscular system, a digestive system, a respiratory system, a circulatory system, a nervous system, a urinary system, a reproductive system, and an outer covering of skin and hair.

**64. Skeletal system.**—The skeletal system includes the bones and the ligaments which bind bones together to form joints. The skeletal system gives the body form and rigidity and forms cavities for the protection of vital organs. Bones and joints together form a complex system of levers and pulleys which, combined with the muscular system, gives the body the power of motion. The relative size and relationship of position of the bones determines the real form or conformation of the horse and his efficiency for any particular work. The trunk or axial skeleton consists of the skull, spinal or vertebral column, ribs, and breast bones. The limbs or appendicular skeleton support the body and furnish the levers of propulsion.

**65. Bones.**—*a*. The skeleton of the horse is made up of about 205 bones. In their living state bones are composed of about one part of organic matter and two parts of inorganic matter. . The latter, which is mineral matter, is largely lime salts. The bones, as you see them in the mounted skeleton, have been freed of organic matter and are white and brittle, but living bone is about twice as strong as a green oak stick of the same size. Bones, according to their shape, are classified as long, short, flat, and irregular.

(1) *Long* bones are found in the limbs, where they support the body weight and act as the levers of propulsion.

(2) *Short* bones occur chiefly in the knee and hock, where they function in the dissipation of concussion.

(3) *Flat* bones, such as the ribs, scapula, and some of the bones of the skull, help to inclose cavities containing vital organs.

(4) *Irregular* bones are such bones as the vertebrae and some bones of the skull.

*b.* All bones are covered with a thin, tough membrane called *periosteum* except at points of articulation where they are covered with *cartilage.*

(1) The periosteum is closely attached to the bone. It covers and protects the bone and influences the growth of the bone to a certain extent. This latter function is of particular interest, for we know that injury to this membrane often results in an abnormal bone growth called an *exostosis,* occurring at the point of injury. Bone growths, such as splints, spavins, and ringbones, are the frequent result of some form of injury to the periosteum. The bone is in part nourished by blood vessels in the periosteum and there are many nerve endings in this membrane.

(2) The articular or joint surfaces of bones are covered with a dense, very smooth, bluish-colored substance called cartilage. The cartilage diminishes the effects of concussion and provides a smooth joint surface offering a minimum of frictional resistance to movement.

**66. Skeletons of horse and man.**—See figure 11. The same letters and figures indicate corresponding parts in each skeleton.

**67. Bones of skull.**—There are 34 bones in the skull and it is divided into two parts, the *cranium* and the *face.*

*a.* The bones of the *cranium* are all flat or irregular bones and surround the *cranial cavity* which contains the brain. This cavity is relatively small considering the size of the animal. The bones join each other in immovable joints. The bone forming what is known as the *poll* has an articulating surface where the head is jointed to the vertebral or spinal column. Together with the bones of the face, the cranial bones form the *orbital* and *nasal cavities.*

*b.* The bones of the face form the framework of the mouth and nasal cavities and include the more important bones of the upper and lower jaws, known as the *maxillae* and *mandible* respectively.

(1) Each *maxilla* has six irregular cavities for the reception of the cheek or molar teeth. From the maxillae forward the face becomes narrower and terminates in the *premaxilla,* which contains cavities for the six upper *incisor* teeth. Inclosed in each maxilla is a cavity known as the *maxillary sinus,* which opens into the nasal passages. This sinus contains the roots of the three back molar teeth and at times becomes infected, due to diseased teeth.

(2) The *mandible,* or lower jaw, is hinged to the cranium on either side by a freely movable joint in front of and below the base of the

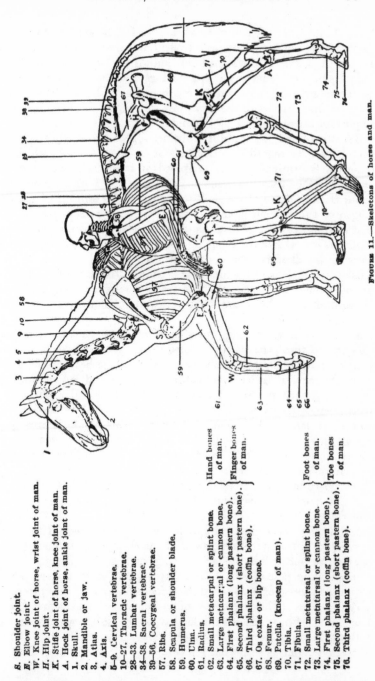

FIGURE 11.—Skeletons of horse and man.

S. Shoulder Joint.
E. Elbow Joint.
W. Knee Joint of horse, wrist Joint of man.
H. Hip Joint.
K. Stifle Joint of horse, knee Joint of man.
A. Hock Joint of horse, ankle joint of man.
1. Skull.
2. Mandible or Jaw.
3. Atlas.
4. Axis.
5–9. Cervical vertebrae.
10–27. Thoracic vertebrae.
28–33. Lumbar vertebrae.
34–38. Sacral vertebrae.
39–56. Coccygeal vertebrae.
57. Ribs.
58. Scapula or shoulder blade.
59. Humerus.
60. Ulna.
61. Radius.
62. Small metacarpal or splint bone.    } Hand bones of man.
63. Large metacarpal or cannon bone.    }
64. First phalanx (long pastern bone).  }
65. Second phalanx (short pastern bone). } Finger bones of man.
66. Third phalanx (coffin bone).        }
67. Os coxae or hip bone.
68. Femur.
69. Patella (kneecap of man).
70. Tibia.
71. Fibula.
72. Small metatarsal or splint bone.    } Foot bones of man.
73. Large metatarsal or cannon bone.    }
74. First phalanx (long pastern bone).  }
75. Second phalanx (short pastern bone). } Toe bones of man.
76. Third phalanx (coffin bone).        }

ear. At its front extremity it has cavities for the six lower incisors. Back of the incisors is a space between the incisors and the six lower molars in each side of the mandible known as the *interdental space*. Injuries to periosteum or possible fracture of the mandible may occur in the interdental space due to rough usage of the bit. The space between the branches of the lower jaw is occupied by the tongue and important salivary and lymph glands.

**68. Vertebral or spinal column.**—The vertebral or spinal column may be regarded as the basis of the skeleton from which all other parts originate. It is composed of irregularly shaped bones bound together with ligaments and cartilage and forms a column of bones from the base of the skull to the tip of the tail. Through the length of this column is an elongated cavity called the *spinal canal* that contains the *spinal cord*, which is the main trunk-line of nerves coming from the brain lying in the cranial cavity. Through this more or less flexible column of bones the powerful impetus of propulsion originating in the hind legs is transmitted to the forequarters of the animal and indirectly it bears the weight of the rider and his equipment. The bones of the vertebral column are divided into five regions as follows:

*a.* The *cervical*, or neck, region contains seven cervical vertebrae. The first of these, the *atlas*, is jointed to the cranium by a hinge-like joint permitting only extension and flexion of the head on the neck. The next cervical vertebra is known as the *axis* and is so jointed to the atlas that it permits of rotation of the head and atlas on the remainder of the neck. The remaining five cervical vertebrae have no special names. The column of bones in this region is arranged, when viewed from the side, in an S-shaped curve. Lengthening and shortening of the neck is brought about by lessening or increasing this curvature. The cervical region is the most flexible part of the vertebral column and from the viewpoint of the student of equitation the possible movements of the head and neck are of great importance.

*b.* The *thoracic* region contains 18 *thoracic vertebrae*. These vertebrae form in part the upper wall of the chest cavity. Each vertebra has on either side an articulating surface for jointing to its corresponding pair of ribs. Each vertebra has on its upper surface a spine or process of bone called the *spinous process*. These processes vary in length. They increase rapidly in length from the first to the fourth and fifth, which are the longest, and form the summit of the withers, and then decrease in length. Movement in this part of the vertebral column is somewhat limited.

*c.* The *lumbar* region contains six *lumbar* vertebrae, sometimes five, especially in the Arab horse. This part of the column forms the framework or the loin. Movement in this part of the vertebral column is much greater than in the thoracic portion.

*d.* The *sacral* region contains five *sacral* vertebrae. These five bones are fused or grown together and may be considered as one bone, the *sacrum*, the highest point of which forms the summit of the croup. The sacrum is jointed very securely to the hip bones on either side and through these joints the propulsive impulses from the hind legs are transmitted to the vertebral column.

*e.* The *coccygeal* region contains from 15 to 21 *coccygeal* vertebrae which form the bony column of the tail. The spinal canal is practically absent in this part of the vertebral column.

The vertebral formula of the horse is C7T18L6S5Cy15–21. The vertebral formula of man is C7T12L5S5Cy4.

**69. Bony thorax (chest).**—The bony thorax is a large cavity formed by the thoracic vertebrae above, the ribs on the sides, and the *sternum* (breastbone) forming the floor. This cavity contains the heart, lungs, large blood vessels and nerves, and part of the trachea and oesophagus. Depth of this cavity with moderate width is desirable.

**70. Ribs.**—The horse has 18 pairs of *ribs*, all of which are jointed to the thoracic vertebrae at their upper ends. The lower ends of the first eight pairs, called *true* or *sternal* ribs, are jointed by means of cartilage to the sternum or breastbone. The last ten pairs, called *asternal* or *false* ribs, are at their lower ends continued by extensions of cartilage which are bound to each other by elastic tissue. The shape and length of the ribs determine the contour of the chest. The ribs form the direct skeletal support of the saddle.

**71. Sternum.**—The *sternum*, or breastbone, is a canoe-shaped bone consisting of seven or eight bony segments connected by intervening cartilage. The sternum forms the floor of the thorax and the front end of the bone forms the bony prominence in the midline of the breast.

**72. Bones of foreleg.**—The bones of the foreleg named from above downward are the *scapula, humerus, radius,* and *ulna, carpal* bones, three *metacarpal* bones, *first phalanx, second phalanx, third phalanx,* and the *proximal* and *distal* (navicular) *sesamoid* bones.

*a.* The *scapula*, or shoulder blade, is a triangular flat bone in the region of the shoulder and lies on the side of the thorax. Along its upper border, or the base of the triangle, is attached a thin, flat, **and** flexible cartilagenous extension. When the leg is extended to the front the edge of this cartilage may slip under the front of the bar of the saddle without injury to the shoulder blade. The direction of this bone is sloping downward and forward. If the direction of this bone approaches vertical the shoulder is said to be straight or upright, which is not favorable for length and freedom of the forward movement of the foreleg. The scapula is attached to the thorax only by muscles, there being no bony union with the sternum, ribs, or spinal column. In man the scapula is jointed to the sternum through the *clavicle* or collarbone, a bone that is entirely absent in the skeleton of the horse. The lower end of the scapula is jointed to the humerus.

*b.* The *humerus* is the bone of the arm and extends downward and backward from the shoulder joint to the elbow. The humerus is surrounded with heavy muscles and is attached by muscles to the wall of the thorax. Because of its muscular protection and position, this bone is not often injured. In man the humerus or arm bone is much freer of the body and has a much greater range of movement in the shoulder joint.

*c.* The *radius* is the bone of the forearm and with the ulna and humerus forms the elbow joint. The *ulna* is a short bone which is fused to the upper part of the radius and also projects above the end of the radius to form the point of the elbow. In man the ulna is comparatively longer and extends, on the little finger side, with the radius to the wrist joint. The long axis of the radius should be vertical.

*d.* The *carpal* bones, or knee bones, correspond to the wrist bones of man. There are seven or eight carpal bones arranged in two rows. The top row articulates with the lower end of the radius and most of the movement of the knee joint is confined to this articulation. The top and bottom rows articulate with each other and the bottom row also with the upper ends of the metacarpal bones. A great deal of concussion transmitted up the bony column from below is absorbed and dissipated by the carpal bones.

*e.* The horse has three *metacarpal* bones. The large middle metacarpal bone (cannon bone) extends from the knee to the fetlock and is sometimes known as the third metacarpal. Because of the great strength of this bone it is seldom fractured although it is one of the most exposed bones of the skeleton. In his early evolutionary state the horse was a fivetoed animal, but during his development to his present form he has lost the two inner and two outer toes and only the two splint bones or *small metacarpals* persist as vestigial remains of the original second and fourth metacarpals. These small metacarpals are located on the internal and external posterior borders of the large metacarpal. Their upper ends articulate with the lower row of carpal bones. As they are only about three-fourths as long as the large metacarpal, they have no direct support at their lower end but where they are in contact with the large metacarpal they are closely bound to it by the strong *interosseous ligament.* Strains of this ligament result in the condition known as splints. After a horse is about 7 years of age this ligament begins to ossify and, in old animals, the splint bones may be firmly fused to the cannon bone. The long axis of the cannon bone should be vertical.

*f.* The *first phalanx,* or long pastern bone, corresponds to the first bone of the long finger of man.

*g.* The *second phalanx,* or short pastern bone, corresponds to the second bone of the long finger of man.

*h.* The *third phalanx,* or coffin bone, corresponds to the bone in the tip of the finger and is completely inclosed in the hoof which is analagous with the fingernail of man. The general shape of the coffin bone is very similar to the shape of the hoof. The three phalanges have their long axis in prolongation of each other and their direction is downward and forward so that the inclosed angle with horizontal in the foreleg is about 50°. If the phalangeal column of bones approach the vertical, the horse is said to have upright or stumpy pasterns, and in such a case greater concussion is imparted directly to the bony column. Upright pasterns are often associated with a straight or upright shoulder. When the slope of the region is greater than average an undue amount of strain is thrown on the flexor tendons and suspensory ligament.

*i.* The *sesamoids* are two pyramidal-shaped bones that form a part of the fetlock joint and articulate with the posterior part of the lower end of the cannon bone. They lie imbedded in ligaments and cartilage and form a bearing surface over which the flexor tendons lie.

*j.* The *distal sesamoid,* or *navicular* bone, is situated back of the coffin bone and articulates with the lower end of the second phalanx. The deep flexor tendon plays over its lower surface. This point is the seat of navicular disease.

**73. Os coxae or hip bone.**—The *os coxae,* or hip bone, is a paired bone and each unites with its fellow of the opposite side at the lowest point to form the floor of the pelvic cavity. Each hip bone is firmly jointed to the sacrum. This girdle of bone is called the pelvic girdle and incloses the pelvic cavity. Each hip bone bears on its side a cavity where the femur, or first bone of the hind leg, is jointed to it. The outer front angle of the hip bone forms the point of the hip, or haunch, which is often injured. The inner front angle, together with the sacrum, forms the point or summit of the croup. The back angle of the hip bone forms the point of the buttock. A long and flat (approaching horizontal) pelvis is most suitable for speed and freedom of movement of the hind legs.

**74. Bones of hind leg.**—The bones of the hind leg named from above downward are the *femur*, *patella*, *tibia* and *fibula*, six or seven *tarsal* bones or bones of the hock, *large metatarsal* (cannon bone), two small *metatarsals* or splint bones, *first phalanx*, *second phalanx*, *third phalanx*, and the *proximal* and *distal* (navicular) *sesamoid* bones.

*a.* The *femur*, or bone of the thigh, corresponds to the thigh bone of man. At its upper end this bone articulates with the hip bone in the hip joint and extends downward, forward, and slightly outward to the stifle joint. Viewed from the side, the inclosed angle between the long axis of this bone and horizontal is about 80°.

*b.* The *patella* is a small bone lying on the front of the stifle joint and articulating with the lower end of the femur. It corresponds to the kneecap of man.

*c.* The *tibia* is the second long bone of the hind leg and lies in the region known as the leg or gaskin. It extends from the stifle joint downward and backward to the hock joint, forming an inclosed angle with horizontal of about 65° to 70°. A position approaching vertical is more favorable for speed of movement than one of considerable slope. This bone along its inner surface has but a thin protective covering of skin and other tissue, and because of its exposed position is the most frequently fractured bone in the horse's skeleton. This bone corresponds to the shin bone of man. The *fibula* in the horse is a small rudimentary bone about two-thirds as long as the tibia and is attached to the upper and outer surface of the tibia. In man this bone, as well as the tibia, extends from the knee to the ankle.

*d.* The hock or *tarsus* of the horse, like the ankle of man, contains six or seven *tarsal* bones arranged in a manner similar to the carpal bones of the knee. The largest of these extends upward from the back of the joint and forms the bony prominence known as the point of the hock, and serves as a point of attachment of the powerful tendon of Achilles.

*e.* The *metatarsal* bones correspond to the metacarpal bones of the foreleg. The hind cannon extends downward and slightly forward at an angle of about 87°. The hind cannon is about one-sixth longer than the fore cannon, and is also more nearly round.

*f.* The *phalanges* and *sesamoids* of the hind leg are very similar to those of the foreleg, except that the phalangeal axis is inclined to be slightly more upright.

**75. Joint or articulation.**—*a. Classification.*—Joints are classified according to structure and mobility into three types.

(1) *Immovable*, in which the opposed surfaces of bone are directly united by connective tissue or fused bone, permitting no movement, such as between the bones of the cranium.

(2) *Slightly movable*, where a pad of cartilage, adherent to both bones, is interposed between the bones and a slight amount of movement is possible due to the elasticity of the cartilage. Many of the joints between the vertebrae are of this character.

(3) *Freely movable*, when a joint cavity exists between the opposed surfaces. The joints of the legs are examples of this type.

*b. Structure.*—The freely movable joints are the truest examples of joints. The ends of the bones entering into a freely movable joint are held in opposition to each other by strong bands of tissue called *ligaments*, which pass from one bone to the other. Ligaments possess but a slight degree of elasticity and have a limited blood supply, which accounts for the fact that they heal very slowly and often imperfectly following an injury. In freely movable joints the ends of the bones are covered with smooth cartilage, which absorbs concussion and provides a smoother bearing for the ends of the bones. In freely movable joints the entire joint is inclosed in a fibrous sac, called the *joint capsule*, which assists the ligaments in holding the bones in position. Its inner surface is lined with a thin secreting membrane called the *synovial membrane*, which secretes a fluid called *synovia* or "joint water." Synovia is a clear and slightly yellowish fluid of much the appearance and consistency of the white of a watery egg. This fluid serves to lubricate the joint in the same way that oil lubricates a bearing. Normally the amount secreted is limited to only the actual amount necessary to prevent friction in the joint. In joints that are inflamed as a result of undue concussion or from other causes, the amount secreted is increased and results in a distention of the joint capsule. Where the capsule is not closely bound to the joint by the ligaments, the distended capsule will pouch out under the skin as a soft swelling. A bog spavin is an example, as are also certain windgalls. Wounds over a joint are always likely to be dangerous for they may have opened the joint cavity. When the joint cavity is opened the synovia flows from the wound and the synovial membrane is stimulated by the loss of the synovia to secrete more. This synovia pouring over the wound surface retards healing and the joint cavity becomes readily infected. An open joint is usually very painful and in a great many instances results in the permanent disability of the animal, even with the best possible care. The hock joint is most frequently opened by accidental injury.

**76. Joints of foreleg.**—The joints of the foreleg named in order from above downward are the *shoulder*, formed by the scapula and humerus; the *elbow*, formed by the humerus, radius and ulna; the *knee*, formed by the radius, carpal bones, and the three metacarpal bones; the *fetlock*, formed by the cannon bone or large metacarpal, two sesamoid bones, and the first phalanx or long pastern bone; the *pastern*, formed by the first and second phalanges (long and short pastern bones); and the *coffin*, formed by the second and third phalanges (short pastern and coffin bones) and the navicular bone.

**77. Joints of hind leg.**—The joints of the hind leg named in order from above downward are the *hip*, formed by the hip bone and femur; the *stifle*, formed by the femur, patella, and tibia; and the *hock*, formed by the tibia, the tarsal or hock bones, and the three metatarsal bones. The remaining joints of the hind legs are named and formed the same as the corresponding joints of the foreleg.

**78. Suspensory ligaments and check ligaments.**—In addition to the ligaments which form a part of the joints, there are certain other important body ligaments.

*a.* The *suspensory ligament* of the foreleg is a very strong, flat ligament arising from the back of the knee and upper end of the cannon bone and passing down the back of the leg, lying in the groove between the splint bones. A short distance above the fetlock the ligament divides into two diverging rounded branches, each branch attaching to the upper and outer part of its corresponding sesamoid bone and then passing downward and forward around the front of the long pastern bone to join its fellow in a point of union with the extensor tendon which attaches to the front of the coffin bone. From the lower part of the sesamoids, bands of ligament pass downward and attach to the back of the long and short pastern bones. From its nature of attachment, it is readily seen that the suspensory ligament is a remarkable sling-like or truss apparatus by which the fetlock is supported, concussion diminished, and the phalangeal axis mechanically held in its sloping position.

*b.* The *check ligament* is a short, strong ligament arising on the back of the upper end of the suspensory ligament, just below the knee, and passing downward and backward for a short distance to where it attaches to the *deep flexor tendon*, which passes down the back of the leg to a point of attachment on the under surface of the coffin bone. When the muscle above is relaxed, it is easily seen that the check ligament by its action really functionally converts the part of the tendon below the check ligament into a ligament which assists the general action of the suspensory ligament.

*c.* The suspensory ligament is considerably more elastic than are the binding ligaments of joints and by its supporting springlike action it absorbs a great deal of concussion. This ligament is most frequently injured in horses that do a great deal of their work at the gallop. The suspensory ligament in the hind leg is very similar to that of the foreleg, but the check ligament is much less perfectly developed.

**79. Plantar ligament.**—The *plantar ligament* is a strong band of ligamentous tissue on the back of the hock bones. It extends from the point of the hock to the upper end of the cannon bone and, by its strong attachments to the small hock bones, braces the hock against the strong pull of the tendon of Achilles. It is of particular importance because it is sometimes injured, resulting in the unsoundness known as *curb*.

**80. Ligamentum nuchae.**—The *ligamentum nuchae*, or ligament of the neck, is a fan-shaped ligament of very elastic tissue extending from the poll and upper surfaces of the cervical vertebrae backward to attach to the longest spines of the thoracic vertebrae (withers). It assists the muscles of the neck in maintaining the head and neck in position. It is of particular interest because the withers or poll is sometimes injured, resulting in the serious conditions of *fistulous withers* and *poll evil*.

**81. Muscular system.**—See paragraph 22.

**82. Structure and action of muscles.**—*a.* All voluntary muscles are composed of a *contractile* portion called the body or belly of the muscle and a *noncontractile* continuation called the *tendon* which is a modified continuation of one end of the body or contractile portion of the muscle. The contractile portion of the muscle is made up of many elongated muscle cells lying side by side lengthwise of the muscle, which when stimulated becomes shorter and thicker. The *tendon* of a muscle is in structure quite similar to that of a ligament and its function is to transmit the power of the muscle to some definite point of movement. The contractile portion has a large blood supply, but the blood supply of the denser tendons is rather limited.

*b.* The body of most muscles is attached to some bone and the point of attachment is called the *origin*, while the tendon may pass one or more joints and attach (*insertion*) to some other bone.

*c.* For almost every muscle or group of muscles having a certain general action, there is another muscle or group of muscles whose action is the exact opposite. The most important examples are the *extensor* and *flexor* muscles of the legs. A muscle is an *extensor* when its action is to extend a joint and bring the bones into aline-ment. A muscle is a *flexor* when its action is to bend the joint. Some muscles, if their points of origin and insertion are separated by two or more joints, may act as a flexor of one joint and an extensor of another joint. Except to establish fixation and rigidity of a part, such opposed muscles do not act simultaneously in opposition to each other, but act successively. There are hundreds of muscles in the body and their actions are very complex, but in this text we will consider only the general action of the important muscle groups.

**83. Tendon sheaths and bursae.**—Many muscles, especially those of the legs, have long tendons which pass one or more joints and undergo changes of direction or pass over bony prominences before reaching their point of insertion. To avoid undue friction at these points and to allow the muscle to act most efficiently, nature has supplied *tendon sheaths* and *tendon bursae* at various points of fric-tion along the course of the tendon. A *tendon sheath* is a synovail sac through which a tendon passes. The inside of the sac secretes synovia and lubricates the tendon. A *tendon bursae* is a synovial sac which is interposed between the tendon and the surface over which it passes in change of direction. It serves the same purpose as a tendon sheath but differs from it in that the tendon is not surrounded by the synovial sac. These tendon sheaths and tendon bursae are found chiefly near joints. The synovial membrane and synovia secreted are the same as those found in joints. Due to chronic ir-ritation from hard work or as a result of injury, the amount of sy-novia secreted may be greatly increased and result in a distension of the sac characterized externally by a circumscribed puffy swell-ing. Such swellings are often seen above the fetlocks where they are called wind puffs or windgalls. While they seldom cause distinct lameness, they are evidence of a so-called "second-handed" condition and indicate that the horse probably is a little stiffened and shortened in his gaits.

**84. Muscles of neck and attachment of foreleg.**—*a.* We have learned from the study of the skeleton that the foreleg of the horse has no bony connection with the remainder of the skeleton. The foreleg is attached to the body by a very complex system of muscles which extend from the leg along the side of the neck to the poll, upward to the withers, backward along the sides of the chest, and back and under the chest to meet at the sternum. The fore part of the horse is really suspended between two uprights, the forelegs, and by this elastic muscular sling a very efficient shock-absorbing mechanism is provided. As the forelegs bear from 9 to 20 percent more of the body weight than do the hind legs, it is easy to understand the importance of this muscular attachment, especially in the riding horse.

*b.* The long muscles that extend from the region of the shoulder to the sides of the neck and to the head are of special interest to the student of equitation, for the manner of the movement of the horse is profoundly influenced by their action. With the shoulders fixed these muscles by their action cause movement of the head and neck and, when the head and neck is fixed by opposing muscular action, these muscles act to advance the shoulder. With the head and neck extended, these muscles are most favorably placed for maximum extension of the shoulder and foreleg with a low and extended action. A high head carriage with shortening of the neck is most favorable for maximum elevation of the shoulder and foreleg, resulting in a higher and shortened stride. Much of the early training of the remount is directly aimed at gaining suppleness and control of the action of this group of muscles.

85. **Muscles of back, loin, and croup.**—The triangular space between the ribs, the transverse processes of the lumbar vertebrae, and the spines of the thoracic and lumbar vertebrae is filled with large muscles. The principal one of this group is the largest and longest muscle of the body, *longissimus dorsi*, extending from the posterior part of the loin along the back and down between the shoulder and thorax to the last cervical vertebrae. These muscles, one on each side, are used extensively when the horse elevates its hindquarters in kicking or when rearing. Acting singly, the muscles flex the vertebral column laterally. In the thoracic region, this muscular pad bears the weight of the saddle when the horse is ridden and distributes the weight evenly to the supporting ribs. The croup and thighs are made up of groups of powerful muscles which are the chief sources of propelling power.

86. **Muscles and tendons of lower leg.**—*a.* The extensor muscles of the foreleg attach mainly to the humerus and radius and lie on the front of the forearm.

(1) The *common digital extensor* originates on the lower end of the humerus and upper part of the radius. At the upper part of the knee the muscle continues as a tendon along the front of the knee, cannon, and pastern regions to its point of insertion on the upper end of the coffin bone. In the pastern region two branches of the suspensory ligament unite with the tendon. This muscle acts as extensor of all joints below the elbow but flexes the latter. This tendon is seldom injured.

(2) The *extensor of the knee* is a strong muscle attached to the humerus and lying on the front of the forearm, having a short heavy tendon which passes over the knee and attaches to the upper end of the cannon bone. It extends the knee joint and flexes the elbow. The tendon passes through a tendon sheath extending from the middle of the knee to about 4 inches above the knee. This region is often bruised in jumping horses, resulting in a synovial distention of the sheath commonly called "jumping knee." While unsightly, it seldom causes lameness.

*b.* The flexor muscles of the foreleg lie on the back of the forearm and like the extensors originate on the humerus, ulna, and radius.

(1) The *superficial digital flexor* originates on the lower end of the humerus and its fleshy portion extends to the lower part of the forearm and from that point continues as a flattened tendon which passes down the back of the leg and below the fetlock divides into two branches which are inserted on either side of the upper end of the short pastern bone. This muscle flexes the knee, fetlock, and pastern. The tendon lies just under the skin on the back of the leg and just back of the deep flexor tendon.

(2) The *deep digital flexor* originates with the superficial digital flexor. The body of the muscle lies on the back of the forearm and from just above the knee continues as the deep flexor tendon and passes down the back of the leg in front of the superficial flexor tendon, passes between the branches of the latter, and continues to its point of insertion on the under surface of the coffin bone. This muscle is the most powerful flexor of the foreleg. In the upper part of the cannon region, this tendon is joined by the check ligament (see par. 78). Where the tendon passes over the back of the sesamoid bones at the fetlock joint, it is inclosed in a tendon sheath. This sheath frequently becomes distended with synovia forming windgalls or wind puffs. This tendon also passes over a bursa where it glides over the navicular bone near the coffin joint, and injury to this bursa results in the condition known as *navicular disease.*

In the cannon region the two tendons described above appear to the eye as one large rounded tendon, but if the foot is raised and the structure examined with the fingers the separate tendons can be readily distinguished. These two muscles and their tendinous extensions, in addition to bringing about movements of the leg, act also as shock absorbing mechanisms. The strains to which they are subjected seldom injure the bodies or bellies of the muscles, but the tendons are not uncommonly injured by strain, particularly in the cannon region, and the resulting inflamed condition is known as *tendinitis*. Either or both tedons may be affected, the deep flexor most frequently.

*c.* The general arrangement and action of the extensor and flexor tendons of the hind leg from the hock joint downward are almost identical with those of the foreleg. Tendinitis in the hind legs is uncommon because of the lesser amount of weight borne and concussion absorbed. Distention of the tendon sheath at and just above the fetlock often occurs, but the navicular bursa is rarely diseased. The navicular bursa of the hind leg, as in the foreleg, is sometimes opened by a nail's penetrating from the under surface of the foot.

**87. Fatigue of muscles.**—*a.* Fatigue of the muscles follows continued work. This is due principally to the consumption of substances from which energy is derived and results in exhaustion. As soon as the accumulated waste products are removed by the blood and lymph, and a fresh supply of nutrition is brought to the muscles, a feeling of fitness again prevails. Hand-rubbing the legs of a horse is beneficial, because the blood and lymph vessels are stimulated to increased activity in the removal of waste products and cause the blood to circulate more freely. Fatigue may also be overcome, in part, by providing a feed of easily digested carbohydrates, which furnishes a maximum of energy.

*b.* A green horse, that is, one not accustomed to steady work, fatigues much more easily than a hardened horse. This is due to the muscles of the former being softer and possibly carrying an excess of fat. It should be remembered that there is a limit to continued muscular effort, and that harmful fatigue can be avoided only by working the horse at a moderate rate in order to keep the proper balance between the products of muscular activity and the ability of the blood to remove its waste material. An animal should never be worked until exhausted, if for no reason other than that it is not economical.

**88. Digestive system.**—The digestive system is really a muscular tube passing through the body and having two external openings, the mouth and the anus. This tube has a total length of about 100 feet, looped on itself many times, dilated at intervals along its course, and provided with several accessory organs. The entire tube is lined with *mucous membrane*. Mucous membrane is a modified form of skin, and this close relationship between the lining of the digestive tube and the covering of the body explains why digestive disturbances are often reflected in skin disturbances. The digestive organs are the *mouth, pharynx, esophagus, stomach, small intestine, large intestine,* and *rectum.* (See fig. 12.)

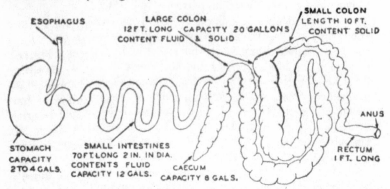

FIGURE 12.—Schematic diagram of digestive system (horse) (not drawn to constant scale).

**89. Mouth.**—The mouth extends from the lips to the pharynx. It is bound on the sides by the cheeks, above by the hard palate, and below by the tongue. Separating the mouth from the pharynx is the soft palate, a fleshy curtain suspended from the back part of the hard palate, which permits the passage of food and water from the mouth to the pharynx but prevents its passage in the opposite direction. The lips pick up loose feed and it is passed into the mouth by the action of the tongue. When the horse is grazing the feed is grasped with the incisor teeth. It is masticated or ground between the molar or cheek teeth and mixed with the *saliva.* The saliva is secreted into the mouth by the salivary glands, the largest of which is the *parotid* lying below the ear and back of the jaw. The horse is by nature a slow eater and requires from 15 to 20 minutes to eat a pound of hay and from 5 to 10 minutes to eat a pound of grain. Hay, when properly masticated, absorbs approximately four times its weight of saliva, and oats a little more than its weight. The saliva moistens and lubricates the mass for swallowing, and as a digestive juice acts on the starches and sugars. The ball of masticated feed, when ready for swallowing, is forced past the soft palate into the pharynx by the base of the tongue. Drinking is performed in the horse by drawing the tongue backward in the mouth, and thus using it as the piston of a suction pump. A horse usually swallows slightly less than one-half pint at each gulp, and the ears are drawn forward at each swallow and drop back during the interval between swallows.

**90. Pharynx.**—The *pharynx* is a short and somewhat funnel-shaped muscular tube between the mouth and esophagus and is also in part an air passage between the nasal cavities and the larynx. The muscular action of the pharynx forces the food into the esophagus. Food or water after entering the pharynx cannot return to the mouth because of the trap-like action of the soft palate and for the same reason a horse cannot breathe through the mouth. Food or water returned from the pharynx passes out through the nostrils.

**91. Esophagus.**—The *esophagus* is a muscular tube extending from the pharynx down the left side of the neck and through the thoracic cavity and diaphragm to the stomach. The swallow of food or water is forced down the esophagus to the stomach by a progressive wave of constriction of the circular muscles of the organ. In the horse this wave of constriction cannot move in the reverse direction and vomiting is not possible. The return of food or water through the nostrils is almost a certain indication that the horse is choked and the esophagus is blocked by a mass of food.

**92. Stomach.**—The *stomach* is a U-shaped muscular sack which lies in the front part of the abdominal cavity and close to the diaphragm. The esophageal and intestinal openings are close together and for this reason water passes rather quickly through the stomach and small intestine to the first of the large intestines, the caecum, sometimes known as the water gut. Considering the size of the animal and the amount of food consumed, the stomach of the horse is relatively very small. The horse in his natural state was a slow but more or less constant eater and did not require a stomach of great storage capacity. The maximum capacity of the stomach is 3 to 4 gallons but it functions most efficiently when it does not contain over 2½ gallons. These facts have a decided influence on our methods of feeding. The small size of the stomach makes it imperative that food be given in relatively small amounts and at frequent intervals. Overloading of the stomach not only lowers its efficiency as a digestive organ but, by pressure against the diaphragm, makes breathing more difficult. The food on entering the stomach is arranged in layers, the end next to the small intestine filling first. The digestive process begins immediately upon receipt of food but no food leaves the stomach until it has been filled to about two-thirds of its capacity. While the animal continues to eat, the partially digested food passes out into the small intestine in a continuous stream. As a result two to three times the capacity of the stomach may pass out during a bulky meal. The emptying process slows up only when feeding stops. The stomach never is completely empty except after complete withholding of food for 1 or 2 days. The contents of the stomach are squeezed and pressed by the muscular activity of the organ but its contents are never churned. The digestive juice secreted by the walls of the stomach is called gastric juice, an acid fluid containing the active digestive enzyme called pepsin which acts on the protein in the food. Some digested food is absorbed by the stomach but as a whole stomach digestion is partial preparatory digestion for more complete digestion in the intestines. The consumption of any considerable quantity of water during the period of stomach digestion tends to disarrange the layering of the food in the stomach and causes as much as one-half of the stomach contents to be washed into the small intestine. For this reason the horse should be *watered first and fed afterward*, unless he is allowed free access to water during his meal. As the food tends to leave the stomach in the order of its receipt, it is advisable to *feed some hay before feeding grain* so that the grain, being held longer in the stomach, undergoes more complete digestion.

**93. Small intestine.**—The *small intestine* is a tube about 70 feet in length, extending from the stomach to the caecum. The small intestine is about 2 inches in diameter and just after leaving the stomach is arranged in a distinct U-shaped curve which in the horse seems to prevent food returning to the stomach after it has once entered the intestine and also tends to close the opening into the intestine when the stomach is over-distended with food. The small intestine lies in folds and coils near the left flank and is suspended from the region of the loin by an extensive fan-shaped membrane called the mesentery. The partially digested food in the small intestine is always quite fluid in character and seems to pass rather rapidly through this part of the digestive tract. Digestion is continued in the small intestine by the action of the bile and pancreatic juice which are secreted by the liver and pancreas, respectively. Some digested food is absorbed in the small intestine.

**94. Large intestine.**—The large intestine is divided into the *caecum, large colon, small colon, rectum,* and *anus.*

*a.* The *caecum* is a large, elongated sack extending from high in the right flank downward and forward to the region of the diaphragm. The openings from the small intestine and to the large colon are close together in the upper end of the organ. This organ is sometimes known as the "water gut" for the reason that water passes rather quickly to the caecum and because its contents are always liquid. Digestion is continued in the caecum and some food is absorbed.

*b*. The *large colon* is about 12 feet in length and has a diameter of 10 to 12 inches. It extends from the caecum to the small colon. This organ is usually distended with food; the greater part of digestion of food by the digestive juices and bacterial action take place in this part of the digestive tract and the greater part of absorption of digested food occurs.

*c*. The *small colon* is about 10 feet in length and 4 inches in diameter and extends from the large colon to the rectum. The contents of the small colon are solid and here the balls of dung are formed.

*d*. The *rectum* is that part of the digestive tract about 12 inches in length extending from the small colon through the pelvic cavity to the *anus*, which is the terminal part of the digestive tract.

**95. Organs of respiration.**—The organs of respiration comprise the *nasal cavity, pharynx, larynx, trachea, bronchi*, and *lungs*. The lungs are the essential organs of respiration; all of the other parts simply act as passages for the air to and from them.

*a*. The *nasal cavity* is bounded by the facial bones and begins at the nostrils, which are held open by cartilages. It is divided into halves by the cartilaginous nasal septum. Each half is partially filled with the thin turbinated bones, which are covered with a very vescular mucous coat. This coat serves to warm the inspired air.

*b*. The *pharynx*, as described before, is common to both the respiratory and digestive tracts.

*c*. The *larynx* is a short tube-like organ situated between the pharynx and the trachea. It regulates the amount of air passing to and from the lungs and helps to prevent the aspiration of foreign bodies. It is the seat of that common disease of the horse known as "roaring", which is a paralysis of the muscles controlling the vocal cords.

*d*. The *trachea* is a long tube connecting the larynx with the lungs and is located in the lower median border of the neck. It is composed of a series of cartilaginous rings held together by elastic fibrous material.

*e*. The *bronchi* are the branches of the trachea which connect the trachea with the lungs. They, in turn, branch into minute tubes, which penetrate every part of the lung tissue.

*f*. The *lungs* are two in number and nearly fill the thoracic cavity. The lung tissue is pinkish in color and will float in water. The lung is made up of innumerable air cells having thin elastic walls which contain capillaries of the pulmonary circulation. This elasticity of the lung tissue permits the organ to contract and expand in the act of respiration. Heaves is caused by a breaking down of the walls of some of the air cells, with attendant loss of elasticity in that part of the lung.

**96. Physiology of respiration.**—Respiration is the act of breathing and is the most vital function of animals. It consists of an exchange of the oxygen in the air for the carbon dioxide in the blood and an interchange of these gases between the blood and the body tissues. The former is external respiration and the latter is internal respiration. External respiration consists of two movements, inspiration and expiration. Inspiration is brought about by a contraction of the diaphragm and an outward rotation of the ribs. Expiration is effected by relaxation of these muscles and contraction of rib and abdominal muscles. The abdominal muscles are used extensively in labored breathing. Since the diaphragm plays such an important part in the respiration movement, it follows that the distention of the digestive tract with bulky food materially interferes with normal breathing, especially when the animal is subjected to fast gaits. The lungs of the average horse contain, when freely distended, 1½ cubic feet of air. The normal horse at rest breathes from 8 to 16 times per minute, and inhales at each respiration approximately 250 cubic inches of air. A horse, while walking, nearly trebles the number of normal respirations, but the normal rate is regained in a very few minutes after the horse stops. If the animal breathes 10 times a minute, during repose, the whole lung is ventilated about once a minute. The amount of air required by the horse depends upon the extent of muscular work being performed. The following table shows the mean amount of expired air obtained from horses at various gaits:

| Gait | Cubic feet expired per hour |
|---|---|
| Repose | 74. 17 |
| Walk | 133. 55 |
| Trot | 287. 87 |
| Canter | 391. 00 |
| Gallop | 849. 10 |

**97. Organs of circulation.**—The organs concerned with the circulation of blood and lymph are the *heart, arteries, veins, capillaries, lymph vessels,* and *lymph glands.*

*a.* The *heart,* the central organ of the system, is situated in the left half of the thorax, between the lungs and opposite the third to sixth ribs. In the ordinary-sized horse, it weighs from 7 to 8 pounds. It is inclosed in a sero-fibrous sac called the pericardium. The heart is divided into four cavities, separated by muscular walls and valves. The action of the heart is to receive the blood and to pump it out to the lungs and body tissues.

*b*. The *arteries* have rather thick elastic walls and carry the blood from the heart to the tissues of the body.

*c*. The *veins* have much thinner walls and, in many cases, are equipped with valves to prevent the blood from flowing back. They carry the blood from the tissues to the heart. The veins of the legs afford an excellent example of valves in veins.

*d*. The *capillaries* are microscopic in size and function as connecting tubes between the arteries and veins. It is through the capillaries that the interchange of oxygen and food between the blood and tissues takes place.

*e*. The *lymphatics* consist of numerous well-defined groups of lymph glands and connecting vessels which are closely related to the arteries. The vessels all unite eventually to form one large duct, which is parallel to the aorta (main artery from the heart) and empties into one of the veins. The lymph glands are located at strategic places along the main vessels and act as filters for the lymph. They assume considerable importance in some diseases; strangles is one disease affecting these organs. The lymph assists in carrying food from the digestive tract to the body and transporting waste back to the blood stream.

**98. Physiology of circulation.**—The heart movements are controlled by an intricate group of nerves. The heart beat is the combined cycle of contraction and relaxation of the organ. In the normal horse at rest, the heart beats from 36 to 40 times per minute. The pulse rate is determined by counting the rate of pulsations in some artery that is easily palpitated; for example, the one at the angle of the lower jaw. The pressure and rate of flow in the veins is very slow when compared with that in the arteries. It is aided by the respiratory movements and muscular contractions. From these facts it is seen that good circulation is made possible by exercise. While the left side of the heart carries on the body circulation the right side pumps impure blood to the lungs to be purified before it returns to the left side of the heart for return to the body tissues. This latter is known as the pulmonary circulation.

**99. Blood.**—The blood is a red alkaline fluid, composed of blood plasma and red and white corpuscles. It clots almost immediately when exposed to the air. The total amount is about one-fourteenth the weight of the body. The white corpuscles are active agents in combating disease germs in the body. The red corpuscles originate in the red bone marrow, liver, and spleen. They carry oxygen from the lungs to the tissues, convey waste away from the tissues, distribute heat, assist in regulating the temperature, and neutralize or destroy bacterial invaders.

**100. Nervous system.**—The nervous system is made up of the brain, spinal cord, ganglia, and nerves, and is the communication system of the body.

*a.* The *brain* and *spinal cord* are the most important parts of the nervous system and are known as the central nervous system. The brain lies in the cranial cavity of the skull. Compared with the size of the animal the brain of the horse is relatively small considering the relative brain size of other animals. Relative size of brain to size of body cannot be considered as an absolute indication of the degree of reasoning intelligence; however, there is a distinct correlation. The horse has been considered as occupying about a midway position in the scale of intelligence of the domesticated animals. The *spinal cord* continues from the brain back through the spinal canal of the vertebral column. The central nervous system might be likened to the switchboard of a telephone system, for it is the directing center of the system which receives and dispatches nerve messages.

*b.* The *ganglia* are secondary nerve centers located chiefly along the spinal cord and might be likened to a subexchange in a telephone system. They receive and dispatch nerve impulses which do not of necessity have to reach the brain. Together with their communicating nerves, they control the involuntary muscles, vital organs, and reflex actions.

*c.* The *nerves* are bands of white tissue emanating from the central nervous system and ganglia and extending to all parts of the body. In general they follow closely the course of the arteries. There are two kinds of nerves, those that convey sensation to the central system, and those that carry back the command impulses of the central nervous system. The nerves may be compared to the wire lines of the telephone system and the large nerves, like the telephone cable, contain many separate lines.

**101. Skin.**—*a.* The skin is the covering tissue that acts as a protection to the surface of the body. Wherever the chance of injury is the greatest, the skin is the thickest; in those parts where sensibility is most required, it is the thinnest. The skin of the back, quarters, and limbs are examples of the first type. An especially heavy protective covering is found on the back. In some horses, this covering is as much as one-quarter of an inch in thickness. The face, muzzle, and those parts not exposed to violence, for example, inside the forearm and thighs, have very thin skin. In spite of this thinness, its strength is remarkable. It is highly sensitive, because it is highly endowed with sensory nerve endings. Accessory organs of feeling are the tactile hairs on the muzzle and the eyelashes. The skin is easily irritated and the horse is endowed with the power of shaking the skin to relieve himself from slight irritations, such as flies. This is accomplished by the aid of the skin muscle (*panniculus carnosus*), which is a thin muscular layer lying directly underneath the skin and attached to it. In health, the skin feels pliable and elastic. The skin of the horse is black except on those parts of the body covered by white hairs where it is white or pinkish in color.

*b.* The skin is divided into two layers:

(1) The epidermis, or outer portion, is nonvascular and contains the openings for the sweat and sebaceous glands and hair follicles.

(*a*) The sebaceous glands are well distributed over the whole surface of the body and secrete an oily fluid. The oily fluid thus produced serves as a protective secretion against the disintegrating influence of water on the skin; to keep the skin supple; to give gloss to well-groomed skin; to prevent penetration of rain; and to save, to some extent, undue loss of heat.

(*b*) The involuntary muscle fibers are attached to the hair roots which cause the hair to stand up when the horse is cold.

(2) The dermis, or inner portion, is a vascular structure and is closely adherent to the underlying fat and skin muscles. It contains:

(*a*) The nerve endings which give to the skin the sense of touch.

(*b*) The hair follicles which grow the necessary hairs.

(*c*) The sweat glands which discharge sweat directly on the surface of the skin. Sweat is a watery, salty, alkaline fluid of characteristic horse-like odor. It serves to keep the skin moist, remove waste, and help regulate the body temperature by evaporation. It is not found to occur over the general surface of the body in any hairy animal other than the horse. The secretion of sweat is continuous. Certain parts of the skin sweat more readily than others. It begins first at the base of the ears, then the neck; the side of chest and back follow. No sweating takes place on the legs. There are two kinds of sweating, namely, insensible, which evaporates as fast as it is formed, and sensible, which is the visible fluid that collects on the skin when the secretion is rapid. The evaporation of sweat from the surface of the skin is a most important source of loss of body heat. Through sweating there is also a loss of protein substance and of mineral matter. Horses that have sweated freely show this, when dry, by a grayish covering on the hairs, resembling fine sand. The loss thus produced accounts for the general reduction of vitality in some horses. For this, clipping is the only preventive. Sweating usually results from work or exercise but may appear as a result of nervousness or excitement. After hard work, horses that have been thoroughly groomed and dried sometimes break out in what is known as a second sweat. This usually indicates extreme fatigue or nervousness and that the horse has not been thoroughly cooled out. Patchy sweating, or sweating continuously in a certain localized area, is sometimes observed. The cause is not definitely known.

**102. Hair.**—Hair covers most of the skin, exceptions being the anal region, genitals, insides of thighs and deep inside of the ear. Even in these regions a few short hairs appear. Hair forms the clothing of the body and its growth is determined by the surrounding temperature. The permanent hair of the body is the hair of the mane and tail, eyelashes, long tactile hairs around the muzzle, and the long hair on the back of the fetlock. The permanent hair is not shed. The general body coat of hair is temporary and is shed twice yearly, spring and fall. The time of shedding is governed by weather conditions or temperature in which the horse is kept. The vitality of the horse seems to be somewhat lowered incident to shedding the coat. This particularly is true during the spring shedding and at this time the skin is much more susceptible to eruptions, irritations, and infections. Mixed sparsely with the general body coat of hair, there will be found a few longer and more rapidly growing hairs that are known as "cat hairs." These hairs are most readily observed when appearing in the growth of the coat following clipping.

**103. Parts of foot.**—The horse's foot is composed of four parts:

*a.* The bones.

*b.* Certain elastic structures of cartilage, or gristle.

*c.* A layer of highly sensitive flesh or quick, the corium, which covers this bony and elastic framework.

*d.* The box, or case of horn, called the hoof, which incloses and protects the sensitive parts.

**104. Bones of pastern and foot.**—The bones of the pastern region and foot form a column extending downward from the fetlock joint into the hoof and are named as follows: the *long pastern bone*, the *short pastern bone*, the *coffin bone*, and the *navicular bone*.

*a.* The *long pastern bone* extends from the fetlock joint above to the pastern joint below. Its upper end joins, or articulates, with the lower end of the cannon bone, forming the fetlock joint. Its lower end articulates with the upper end of the short pastern bone, forming the pastern joint.

*b.* The *short pastern bone* follows the direction of the long pastern bone downward and forward and lies between the pastern and coffin joints, its lower end being within the hoof.

*c.* The *coffin bone* is of irregular shape, is situated within the hoof, and is similar to the hoof in shape.

(1) The surface of the front and sides is known as the *wall surface*. It has a number of small openings for the passage of blood vessels and nerves and is roughened to give attachment to the sensitive *laminae* which cover it.   On each side of this surface is a groove running forward to an opening, through which an artery and a nerve enter the bone and a vein leaves it.

(2) At the top of this surface, in front, is a projection called the *extensor process*, to which is attached the extensor tendon of the foot. On each side of the coffin bone is an extension to the rear called the wing.   The lateral cartilages are attached to the outer and upper borders of the wings and the ends of the navicular bone are attached to the inner surface.

(3) The lower surface of the coffin bone, called the *sole surface*, is concave, half-moon shaped and smooth, except at the back part, which is roughened for the attachment of the deep flexor tendon of the foot. It is called the *tendinous surface*.   The upper surface, called the *articular surface*, articulates with the short pastern bone and navicular bone and with them forms the coffin joint.

*d.* The *navicular bone* is of irregular shape.   It is situated behind and below the short pastern bone and behind the coffin bone, forming a joint with both.   The extremities of the bone are attached to the wings of the coffin bone.   The lower surface is covered with cartilage, which forms a smooth surface for the movement of the deep flexor tendon, which bends the joint.   Because of its shape the bone is frequently called the shuttle bone.

**105. Elastic structures of foot.**—All the structures of the foot, except the bones, are more or less elastic or springy, and yield when pressure is applied, but certain parts have a very high degree of elasticity, their special use being to overcome the effects of concussion or jar when the foot strikes the ground, and to prevent injury.   These parts are the *lateral cartilages* and the *plantar cushion.*

*a.* The *lateral cartilages* are two large elastic plates of cartilage, one attached to the top of each wing of the coffin bone.   They extend backward and upward so far that their borders may be felt under the skin above the coronet at the heels.

*b.* The *plantar cushion* is a very elastic wedge-shaped pad, which fills up the space between the lateral cartilages on the sides, the frog below, and the deep flexor tendon of the foot above. The point, or front part, of the plantar cushion extends forward to the ridge, which separates the sole surface from the tendinous surface of the coffin bone, and lies just below the lower end of the deep flexor tendon. The base, or back part, is covered by the skin above the heels. If the frog comes in contact with the ground when the foot is planted, the plantar cushion acts as a buffer and prevents jar.

**106. Sensitive structures of foot.**—Over the bones and elastic parts of the foot is found a complete covering of very sensitive flesh called the corium. From each part of this layer of flesh some portion of the hoof is secreted or grown. The sensitive parts are the *coronary band*, the *perioplic ring*, the *sensitive laminae*, the *sensitive sole*, and the *sensitive frog.*

*a.* The *coronary band* is a thick band of tough flesh, nearly an inch wide, extending entirely around the top of the hoof from one bulb to the other, and lying in a groove called the coronary groove on the inner surface of the wall at its upper border. The surface of the coronary band is covered with small hair-like projections, called villi, from which is grown the horny wall of the hoof.

*b.* The *perioplic ring* is a narrow band of flesh running around just above the coronary band and separated from it by a faint groove in the wall. From the fine villi on the surface of this ring the delicate fibers grow which form the *periople* or varnish-like horn covering of the hoof which assists in the prevention of evaporation of moisture from the wall.

*c.* The *sensitive laminae*, or fleshy leaves, cover and are firmly attached to the wall surface of the coffin bone and to the lower part of the outer surface of the lateral cartilages. From these delicate leaves of flesh grow the *horny laminae*, or inside lining of the horny wall.

*d.* The *sensitive sole* covers the sole surface of the coffin bone, is covered with villi, and grows the horny sole.

*e.* The *sensitive frog* covers the lower surface of the plantar cushion and from its villi the horny frog is secreted.

**107. Hoof.**—The *hoof* is the outer horny covering of the foot. It is divided into three parts, the *wall*, *sole*, and *frog*. In the healthy foot these parts are firmly united.

*a.* The *wall*, except the bar, extends from the edge of the hair to the ground and is divided into the *toe*, *quarters*, and *buttress*.

(1) The *toe* is the front part of the wall. It is steeper in the hind foot than in the fore.

(2) The *quarter* extends backward on each side from the toe to the buttress.

(3) The *buttress* is the back part of the heel and may be defined as the angle formed by the union of the wall and bar.

(4) The *bar* is that part of the wall which extends inward and forward from the buttress to within about an inch of the point of the frog. The hoof is thus made stronger by the ends of the wall extending inward to form the bars. The bars are weight carriers, and they also act directly on the wall to produce expansion when weight is placed on the frog.

(5) The outer surface of the wall is covered by a thin varnish-like coat of fine horn, called *periople*. The inner surface is covered with from 500 to 600 *laminae*. These are thin plates of horn running downward and forward. Between them are fissures into which dovetail the sensitive laminae. The horny laminae and the sensitive laminae are firmly united. This union binds the wall of the hoof to the coffin bone and its cartilages, suspends the weight of the horse from the wall as in a sling, and thus prevents the bones from descending on the sole.

(6) On the upper border of the wall is the coronary groove, in which lies the coronary band. The lower border is known as the *bearing surface*. It is the part that comes in contact with the ground in the unshod foot and to which the shoe is fitted in the shod foot.

*b.* The *horny sole* is a thick plate of horn, somewhat half-moon shaped.

(1) The upper surface is arched upward and is in union with the sensitive sole from which the horny sole grows. The lower surface is hollowed and is covered with scales or crusts of dead horn, which gradually loosen and fall off.

(2) The outer border of the sole is joined to the inner part of the lower border of the wall by a ring of soft horn called the *white line*. This line shows where the nail should be started in shoeing.

(3) The inner border is V-shaped and is in union with the bars, except where the sole joins the point of the frog. The sole protects the sensitive parts above.

*c.* The *frog* is a wedge-shaped mass filling the V-shaped space between the bars and sole and extending downward more or less below the bars.

(1) The lower surface has two prominent ridges, separated behind by a cavity called the *cleft*, and joining in front at the point

of the frog. These ridges terminate behind in the *bulbs* of the
frog. Between the sides of the frog and the bars are two cavities
called the *commissures*.

(2) The upper surface of the frog is the exact reverse of the lower.
It has in the middle a ridge of horn called the *frog stay*, which assists
in forming a firm union between the horny and sensitive frog.

(3) The function of the frog is to assist the plantar cushion in
breaking the jar or concussion, to prevent slipping, and to produce
expansion and contraction upon which the normal blood circulation
in the foot depends.

**108. Dissipation of concussion.**—The concussion borne by the
foot is lessened by a combination of functions of its varied structures.
When the weight of the horse is transmitted down the bony column
of the leg, the following things take place: Except possibly at the
walk, the weight, or at least a great portion of the weight, is first
received by the frog. The frog spreads and moves the bars outward,
carrying the heels and the posterior part of the quarters outward.
Simultaneously, the frog transmits the jar to the plantar cushion,
which spreads and carries the lateral cartilages outward. The frog
and plantar cushion, by virtue of their elasticity, receive the major
portion of the jar. At the same time the weight is initially borne
by the wall and the bars. The end of the bony column is hung in
a sling in the wall and bars by the dovetailing of the sensitive laminae
into the horny laminae. As the weight comes downward, these
leaves give way slightly and allow the coffin bone to approach the
ground; this in turn causes the sole to be somewhat lowered. The
arrangement of the deep flexor tendon over to the navicular bone
affords a means by which a portion of the shock is absorbed. The
spreading movement of the elastic structures is known as *expansion*.
When the weight is removed, these structures return to their normal
positions. This is known as *contraction*.

**109. Blood supply.**—The sensitive structures, especially the
corium, are highly vascular and filled with a network of veins. The
arterial circulation is sufficient unto itself, but the venous circulation receives a mechanical aid from the movements of the foot.
When contraction takes place, the plexuses fill with blood; later,
during expansion, the blood is forced out of the veins. These movements of the foot materially aid in the circulation.

**110. Moisture.**—The horn is made up of a network of tubules
that are cemented together. The moisture is contained primarily
in these tubules. It is derived internally from the blood supply
and externally from moist standings and the soil. The natural hard-

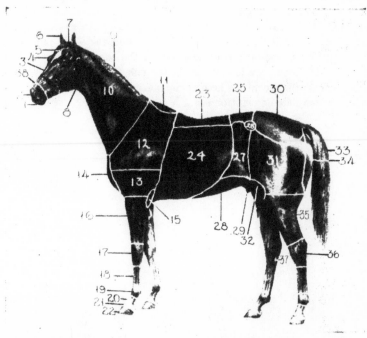

1. Lips, upper and lower.
2. Nostril.
3. Face. From muzzle to a line connecting inner corners of eyes. Bounded on sides by lines from outer corners of eyes to corresponding nostril.
4. Eye. Includes eyelids.
5. Forehead. From upper border of face to poll. Bounded on sides by line from outer corner of eye to base of ear.
6. Ears.
7. Poll. Prominence between the ears.
8. Throat.
9. Crest. Upper border of neck bearing the name.
10. Neck.
11. Withers.
12. Shoulder.
13. Arm.
14. Breast. A single region bounded by the neck, region of the arm, and below by horizontal line at level of elbow joint.
15. Elbow. Corresponds to ulna.
16. Forearm.

17. Knee. Corresponds to knee joint.
18. Cannon.
19. Fetlock or fetlock joint.
20. Pastern.
21. Coronet. Corresponds to coronary band.
22. Hoof.
23. Back.
24. Costal region.
25. Loin.
26. Point of hip.
27. Flank.
28. Abdomen or belly.
29. Sheath.
30. Croup.
31. Thigh.
32. Stifle. Corresponds to stifle joint.
33. Tail.
34. Buttocks.
35. Leg.
36. Hock.
37. Chestnut. (Also on foreleg above knee.)
38. Muzzle. Includes lips, nostrils, and nose, or space between the nostrils.

FIGURE 13.—External regions of horse.

ness of the horn and the periople on the wall serve to prevent undue evaporation. The wall is about one-fourth water, the sole one-third, and the frog one-half water.

111. **External regions of horse.**—In order to insure a uniformity of phraseology for various official papers, and for other purposes of description, a standard nomenclature of the external regions of the horse has been developed which is generally used by horsemen throughout the world. These regions are shown in figure 13. (For a more complete description see AR 40–2250.)

# Minor Surgery and Medical Aid

## Section I

## OPERATING ROOM AND SURGICAL TECHNIQUE

**112. Operating room.**—*a.* By operating room is usually meant not only the room or rooms where operations are actually performed, but all the other rooms connected and associated with them, all of which constitute the operating suite. This section of a hospital is a most important place, and upon its equipment and care depends to a considerable extent the success or failure of an operation. Surgeons may, however, be required by necessity to perform operations under conditions far from satisfactory in combat. However, whenever possible, operations of a major character should be performed in hospitals where the patient can be safeguarded by all possible aseptic conditions.

*b.* The administration of the operating room is one of the duties of the chief of the surgical service. He issues the necessary instructions to nurses and attendants regarding procedures and technique.

*c.* The operating suite of a modern hospital should be in a location as free from miscellaneous hospital traffic and noises as possible. It consists of the operating room or rooms and various accessory compartments arranged in a convenient order. There are usually at least two operating rooms so that one is always ready for use while the other is being cleaned or repaired, the main room being used for clean surgery and the other one for the dirty or pus cases. In an emergency both may be used simultaneously.

*d.* The actual size of an operating room should be determined by the number and character of operations to be performed and the space available; it should be large enough to prevent crowding, yet not so large that it is difficult to clean, ventilate, or heat.

**113. Lighting.**—When natural light is used, a northern exposure is preferable because there is less variation in the intensity of the light from that direction. However, if large north windows are used in a cold climate, one must consider the danger of placing the operating table too close to the window. Little dependence is now placed on natural light, since artificial light is much more dependable and easily controlled. Overhead adjustable top lights are now made with the rays focused from a number of reflectors to reduce shadows on the field of operation to a minimum. These are even more effective when the new spot-beam portable light is used in conjunction with them. Emergency lights are also available to work with batteries should the electric current fail.

**114. Heating and ventilation.**—The temperature of the operating room is kept at about 80° F. during operations and the ventilating system should be capable of maintaining this temperature during the coldest weather likely to occur in the locality. Many of the modern hospitals are equipped with an air-conditioning unit. Direct or natural ventilation is used chiefly in small hospitals, and must be as nearly perfect as possible. Fresh, clean, warm, moist air should be constantly provided and drafts avoided.

**115. Equipment.**—*a.* An operating table with all accessories, adjustable as to height and the various standard positions, is desirable, but this type of table is expensive, and quite as good work may be performed on one of a simple design, provided proper forethought is given the type of operation and the required position of the patient. On the table there should be a soft pad about 1½ inches thick covered with rubber sheeting and over all a linen sheet. In addition to the operating table but few pieces are necessary. There should be two or three tables with glass or polished metal tops, preferably metal, for surgical dressings and instruments to be used during the operation; one single and one double hand basin stand; an irrigating stand; two enamel buckets and a set of glass shelves for solutions, ligatures, drains, pins, etc. All the operating room equipment should be of simple, sturdy, easily cleaned design and should be painted with a durable white enamel.

*b.* Each table in the operating room holds certain specified articles placed in a definite way so that no time is lost in hunting for the desired article.

(1) On the large table are kept special instruments, reserve instruments, reserve sutures, and linen. At the far end is laid out the preparation equipment for sterilization of the operative field.

(2) There is a basin stand near the foot of the operating table within easy reach of the instrument nurse containing sterile water for dipping the suture materials or for soaking tape sponges.

(3) The instrument tray or table which extends over the operating table holds instruments arranged in regular order. This table routinely holds knives, various scissors, plain and toothed thumb forceps, curved and straight hemostats, Allis forceps, Kocher forceps, gauze sponges, stick sponges, various retractors, probes, and grooved directors.

(4) A stand with a hand basin for sterile water is behind the surgeon for rinsing his gloves during the operation if necessary.

(5) Conveniently located, either in the scrub room or in the operating room near the entrance from the scrub room, are placed basins for solutions to sterilize the previously scrubbed hands of the surgeon and assistants.

(6) A table is provided near the entrance from the scrub room to hold sterile gloves and gowns.

(7) The anesthetist's table for general anesthesia, in addition to the articles necessary for the administration of the anesthetic and an extra supply of the anesthetic, should have the following equipment on it and immediately available for use in an emergency:

(*a*) Wooden mouth gag.

(*b*) Tongue forceps.

(*c*) A curved needle threaded with silk, sterilized, and in a sterile package.

(*d*) Sterile hypodermic syringes with the following drugs in sterile solution in appropriate containers:

Caffeine sodium benzoate.

Atropine sulfate.

Epinephrine hydrochloride (adrenalin).

(*e*) Tracheotomy set.

(*f*) Gauze strips.

(*g*) Forceps (to hold gauze sponge).

(*h*) Watch or small clock.

(*i*) Pus basin.

(*j*) Blood-pressure apparatus.

(*k*) Stethoscope.

(*l*) Anesthetist's chart.

This equipment should be within easy reach and it should be unnecessary to ask for any of these important articles during anesthesia, as delay in meeting an emergency may result in disaster. Some cases require washing out of stomach during or upon completion of operation. It is essential, therefore, that a stomach tube and Levine tube be available in the operating room.

**116. Cleanliness.**—The walls and floor of the operating room are usually built of waterproof material with a smooth surface and so constructed that sharp, dirt-collecting angles are avoided. The floor should be washed daily with soap and warm water and all surfaces that might collect dust wiped with a damp cloth, the glass-topped tables, that are usually draped sterile, being wiped with a cloth dampened with alcohol. Once a week the walls are thoroughly scrubbed with soap and water, special care being taken to scrub and clean all corners and crevices. Blood or other stains that may get on the floor during an operation should be removed as quickly as possible, and, if a second operation is to be performed immediately, the floor, if necessary, should be cleansed by hand.

**117. Adjoining rooms.**—The rooms, other than those used for operating, that comprise the operating suite are usually the anesthetizing room, the wash or scrub-up room, the sterilizing room, the instrument room, the surgical dressings room, the storeroom, and the utility room.

*a.* The anesthetizing room is suitably equipped for the administration of anesthetics.

*b.* In the wash or scrub-up room there should be at least two lavatories, with foot or knee control for the hot and cold water, a shower bath and toilet, and clothes lockers for the use of the surgeon and his assistants when they change into operating suits. It is well also to have in this room a basin stand for the solutions used to disinfect the hands after the preliminary scrubbing, in order that the surgeon and his assistants can receive their operating gowns and proceed without delay.

*c.* The sterilizing room is provided with all equipment necessary to sterilize properly instruments, utensils, dressings, water, etc. Despite the fact that this equipment is sturdily constructed, constant care must be taken that it is always in working condition and the printed directions furnished by the manufacturers exactly observed. Operation of this equipment will not be intrusted to an inexperienced or careless person, thereby endangering the lives of patients.

*d.* An instrument room, while not a necessity, is advantageous. However, as a rule, unless the clinic is large, suitably designed glass cabinets placed in the surgical-dressings room will suffice.

*e.* The surgical-dressings room should be constructed similarly to the operating room. In this room are made, prepared, and stored, after sterilization, the various surgical dressings and packages of linen, such as gowns, sheets, towels, etc., used in operations. Here cleanliness is of paramount importance. Ample locker and shelf space should be provided, and also a large smooth-topped work table.

*f.* There should be a storeroom solely for the storage of operating room supplies. Much valuable time may be lost unless such a room is provided and kept fully stocked for emergencies.

*g.* The utility room, in which all cleaning equipment used in the operating suite is stored, should have in it a large, deep sink with running hot and cold water, in which the linen used during operations may be soaked and the greater part of blood stains removed before sending to the laundry. The utility room is an integral part of the operating room equipment, and as such must be scrupulously cared for.

**118. Surgical technique.**—*a.* Before an operation, it is necessary to make sterile and to keep sterile the patient's skin, the hands and clothing of the surgeon and his assistants, and all instruments and materials that come in contact with the wound or are handled by the surgeon and his assistants.

*b.* During the operation the surgeon and his assistants must not touch anything that is not sterile. A great responsibility rests upon the operating room personnel, because the most perfect surgery may be a complete failure if there is the smallest break in the aseptic technique for which they are responsible.

*c.* By aseptic surgery is meant that mode of surgical practice in which everything used at the time of operation and at subsequent dressings, as well as the wound, is free from pathogenic bacteria and is sterile, or surgically clean. To maintain that condition requires constant vigilance before, during, and after an operation, and no failure of technique, however trivial, must be allowed to pass uncorrected.

*d.* Infection is the word used to describe the condition which exists when infectious organisms gain access to the tissues of the body in such numbers that their presence is manifested by characteristic symptoms, such as inflammation, suppuration, putrefaction, etc.

*e.* Inflammation is the first objective or outward symptom of infection and is characterized by local pain, heat, redness, swelling, and disordered function. The general or subjective symptoms of inflammation vary greatly, depending upon the amount and location of the tissues involved, the physical condition of the patient, and the disease-producing power of the infecting organism. Fever is the most constant subjective symptom of inflammation, but it may be so slight that it escapes notice or it may be so severe that recovery of the patient seems doubtful. Aseptic treatment and careful observation of wounds is imperative, in order to prevent infection, and if infection does occur it may be recognized promptly and appropriately treated.

*f.* Suppuration is the result of inflammation and is due to the liquefying action of pyogenic (pus-producing) organisms on the exudates of tissues damaged by inflammation and also upon the tissues themselves, forming pus.

*g.* When a wound has become so infected that the inflammation does not subside and pus forms, it is termed a "septic" wound. Frequently, as a result of the passage of bacteria from a septic wound into the blood stream or of the absorption of the toxins (poisons) elaborated by the bacteria, grave general symptoms are caused and sepsis or septicemia (blood poisoning) is said to be present.

*h.* The word putrefaction refers to that condition when inflammation has so far progressed that the tissues have been devitalized and a foul or putrid odor arises from the wound. The putrid odor is due to the action of putrefactive bacteria.

*i.* The micro-organisms producing pus are know as pyogenic bacteria. The various varieties of the staphylococcus and streptococcus are the causative agents in the majority of surgical infections. Other organisms are, however, occasionally demonstrable. The staphylococcus is the most common cause of infection. It rarely causes alarming constitutional symptoms, and as a rule such an infectious process remains quite localized. The streptococcus is more virulent and tends to invade the whole system. Infection of wounds by one type of organism is quite rare; two or more varieties usually are present and the coincident symptoms are dependent upon the predominating bacterium, either because of its virulence or numbers.

It is well to note that the encapsulated spores of the Bacillus anthracis are the most difficult of all germs to kill, and any process which will render them harmless (and they must be dead to be harmless) may be relied upon to accomplish the same result as regards the other bacteria. The prevention of infection is the best treatment known for this condition. Infection is prevented through the employment of measures that destroy infectious bacteria and their spores, or inhibits or stops their growth. These measures make up that process in surgical technique known as sterilization.

*j*. Sterilization is the process of rendering anything sterile by destroying infectious organisms and their spores, and is accomplished by mechanical, thermal, and chemical methods. Sterilizing agents are substances which destroy or remove or prevent the growth of infectious organisms.

(1) The methods used in mechanical sterilization, while not dependable, are important preliminary steps to more complete methods of sterilization. The most important of the mechanical methods of sterilization are scrubbing and irrigation.

(*a*) A thorough scrubbing with hot water, soap, and brush is frequently of great importance, as it removes dirt which may harbor harmful bacteria from the walls and floors of operating and treatment rooms, from instruments and utensils, the hands of the surgeon and those assisting at operations and dressings, and the skin of the patient. Instruments and utensils should always be cleaned and scrubbed immediately after use, as that removes most of any bacteria present and makes subsequent sterilization more easily effective.

(*b*) The irrigation of wounds with sterile water or other aqueous solutions to float off or dislodge by force dirt and bacteria, or to bring solutions in contact with parts of a wound which are not otherwise accessible, has a distinct place in surgical practice. Irrigation is a splendid mechanical cleanser and, in many cases, will remove infectious organisms when other methods fail.

(2) Thermal sterilization, or sterilization by heat is the most efficient agent of sterilization, and, when properly used, is almost certain in its germicidal action. Moist heat is used as a sterilizing agent in two forms—boiling water, and live steam under normal and increased pressure.

(*a*) Boiling water is the simplest method of sterilization, and is used chiefly for sterilizing instruments (except those with lenses), metal utensils, enamelware, and other objects which are not injured by heat and moisture. These articles should be boiled for 20 minutes in water containing about 1 percent (3 teaspoonfuls to the quart) of sodium carbonate, which is added to prevent rusting, to raise the boiling point of the water, and to dissolve any organic matter that may be present. In emergencies surgical dressings may be boiled, but it is far more satisfactory to have them dry at the time of operation. Glassware is boiled 20 minutes in water without sodium carbonate.

(*b*) Live steam is air-free steam and for sterilization purposes is used under normal or increased pressure. Steam under increased pressure is termed superheated steam and is the best method of sterilization. Steam at normal pressure is but little used at the present time.

(*c*) An autoclave is a sterilizer in which steam under pressure (superheated steam) is used. A vacuum first is created to insure penetration of the steam, and when the proper reading of negative pressure (vacuum) is registered in the gage, superheated steam is admitted to the chamber and the articles therein subjected to a steam pressure of 20 pounds for three-quarters of an hour. At the end of this time all organisms will have been killed and the dressings or other articles rendered safe to use, but they are wet. A second vacuum then is induced and maintained until they are dry. One such sterilization ordinarily is sufficient to preclude the possibility of infection, but if there exists the slightest doubt as to the asepsis of the sterilized material the process may be repeated two or three times, despite the fact that anthrax spores are killed by live steam in 12 minutes. This method of repeated sterilization, either by steam or boiling, is termed fractional sterilization.

(*d*) The method of sterilization in which dry heat is used includes the use of the actual cautery, a flame, or hot air. Hot air is fairly satisfactory and it will kill anthrax spores in about 3 hours at 140° C. The cautery is a positive germicide, but causes extensive destruction of the tissues. Sterilization by a flame is rarely, if ever, used in surgery, but may be used for rapid sterilization of platinum loops, needles, and other small instruments.

(3) Chemical sterilization will kill bacteria and spores, but in order to do this promptly they must be used in such strong solutions that the tissues to which they are applied may likewise be destroyed. Such a result is usually undesirable and the use of chemicals as sterilizing agents is confined chiefly to the sterilization of instruments which boiling or steam would ruin, or in weak solution as an adjunct to the mechanical method of sterilization. Chemical solutions of appropriate strength are used in the sterilization of instruments, materials, and utensils, the skin of the patient, the oper-

ator's hands, and the walls and floors of rooms. When used in contact with the tissues the aid is to secure complete sterilization without causing damage to the tissues, but no such ideal aniseptic has yet been found. The following are some chemicals used in sterilization :

(*a*) Alcohol, 70 percent, is commonly used to disinfect the hands of operators, for disinfecting cutting and sharp instruments, for cleansing and drying the skin of the operating field before the application of iodine, and as a solvent or diluent for various antiseptics.

(*b*) Iodine, in strengths varying from 3½ to 7 percent, is a reliable germicide and is used for sterilizing wounds and in preparation of the skin. In the presence of water the iodine is precipitated and it will not penetrate if the skin or tissues are wet. When used for skin sterilization it is usually preceded by an application of benzine or ether to remove the sebaceous matter and dry the skin. After the iodine has dried it is customary to remove the excess with alcohol to prevent the burning or blistering of the skin.

(*c*) Bichloride of mercury is now seldom used in contact with the body although some operators use it in preparation of ·their hands. In weak solutions it has a powerful germicidal action on superficial bacteria, but is of little value as a germicide in deep wounds because it combines with the proteins in the tissues to form an insoluble albuminate of mercury which markedly hinders its action and penetrative power. A 1–500 solution in alcohol is useful in sterilizing rubber goods. As mercury has corrosive action on metals it should never be used to sterilize instruments.

(*d*) Phenol (carbolic acid) in saturated solution is used for sterilization of cutting instruments which would be injured by boiling. They are submerged in the solution for 15 minutes, washed in sterile water, and placed in alcohol until needed. It is also used for sterilization of tissues, such as the stump of the appendix, where deep penetration is not required, and as a local cauterizing agent. Phenol dressings should not be used because of the danger of subsequent gangrene.

(*e*) Dakin's solution is a solution of sodium hypochlorite of strength between 0.45 and 0.5 percent. In contact with the tissues it gives off nascent chlorine, which destroys bacteria and dissolves the necrotic tissue in which they grow. It is rapidly decomposed by light and heat and should be titrated daily to insure the proper strength. When used according to the Carrel technique in a properly prepared wound, it is of great value.

(*f*) The chloramine group of disinfectants also act by liberation of chlorine. They are more stable than Dakin's solution and give off their chlorine more slowly, but they lack the important solvent action on the necrotic tissue.

(*g*) Potassium permanganate is an excellent deodorizer and, in addition, is a good disinfectant for the hands in saturated solution.

(*h*) Boric acid is a very mild antiseptic and generally is used in saturated solution (4 percent) for the irrigation of infected wounds or the sterilization of instruments which heat in any form would destroy.

(*i*) Formaldehyde is a germicide and is used as a gas or in solution. It is very irritating to the tissues and seldom is applied in a dressing; in weak solution (4 percent) it is a satisfactory sterilizing solution for instruments. Formaldehyde solution is a satisfactory method of sterilizing instruments which heat would injure, as catheters, cystoscopes, and similar articles. Mercury oxycyanide solution 1–1,000 is also used for catheters, cystoscopes, etc.

(*j*) Various substances that color or dye the skin, such as picric acid, mercurochrome, gentian violet, merthiolate, and acriflavine are also used as disinfectants.

*k.* The sterilization of equipment is accomplished as follows:

(1) Large packs are sterilized for 60 minutes under 20 pounds pressure with 20 to 30 minutes vacuum allowed for drying. Small packs are sterilized for 30 minutes under 20 pounds pressure with 15 to 20 minutes vacuum allowed for drying. Enamelware and glassware are sterilized for 20 minutes under 30 pounds pressure with no vacuum. Rubber goods are sterilized for 15 minutes at 20 pounds pressure and 15 minutes vacuum. Solutions in flasks are sterilized separately for 15 minutes at 20 pounds pressure. Pressure, at conclusion of sterilization period, is allowed to decrease gradually. No vacuum is used on solutions. Sharp instruments are sterilized in cresol 1 hour and boiled for 1 minute. Sharp instruments can be sterilized by placing in cresol for 30 minutes, rinsed in plain sterile water, and placed in 70 percent alcohol for 30 minutes. Other instruments are placed in trays and boiled for 20 minutes. A 1-percent solution of sodium carbonate (3 teaspoonfuls to the quart) raises the boiling point about 5°, prevents rust, and removes grease and other organic matter. Gloves are cleaned, inspected for holes, dried, then powdered well and evenly on both sides with talc. The cuffs are turned back 2 inches. Each pair is placed in a muslin envelope of 4 thicknesses with a small powder bag. This is wrapped

in a muslin cover and sterilized for 15 minutes under 20 pounds pressure.

(2) Both chemical and bacteriological controls are used to insure proper sterilization, and laboratory cultures of all packages are frequently taken.

(3) Basins are boiled in a special sterilizer for 30 minutes.

(4) The suture materials which are dispensed in tubes have been rendered sterile by the manufacturer. The tubes themselves are sterilized in two ways. If the tubes are marked "boilable" they are sterilized by boiling with instruments for 20 minutes. If they are not marked "boilable", they are stored in 5 percent phenol or cresol solution and then placed in 70 percent alcohol for 20 minutes just prior to operation.

(5) Suture materials such as silk and linen not dispensed in tubes are sterilized in the autoclave under 20 pounds pressure for 15 minutes or boiled with instruments. Horsehair, silkworm gut, silver wire, etc., are sterilized by boiling for 20 minutes prior to operation.

**119. Surgical dressings.**—*a.* Surgical dressings commonly are made from gauze, cotton, flannel, rubber, linen, etc., by the operating room force. The gauze and cotton should be of good quality and capable of rapidly absorbing fluids.

*b.* It sometimes happens that the gauze, as received from the manufacturers, is sized (coated with a starch preparation which makes it unfit for surgical use) and such gauze must be boiled in a 1 percent solution of sodium carbonate in order to remove the sizing.

*c.* Sponges are used for many purposes and are made of gauze, either rolled in a ball or flat. The flat sponges are of various sizes, 2 by 2, 4 by 4, and 4 by 8 inches, and are usually of from 6 to 8 thicknesses of gauze. All raw edges are turned in. Sponges are wrapped in double muslin wrappers for sterilization.

*d.* Packs, or taped sponges, are used for surrounding the field within the abdomen. They are made of 6 or 8 layers of gauze, with all the raw edges turned in and sewed. To avoid leaving them in the abdomen, a tape is sewed to one corner, and to this a metal ring is secured. The common sizes of packs are 4 by 18, 8 by 18, and 12 by 12 inches. For sterilization they are placed in double muslin covers, each package containing a definite number and so labeled. During the operation the nurse or attendant in charge of them must know the exact location at all times of every pack that has been issued.

*e.* Pads are 8 by 10 and 12 by 16 inches and are of absorbent cotton wrapped in an outer covering of gauze. They are used in wound dressings for absorbing fluids and to protect the tissues from pressure.

*f.* Sheets and towels are folded in a certain manner and wrapped, a definite number in each package, in double muslin covers for sterilization.

*g.* Caps and masks are worn to prevent infection by dandruff or secretions from the mouth and nose. They are inclosed in muslin wrappers, sterilized, and placed in the surgeon's dressing room.

*h.* Operating suits are worn in place of their outer clothing by surgeons and attendants during operations. They may be used as they come from the laundry.

*i.* Operating gowns are of standard type in the Army and are worn by all persons present at an operation. When putting on a sterile gown one should avoid touching the ungloved hand to its outside.

*j.* In preparation for emergencies a hospital should have on hand a considerable quantity of sterile goods. They may be placed in metal drums or in packages, each containing a standard outfit for an operation. These should be sterilized once a week if not used.

**120. Sutures and ligatures.**—*a.* There are two principal kinds of sutures and ligatures, absorbable and nonabsorbable. The principal varieties of absorbable sutures are plain gut, chromic gut, and kangaroo tendon. Gut sutures are made from the submucous coat of the intestine of the sheep; they are used in the deep tissues such as peritoneum, muscle, and fascia. The plain gut is supposed to last from 8 to 10 days in the tissue. Chromic gut sutures are prepared to last 10 and 20 days in the tissue, but the rate of absorption is variable. Sutures come in various sizes from 000 to 3. They are usually issued in plain glass tubes which may be sterilized by boiling or submerging in a special suture sterilizing solution such as potassium-mercuric-iodide solution 1–8,000 in 95 percent alcohol. Kangaroo tendon is much stronger and heavier than the gut and lasts about 30 days in the tissue.

*b.* The atraumatic intestinal suture is attached to the needle in such a manner that the perforation made by the needle is not enlarged or traumatized by the entrance of the suture itself. These sutures are made in both plain and chromic from size 0000 to 2 and may be used for all membranes where minimized suture trauma is desirable.

*c.* Nonabsorbable sutures are made of silk, linen, silkworm gut, horsehair, dermol, silver wire, and other materials.

**121. Instruments.**—*a.* Most surgical instruments are made of special steel, and are nickel-plated or of stainless steel. They are kept in a special cabinet when not in use.

*b.* After an operation all metal instruments should be washed carefully in cold water with a brush to remove all blood and other foreign matter, then boiled. They should be then dried and carefully examined for dirt in the crevices and breaks in the plating and sharpened if necessary. They are then wiped with warm liquid petrolatum or typewriter oil to prevent rusting and placed in the instrument cabinet.

*c.* The instruments required for an operation vary greatly according to the nature of the operation and the ideas of the surgeon. The following is suggested as a basic outfit for ordinary operations (others may be added as desired) : 2 scalpels; 3 scissors (1 curved Mayo, 1 straight Mayo, and 1 blunt for suture scissors) ; 2 plain thumb forceps; 2 rat-toothed thumb forceps; 12 small (Kelly Rankin) straight hemostats; 12 curved Kelly hemostats; 8 Allis intestinal forceps; 12 Ochsner straight forceps, 6½-inch; 6 large Ochsner straight forceps, 7¼-inch; 6 mosquito forceps; 12 towel clips; 2 large retractors; 2 Army type retractors; 1 grooved director; 1 silver probe; 12 sponge holders; 3 curved hysterectomy forceps; 3 needle holders; needle kit containing all types of needles (straight intestinal, straight skin, curved cutting, curved intestinal, Mayo needles) ; plain and chromic gut; assorted glass syringes and hypodermic needles; 3 medicine glasses; skin clips and forceps or dermol for the skin; 12 laparotomy rings; and 2 tumblers.

**122. Operating personnel.**—*a.* In the Army this consists of the operating surgeon and the medical officers who assist him, the operating room nurse, the anesthetist, and two or more enlisted men.

*b.* The operating surgeon is in general charge. He is responsible for the patient's life and for the successful outcome of the operation. He is held accountable for all mistakes and accidents, no matter whose fault it may be, that may cause an unfavorable outcome.

*c.* To the operating room nurse is delegated the authority necessary for the routine administration of the operating suite. This involves numerous details such as the care and accounting for all property, cleanliness, sterilization, preparation for operations, and supervision and instruction of enlisted men.

*d.* (1) The anesthetist is usually a nurse who has had special training in this branch. She is responsible to the operating surgeon for the general condition of the patient during the administration of an anesthetic.

(2) Since local and spinal anesthesia have become so popular, many surgeons prefer to be their own anesthetists. The operating room nurse, in case no regular anesthetist is assigned, sits at the patient's head during the operation and keeps a record at frequent intervals of the blood pressure, pulse, and respirations.

*e.* The enlisted men are detailed to the operating room for the purpose of instruction and training. The principal characteristics of a good operating room attendant are dependability, faithfulness in the most minute details of his work, an even temper which will enable him to work quickly and accurately in emergencies, intelligence to understand the reason for everything he does, and a devotion to the welfare of the patient.

**123. Preparation for operation.**—*a.* Each one of the operating room personnel removes his outer clothes, puts on his operating clothes, and then proceeds to the scrub-up room. Here the hands and forearms are scrubbed for 15 minutes with hot water and green soap and rinsed and soaked in 70 percent alcohol. This washing should be done in a methodical way so that each side of the fingers and every part of the hands and forearms are scrubbed thoroughly. It is essential that persons engaged in surgical work keep their nails short and clean. After scrubbing and rinsing in alcohol, the surgeon enters the operating room where he is handed a hand towel with which he dries only his hands, leaving his forearms untouched by the towel. He then puts on a sterile gown and sterile rubber gloves. When fully prepared as above, and while waiting for the start of the operation, the surgeon and his assistants must hold their hands, covered with a sterile towel, above their waist.

*b.* The field of operation is shaved before the patient enters the operation room, although sometimes this is done in the operating room. If a general or spinal anesthetic is used, the skin preparation is done after the patient is anesthetized. With local or block anesthesia, the field is prepared before the injection of the anesthetic is given.

*c.* If a spinal anesthetic is used, special material and apparatus are necessary which should be laid out on a table. The spinal kit consists of the following articles: one 5-cc. hypodermic syringe; one 2-cc. hypodermic syringe; two spinal needles; one hypodermic needle; one mixing needle; one ampule saw; one sacral sheet; sponges, etc.; 100, 120, 150 milligrams of novocaine crystals or other drug as desired by the operating surgeon. After the spinal injection the table is tilted according to instructions from the anesthetist.

*d.* There are many ways of preparing the skin. A simple and very satisfactory one is to scrub the skin with a gauze "prep" sponge wet with ether to remove grease and moisture, and then paint the skin thoroughly with 3.5 percent iodine and allow to dry. After the iodine is completely dry paint the skin with a second coat, beginning in the middle of the field and progressing outward to the edges of the previous coat and remove with alcohol on sponges. Drape with sterile towels and sheets, so that only the prepared skin is exposed. Other common disinfectants used in the Army for skin preparation are merthiolate, mercurochrome, Scott's solution, etc.

*e.* Following is a summary of the routine preparations for an operation:

(1) The operating room nurse, the anesthetist, and the surgeon are notified as to the time and nature of the operation.

(2) The attendant in charge of the instruments selects those needed and puts them in the sterilizer with the necessary utensils.

(3) The cutting instruments are placed in a sterilizing solution.

(4) All hands assist in placing the furniture and equipment in proper order, and all glass-topped tables, Mayo tables, overhead lights, and portable lights are wiped with a towel wet with alcohol.

(5) The attendant in charge of sterile supplies selects the packages of sterile goods and places them on the proper tables.

(6) The nurses or attendants proceed to scrub up and put on sterile gowns and gloves.

(7) Nurses or attendants drape, with sterile sheets, the table for gowns and gloves, the instrument table, the surgical dressing table, the basin stands, and spinal anesthetic table.

(8) The trays of sterile instruments are brought in from the sterilizer and are arranged in proper order on the instrument table and draped with a sterile towel until needed.

(9) The basin and utensil set is opened and the contents placed in their proper places.

(10) The sterile packages are opened and an attendant places their contents in the proper place on the surgical dressing table.

(11) Nurse or attendant sorts and arranges the extra instruments on a table and prepares the sutures and ligatures. (Sutures are no longer placed in a damp towel, but in a dry one, as it has been discovered that continued soaking causes them to lose their tensile strength and greatly increases the danger of contamination. They are dipped in warm water for a few seconds immediately before handing them to the operator.)

(12) If spinal anesthesia is to be used, the spinal kit is opened.

(13) All tables and stands containing sterile articles are draped with sterile towels or sheets until they are needed.

(14) The patient is wheeled into the operating room.

(15) By this time the surgeons and assistants are dressed and scrubbed and ready to put on sterile gowns and gloves.

(16) The patient's skin is then prepared by the assistant in the manner previously described.

(17) The patient is then draped with towels and laparotomy sheets by the assistant and nurse or attendant.

(18) The instrument table is rolled into place as well as the basin stands.

(19) The surgeon and his assistants assume their proper places.

(20) The nurse or attendant hands the surgeon the scalpel; the incision is made, after which the skin knife is discarded, and the operation proceeds.

## Section II

## BANDAGING AND DRESSING

**124. General.**—Bandaging is an art which develops only after extensive practice. The coach-and-pupil method is a very good method for beginners. Each pair alternate as the coach and pupil.

**125. Uses.**—*a.* To retain dressings, in keeping medications to affected parts.

*b.* To give support to dependent parts of the body as the arms, scrotum, etc.

*c.* To apply pressure in control of hemorrhage, to assist in absorption of fluids and as tourniquets.

*d.* To keep foreign matter out of wounds.

*e.* To absorb wound secretions, as pus, etc.

*f.* For immobilization in combination with splints.

**126. Acknowledgment.**—The illustrations and most of the text in this section are taken from the *Handbook of the Hospital Corps, U. S. Navy*, and the courtesy of the Bureau of Medicine and Surgery in permitting the use of that handbook is acknowledged.

**127. Rules for bandaging.**—*a.* In applying a roller bandage, the roll should be held in the right hand so that the loose end is on the bottom; the outside surface of the loose or initial end is next applied to and held on the part by the left hand; and the roll is then passed around the part by the right hand which controls the tension and application of the bandage. Two or three of the initial turns of a roller bandage should overlie each other in order to secure the bandage and keep it in place. In applying the turns of the bandage, it is often necessary to transfer the roll from one hand to the other.

*b.* Bandages should be applied evenly, firmly, and not too tightly. Excessive pressure may cause interference with the circulation and may lead to disastrous consequences. In bandaging an extremity, it is therefore advisable to leave the fingers or toes exposed in order that the circulation of these parts may be readily observed. It is likewise safer to apply a large number of turns of a bandage rather than to depend upon a few too firmly applied turns to secure a splint or dressing.

*c.* In applying a wet bandage, or one that may become wet in holding a wet dressing in place, it is necessary to allow for shrinkage. The turns of a bandage should completely cover the skin, as any uncovered areas of skin may become pinched between the turns with resulting discomfort.

*d.* Bandages should be applied in such a manner that skin surfaces are not brought in contact, as perspiration will cause excoriation and maceration of the skin.

*e.* In bandaging an extremity, it is advisable to include the whole member (arm and hand, leg and foot), except the fingers and toes, in order that uniform pressure may be maintained throughout. It is also desirable in bandaging a limb that the part be placed in the position it will occupy when the dressing is finally completed, as variations in flexion or extension of the part will cause changes in the pressure of certain parts of the bandage.

*f.* The initial turns of a bandage of an extremity (including spica bandages of the hip and shoulder) always should be applied securely, and when possible, around the part of the limb that has the smallest circumference. Thus in bandaging the arm or hand, the initial turns usually are applied around the wrist, and in bandaging the leg or foot, the initial turns are applied immediately above the ankle.

*g.* The final turns of a completed bandage usually are secured in the same manner as are the initial turns, by the employment of two or more overlying circular turns. As both edges of the final circular turn are necessarily exposed, they should be folded under to present a neat, cuff-like appearance. The terminal end of the completed bandage is turned under and secured to the final turns by either a safetypin or adhesive tape. When these are not available, the end of the bandage may be split lengthwise for several inches, and the two resulting tails secured around the part by tying.

*h.* When the turns of a bandage cross each other, as in the figure-of-eight, the spiral reverse, and the spica, the line of crossing should be straight, and if practicable, should be in the center line of the part bandaged, but the line of crossings should not be over a bony prominence. The exposed portions of the turns should be of approximately the same width.

*i.* In removing a bandage, it may be cut, preferably with bandage scissors. In doing so the operator should be careful to avoid interference with the underlying dressing and the affected area.

*j.* If the bandage is removed without cutting, its folds should be gathered up in first one hand and then the other as the bandage is unwound. This procedure will facilitate removal and the rewinding of the bandage, if that be desirable.

**128. Application of bandages and their uses.**—*a. Circular bandage.*—After anchoring the initial turns of the bandage, a series of circular turns is made around the part. Each turn should overlie accurately the turn beneath it, neither ascending nor descending. This bandage is used for retention of dressings to a limited portion of an extremity, the neck, or the head; compression to control venous hemorrhage and to promote venous stasis.

*b. Spiral bandage.*—After anchoring the initial turns, each turn is applied in a spiral direction in such a manner as to overlie one-third of the preceding turn. As usually applied to an extremity, the upper edge of each turn of an ascending spiral is tighter than the lower edge with resulting inequality of pressure. For this reason, many surgeons object to its use on an extremity. This bandage is used for retention of dressings of the arm, chest, and abdomen (fig. 14).

*c. Oblique bandage.*—A series of oblique turns is applied around a part in such manner as to have an uncovered area between turns. The width of the uncovered area should be uniform throughout. This bandage is used for retention of thick dressings or of temporary dressings which require frequent removal.

*d. Recurrent bandage.*—In applying this bandage, the roller, after securing the primary turns, is carried completely over a part to a point opposite its origin, and then reflected and brought back to the starting point where it is secured by one or more circular turns (fig. 15). In the recurrent bandage of the hand, the bandage is secured at the wrist, carried over the back of the hand, around the tips of the fingers, across the palm to the wrist. Held at this point by the disengaged hand of the operator, the bandage is carried across the palm around the tips of the fingers, across the back of the hand to the wrist, where it is held by the thumb of the operator's disengaged hand. Each turn overlies one-third of the preceding turn. The original turn over the fingers may cover the middle and ring fingers, with each succeeding turn applied alternately over the other fingers first to one side and then to the other of the middle finger ; or the original turn over the fingers may be applied over the first finger

FIGURE 14. — Spiral band-
age. (Owen.)

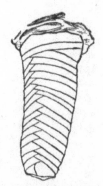

FIGURE 15. — Recurrent
bandage of stump.
(Wharton.)

or over the little finger, each subsequent turn covering a portion of the remaining exposed fingers. The reflected portion of the bandage at the wrist is then secured by a number of circular turns. It is customary to complete such a bandage with a figure-of-eight bandage enclosing the entire hand.

*e. Figure-of-eight bandage.*—This is undoubtedly the most useful bandage and, with its various modifications, probably is employed more frequently than any other type. The enlisted man should perfect himself in the application of this bandage, as, with a few exceptions, the majority of bandages are applied on the principle of the figure-of-eight. Its name is derived from the fact that the turns are applied so as to form a figure 8. Although it is employed commonly in bandages of the joints (elbow, knee, and ankle), it frequently is applied in bandaging the neck and axilla, head and neck, and head and jaw. If properly applied, it may be used very successfully in bandaging the extremities.

(1) *Hand and wrist.*—After anchoring the bandage with two circular turns about the wrist, the bandage is carried across the back of the hand to the base of the fingers, then into the palm, across the palm to the back of the hand, and across the back of the hand to the starting point at the wrist, where one circular turn is made. This general course is followed with several similar turns, each one overlying about one-third of the preceding turn on the back of the hand. After a sufficient number of turns has been made, the bandage is terminated with a circular turn around the wrist. This bandage is used for retention of dressings on the back of the hand or in the palm (fig. 16).

FIGURE 16.—Figure-of-eight bandage.   (Wharton, modified.)

(2) *Forearm.*—This bandage may be the continuation of the figure-of-eight of the wrist and hand, or may be started with primary circular turns of the wrist. The bandage is carried obliquely upward across the back of the forearm and around the arm in its natural course, where it forms the upper loop of the figure-of-eight. The bandage then is carried in an oblique direction downward across the back of the arm, where it crosses the upward turn of the bandage. Then it is carried around the lower end of the forearm to complete the lower loop of the figure-of-eight. The same process is repeated several times until the elbow is reached, each turn overlapping the upper one-half or three-quarters of the preceding turn. The bandage is terminated finally with two or more circular turns at the elbow. The final cir-

cular turn, with both upper and lower edges of the bandage folded under, should be applied firmly and should present a neat, cuff-like appearance at the upper end of the completed bandage (fig. 16). During the application of this bandage, there is always considerable slack in one edge of the bandage where it is carried around the arm. As the bandaging proceeds, however, these loose edges are covered by the ascending turns of the bandage. It is used for retention of dressings and covering of splints.

(3) *Elbow.*—With the elbow in the desired position, the initial end is secured by circular turns around the forearm just below the elbow. The bandage then is carried upward over the flexure of the elbow in an oblique direction and passed around the arm just above the elbow, where a circular turn is made, and then is carried obliquely downward across the flexure and passed around the forearm. This procedure is repeated, with each turn overlying the preceding turn, the turns on the forearm ascending and those on the arm descending until the entire joint is covered. The final turn is a circular one around the elbow joint itself. This bandage may be started with a circular turn around the joint followed by figure-of-eight turns covering the upper part of the forearm and the lower part of the arm. It is used for retention of dressings around the elbow joint.

*f. Spiral reverse bandage of the arm.*—This bandage is in reality a modification of the figure-of-eight, in that only the lower loop or one-half of the figure-of-eight is completed. After anchoring the

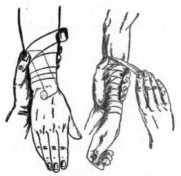

FIGURE 17.—Spiral reverse.     (Eliason.)

primary turns, the bandage is carried obliquely upward on the back of the arm. When this turn reaches the center line of the arm, the thumb of the disengaged (usually the left) hand is placed upon the body of the bandage to hold it securely in place upon the arm. The operator then unrolls about 5 or 6 inches of bandage which is held slack and is folded upon itself by changing the position of the hand holding the roller from supination to pronation. The bandage then is carried obliquely downward across the arm to a point opposite that from which the ascending turn started. It then is tightened slightly to conform to the part accurately, then is carried around the limb and the procedure is repeated. It is necessary to retain the thumb upon the point of reverse until the succeeding turn reaches that point. As in the figure-of-eight, each turn should overlie at least one-third of the preceding turn and the reverses should be in a straight line (fig. 17).

g. *Complete bandage of the hand.*—After securing the initial turns around the wrist, a recurrent bandage of the hand is applied. The bandage then is carried obliquely across the back of the hand to the tip of the index finger. A circular turn is made around the ends of the fingers. The fingers and hand then are covered by a figure-of-eight or spiral reverse bandage which finally is completed by two or more circular turns around the wrist. This bandage may or may not be applied to include the thumb. It is used for retention of dressings of the hand (fig. 18).

h. *Demigauntlet bandage.*—Using a 1-inch bandage, secure the initial turns at the wrist and carry the bandage across the back of the hand to the base of the thumb, around the thumb, across the back of

FIGURE 18.—Complete bandage of hand. (Wharton.)

FIGURE 19.—Demigauntlet of hand. (Wharton.)

FIGURE 20.—Gauntlet bandage of hand. (Wharton.)

the hand to the wrist, where a circular turn is made. The same procedure is repeated successively for each finger and the bandage finally terminated with a circular turn around the wrist. It is used for retention of dressings on back of hand (fig. 19).

i. *Gauntlet bandage.*—The demigauntlet bandage may be extended to include the entire thumb and fingers with either simple spiral turns or spiral reverse turns of each digit (fig. 20).

*j. Spica bandage of right shoulder (ascending).*—After securing the initial end by two circular turns around the arm opposite the axillary fold, the bandage is carried diagonally across the arm and front of the chest to the axilla of the opposite side, then around the back of the chest, across the arm, and across the upward turn to the point of origin. After carrying the bandage around the arm, this procedure is repeated, each turn overlying about two-thirds of the preceding turn until the entire shoulder is covered. The turn should cross in a straight line extending up the center line of the arm over the point of the shoulder. Likewise the turns across the chest and back should overlap each other uniformly, and the turns in the opposite axilla should overlap each other exactly. The bandage may be secured by either a pin or adhesive tape. It is used for retention of dressings of shoulder and axilla and of shoulder cap (fig. 21).

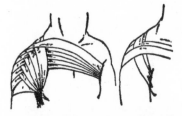

FIGURE 21.—Spica and spica loops of the shoulder. (Eliason.)

FIGURE 22.—Ascending and descending spica. (Eliason.)

*k. Bandages of the lower extremity.*—The bandages described in the preceding paragraphs may be applied to the corresponding parts of the lower extremity. However, descriptions of a few of the special bandages of the lower extremity are as follows:

(1) *Spica bandage of the groin (ascending).*—After securing the initial turns around the upper part of the thigh just below the groin, the bandage is carried obliquely upward across the lower abdomen to the iliam crest of the opposite side, transversely across the back, then downward obliquely across the front of the thigh, across the upward turn of the bandage, and around the thigh to the point of origin, thus completing a figure-of-eight. This is repeated several times until the entire groin is covered, each turn overlying about two-thirds of the preceding turn. The same care in regard to the line of crossings of the turns and to the uniform overlapping of the bandage on the abdomen should be observed as is noted in the description of the spica bandage of the shoulder. It is used for retention of dressings in region of the groin (fig. 22).

(2) *Spica bandage of the foot.*—The initial end is secured by two circular turns around the leg just above the ankle. The bandage then is carried across the dorsum of the foot to the base of the toes where a circular turn is made around the foot. After two or three spiral reverse turns are made, the bandage is carried across the dorsum of the foot, backward alongside of the heel, around the heel, forward along the other side of the heel across the preceding upward turn on the dorsum of the foot, and around the foot to the starting point of the turn. This process is repeated, the turns gradually ascending on both the foot and the heel, the crossings of bandage being in the midline of the dorsum of the foot. The bandage finally is carried upward around the ankle and secured by two or more circular turns at its original starting point. It is possible to apply this bandage without the use of the spiral reverse turns by employing the figure-of-eight throughout. It is used for retention of dressings on the foot and support for sprained ankle (fig. 23).

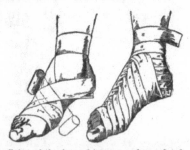

FIGURE 23.—Spica of the foot; first step and completed.   (Eliason.)

(3) *Bandage of foot, not covering the heel.*—After securing the initial end by two circular turns around the leg just above the ankle, the bandage is carried obliquely across the dorsum of the foot to the base of the toes where a circular turn is made around the foot. The bandage is carried up the foot by a few spiral reverse turns crossing in the center line, and then applied as a figure-of-eight around the ankle and instep. The bandage may be terminated just above the ankle or be extended up the leg as far as may be necessary. It is frequently practicable to apply this bandage without employing the spiral reverse turns, the figures-of-eight being applied following the circular turns at the base of the toes. It is used for retention of dressings of foot. This bandage usually is employed in application of bandages covering the entire leg.

*l. Special bandages.*—(1) *Velpeau bandage.*—The fingers of the affected side are placed upon the opposite shoulder, a pad placed in the axilla, and the skin surfaces separated by sheet wadding. Place the initial end of the bandage on the shoulder blade of the sound side, carry the bandage across the outer portion of the affected shoulder, downward over the outer and posterior surface of the flexed arm, behind the point of the elbow, obliquely across the back of the forearm and chest to the opposite axilla, and around to the point of origin. After repeating this turn once, the bandage is carried from the point of origin across the back and side of chest, in front of the flexed elbow and transversely across the front of the chest. Then it is carried around the other side of the chest, diagonally across the back to the affected shoulder. The first turn then is repeated, followed by a second circular turn around the chest and

  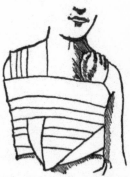

Figure 24.—Velpeau bandage; start (Eliason), posterior view (Eliason), and completed (Wharton).

flexed arm. Each vertical turn over the shoulder overlaps two-thirds of the preceding turn, ascending from the outer part of the shoulder to the neck and from the upper posterior surface of the arm inward toward the point of the elbow. Each transverse turn also overlies one-third of the preceding turn. These transverse turns are continued until the last turn covers the wrist. The bandage is finally secured with pins, both where it ends and at various points where the turns of the bandage cross each other. (The initial turns of this bandage may be secured by circular turns around the chest under the arm of the affected side.) It is used for fixation of arm in treatment of fractured clavicle and fixation of humerus after reduction of dislocated shoulder joint (fig. 24).

(2) *Barton bandage.*—With the initial end of the bandage applied to the head just behind the right mastoid process, the bandage is carried under the bony prominence at the back of the head, upward

and forward back of the left ear, obliquely across the top of the head, downward in front of the right ear, under the chin, upward in front of left ear, obliquely across the top of the head, crossing the first turn in the midline of the head, thence backward and downward to the point of origin behind the right mastoid. Then it is carried around the back of the head under the left ear, around the front of the chin, under the right ear to the point of origin. This procedure is repeated several times, each turn exactly overlying the preceding turn. The bandage is secured with a pin or strip of adhesive tape, and either a pin or adhesive may be applied at the crossing on top of the head. It is used for fracture of lower jaw and retention of dressings of chin (fig. 25).

FIGURE 25.—Barton bandage.   (Wharton.)

(3) *Recurrent bandage of head.*—The initial turns are applied around the head, passing around the nape of the neck, above each ear and around the forehead. When the bandage has reached the center of the forehead on the third turn, its free margin is held by a finger of the left hand and the bandage is reversed and carried over the top of the head in the center line to the nape of the neck. With an assistant holding the bandage at the latter point, it is reflected forward over the top of the head covering the right half of the preceding turn. When it reaches the forehead in the midline, it again is reflected over the top of the head, overlying the left half of the first turn. At the nape of the neck in the center line, it is again reflected and carried forward overlying the outer half of the second turn. This process is repeated until the entire head is covered, the turns alternating to the right and left of the center line. The bandage finally is completed by several circular turns overlying the original turns and fixing the ends of antero-posterior turns at the nape of the neck and on the forehead, where pins should be applied to provide additional security. Uses: Retention of dressings of wounds of

the scalp, of fractures and operative wounds of the skull (fig. 26). This bandage may be applied with the turns over the head in a transverse direction extending from ear to ear.

(4) *Crossed bandage of one eye.*—The initial extremity is secured by a circular turn around the head below the bony prominence at the back, above both ears and across the forehead. The bandage then is carried from the back of the head, below the ear, obliquely across the outer part of the cheek to the base of the nose at its junction with the forehead, over the opposite side of the head and downward behind the mastoid process. A circular turn then is carried around the head, overlying exactly the original turns. A

FIGURE 26.—Recurrent turns.
(Eliason.)

FIGURE 27.—Crossed bandage (figure-of-eight) of one eye and of both eyes.
(Eliason.)

second turn under the ear and across the face and head then is applied, overlapping the upper two-thirds of the preceding turn. These alternating turns are repeated until the eye (and if more comfortable, the ear on the same side) is completely covered. The bandage is completed with a final circular turn around the head. It is used for retention of dressings of the eye (fig. 27).

(5) *Crossed bandage of both eyes.*—The initial turns are applied as for one eye and the bandage carried forward below the right ear, diagonally upward across the cheek to the base of the nose and over the opposite side of the head above the left ear, and downward behind the left mastoid process. Then a circular turn is applied. When the roller reaches the back of the head below the bony prominence, it is carried obliquely forward and slightly upward over the right ear across the forehead and downward over the left eye, the lower margin of the bandage crossing the previous turn at the junction of the nose with the forehead. The bandage then is carried across the left cheek below the left ear and backward to the nape of the neck. Then a circular turn is made, followed by a repetition of the previous turns across the eyes, each circular turn

accurately covering its predecessor and each oblique turn overlying the upper one-half of the preceding turn until both eyes are completely covered. The ears may or may not be included in the bandage, which is completed by two circular turns around the head. Pins are placed at the interesections of the bandage (fig. 27).

(6) *Sayre's dressing.*—This consists of two strips of adhesive plaster 3 inches wide and 2 yards long. Two circular turns of a flannel bandage 4 inches wide are applied to the arm of the affected side just below the axillary fold. The end of one adhesive strip is looped around the arm (overlying the flannel bandage) and pinned, with the loop sufficiently large not to constrict the arm. With the

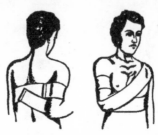

FIGURE 28.—Sayre's dressing for fracture of the clavicle, showing application of first and second strips. (Wharton.)

arm drawn upward and backward, the strip of plaster is carried across the back and around the opposite side of the chest. It may end here or be carried completely around the chest. The hand of the injured side now is placed as near as possible to the shoulder of the sound side, the skin surfaces being separated by sheet wadding. The end of the second strip is applied over the scapula of the affected side (some surgeons start this strip at the top of the posterior surface of the arm of the affected side; others apply the initial end of this strip on the shoulder of the sound side) and is carried downward on the posterior surface of the arm of the affected side, under the point of the elbow, diagonally across the chest on the posterior surface of the forearm and hand over the sound shoulder down the back where it joins the first strip of plaster. A small hole is cut in this strip to receive the point of the elbow, which must be protected by a layer of cotton or sheet wadding. Then the entire dressing is covered with a Velpeau bandage. It is used for treatment of fractures of the clavicle (fig. 28).

(7) T-*bandage.*—This bandage consists of a horizontal bandage to which is attached, about its middle, a vertical bandage of approxi-

mately one-half the length of the horizontal bandage. The horizontal portion is employed to secure the bandage to the body, the vertical portion being used to retain dressings. This bandage is very useful in retaining dressings about the perineum and anal region. When used for this purpose, the horizontal band is applied around the abdomen above the iliac crests in such manner that the vertical portion is placed exactly in the midline of the back directly over the spine. The vertical portion then is brought forward between the thighs and secured to the horizontal portion in front of the abdomen, The vertical portion may be split longitudinally to form two strips of equal width.

(8) *Double* T-*bandage.*—This differs from the T-bandage in having two vertical strips instead of only one. The horizontal portion may be of any desired width. It frequently is used for the retention of dressings of the chest, breast, and abdomen. When so employed, the two vertical strips are carried over the shoulders from the back to the front and secured by pins to the horiztonal portion.

(9) *Tailed bandage.*—(*a*) The four-tailed bandage is made readily by splitting a strip of muslin or other material of the desired width, lengthwise, within a few inches of the center of the strip. This provides a bandage with a body and four tails.

(*b*) The many-tailed bandage is prepared in a similar manner, by splitting the muslin or other material into several strips, having a sufficiently large area in the center for the retention of dressings, etc. The number of tails on each side should be the same.

(10) *Plaster of paris bandage.*—These bandages are prepared by impregnating the meshes of crinoline with plaster of paris of the extra calcined, dental variety. A strip of crinoline about 3 or 4 inches wide and usually 4 or 5 yards long, is placed on a table. Plaster of paris then is dusted upon the strip and evenly rubbed into the meshes of the fabric. A very satisfactory method of preparing this bandage is by constructing a wooden box 12 inches long, 6 inches wide, and 3 inches deep, and at each end, just above the bottom of the box, cutting a slit 5 inches long and $\frac{1}{8}$ to $\frac{1}{4}$ inch wide. The end of the bandage is drawn into the box through one slit across the bottom of the box and out of the box through the other slit. A sufficient quantity of the plaster of paris to cover the bandage with a layer of powder 1 inch deep is placed in the box. As the bandage is drawn through, plaster of paris is rubbed into the meshes with the hand or preferably with a smooth piece of wood approximately 4 inches in length. The bandage may be loosely rolled into a cylinder as it emerges from the box. If the bandages

are not to be used within a few hours, they should be wrapped in paper to prevent absorption of moisture.

(*a*) *Application.*—The part to be encased in plaster of paris should be covered with a suitable bandage of soft material, preferably flannel. The bony prominences should be well protected with cotton. Care should be taken to remove all creases in the dressing and bandage. Two rolls of the plaster of paris bandage are placed in warm water. When bubbles cease to arise from the bandage one roll is removed from the water, the excess water being expressed by grasping the roll at its two ends and exerting pressure with the hands. This method prevents the loss of a considerable amount of plaster through the ends of the roll.

NOTE.—As soon as a bandage is removed from the water replace it with another bandage.

The bandage should be applied rapidly and evenly to the limb. No special form of bandage is necessary as it is sufficient that the part be properly covered. The second bandage is applied as soon as the first has been completed. During the application of the bandage it should be rubbed with the hands in order to provide a smooth, even surface. It also is desirable to rub some loose plaster into the dressing. When the final roller has been applied, the surface of the completed dressing should be rubbed evenly with liquid plaster prepared by addition of water to dry plaster until it has the consistency of thick cream. In many cases, such as compound fractures, it is frequently necessary to provide access to certain areas of the encased limb. After the bandage has partially set, a "window" or trap may be cut in the bandage over the desired area. Removal of a plaster of paris bandage may be accomplished with the aid of a plaster saw. If none is available, the plaster may be softened with a small amount of peroxide of hydrogen, hydrochloric acid, or vinegar, and then may be cut with a knife.

(*b*) *Uses.*—This bandage is used for fixation of fractures; ambulant treatment of fractures; fixation and treatment of injuries and diseases of joints.

(11) *Starched bandage.*—This bandage may be obtained already prepared or it may be prepared in the following manner: Starch is mixed with cold water until a thin, creamy mixture results. This is heated to form a clear mucilaginous liquid. The part should be covered with a flannel bandage over which a gauze bandage is applied. The starch then is rubbed evenly into the meshes of the material. A second gauze bandage is applied and again treated with the starch mixture. This may be repeated until the desired thickness of the bandage is obtained. Bandages impregnated with starch may be

moistened and applied wet to a part. This type of bandage is occasionally useful in the treatment of sprains of the thumb or fingers.

(12) *Triangular bandage.*—This bandage, also known as the handkerchief bandage, is used for the temporary or permanent dressing of wounds, fractures, dislocations, etc., and for slings. It is very valuable in first-aid work as it is quickly and easily applied, stays on well, and can be improvised from any kind of cloth, as a piece of a shirt, an old sheet, a large handkerchief such as the Navy uniform neckerchief, etc. Unbleached muslin is generally used in making triangular bandages, although linen, woolen, silk, etc., will answer the purpose. In making them, a square of material about 3 by 3 feet or slightly more is folded diagonally to make one bandage or may be cut along the fold to make two bandages. The long side of the triangle is called the "base", the point opposite the base is called the "apex", and the points at each end of the base are called the "ends" or "extremities." These bandages may be used either as a triangle or as a cravat, the latter being made from the triangle by bringing the apex to the base and folding it upon itself a sufficient number of times to obtain the width desired (fig. 29). The names of these bandages indicate the part of the body to which the base is applied, the location of the apex, and the shape. For example, in the fronto-occipital triangle the base of a triangular bandage is applied to the forehead and the apex is carried to the occiput, and in the mento-vertico-occipital cravat the middle of the base is placed under the chin and the ends carried over the vertex of the skull to the occiput. A few of the more commonly used triangular bandages are as follows:

(*a*) *Fronto-occipital triangle.*—Place the middle of the base of the triangle on the forehead so that the edge is just above the eyebrows and bring the apex backward over the head, allowing it to drop over the occiput. Bring the ends of the triangle around to the back of the head, above the ears, cross them over the apex at the occiput, and carry them around to the forehead and there tie them in a square knot. Finally turn up the apex toward the top of the head and pin with a safety pin or turn up the apex and tuck it in behind the crossed part of the bandage. It is used to retain dressings on the forehead or scalp (fig. 30).

(*b*) *Triangle of chest or back.*—Drop the apex of the triangle over the shoulder on the injured side and bring the bandage down over the chest (or back) to the level desired and so that the middle of the base is directly below the shoulder. Carry the ends around the body and tie in a square knot on the back. Finally, bring the apex down on the back (or chest) and tie it in a square knot to one of the ends.

It is used to retain dressings on burns or wounds of the chest or back (fig. 31).

(*c*) *Brachio-cervical triangle, or arm sling.*—The arm to be put in the sling should first be bent at the elbow so that the little finger is about a hand's breadth above the level of the elbow. Drop one end of the triangle over the shoulder on the uninjured side and let the bandage hang down over the chest with the base toward the

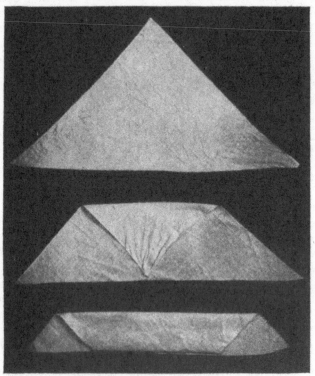

FIGURE 29.—Folding cravat from triangle.

hand and the apex toward the elbow. Slip the bandage between the body and the arm, carry the lower end up over the shoulder on the injured side, and tie the two ends together at either side of the neck, using a square knot. Draw the apex of the bandage toward the elbow until it is snug, bring it around the elbow to the front, and after folding back a little, fasten it to the front of the bandage with a safetypin. The lower end of the bandage may be passed between the arm and the body and under instead of over the injured

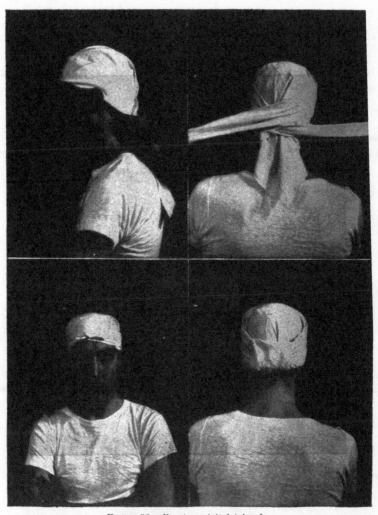

FIGURE 30.—Fronto-occipital triangle.

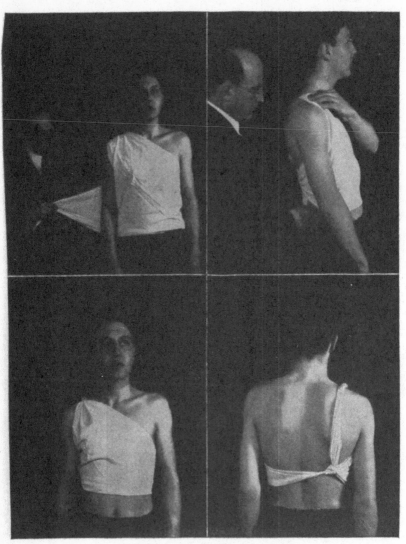

FIGURE 31.—Triangle of chest or back.

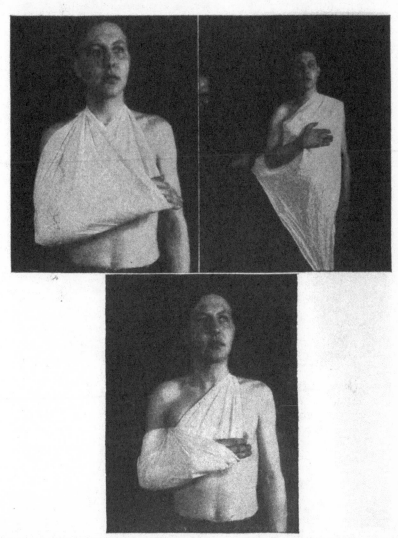

FIGURE 32.—Brachio-cervical triangle or arm sling showing lower end passing between arm and body.

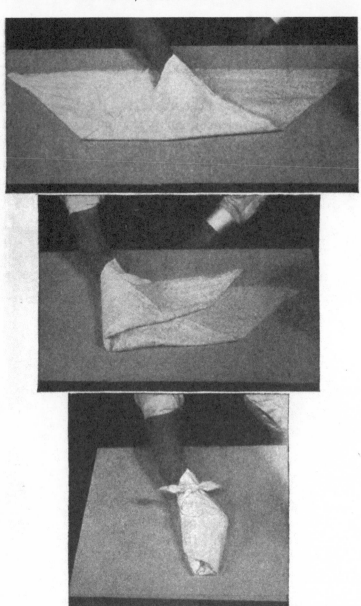

FIGURE 33.—Triangle of hand.

shoulder before tying to the other end. The ends of the fingers should extend slightly beyond the base of the triangle (fig. 32).

(*d*) *Triangle of hand.*—Place the middle of the base of the triangle well up on the palmar surface of the wrist, carry the apex around the ends of the fingers and over the dorsum of the hand to the wrist or forearm, fold each half of the part at the sides of the hand back toward the opposite side of the wrist, cross the ends around the wrist, and tie in a square knot. It is used to retain dressings of considerable size on the hand (fig. 33).

(*e*) *Triangle of foot.*—Place the middle of the base of the triangle on the ankle well above the heel, carry the apex around the ends of the toes and over the dorsum of the foot to the ankle, fold each half of the part at the sides of the foot back toward the opposite side of the ankle, cross the ends around the ankle, and tie in a square knot. It is used to retain dressings of considerable size on the foot (fig. 34).

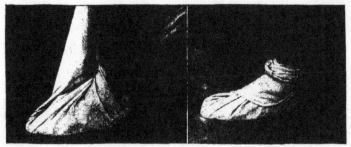

FIGURE 34.—Triangle of foot.

(*f*) *Gluteo-femoral triangle.*—To apply this bandage requires two bandages, one a triangle, the other a cravat. First fasten the cravat around the waist. Place the base of the triangle in the gluteo-femoral fold and carry the ends around the thigh to the front where they are tied with a square knot. The apex is then carried upward and passed under the cravat around the waist, turned down and fastened to the triangle with a safetypin. It is used to retain dressings on the buttock or hip (fig. 35).

(13) *Cravats.*—(*a*) *Mento-vertico-occipital cravat.*—After making a triangle into a cravat of the proper width, place the middle of the cravat under the chin, carry the ends upward in front of each ear to the vertex of the skull, crossing them there, and continuing downward to the occiput where they are tied in a square knot. Uses: To retain dressings on the chin, cheeks, and scalp, and as a temporary dressing to secure fixation of the parts in fracture or dislocation of the jaw (fig. 36).

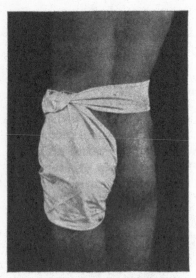

FIGURE 35.—Gluteo-femoral triangle.

FIGURE 36.—Mento-vertico-occipital cravat.

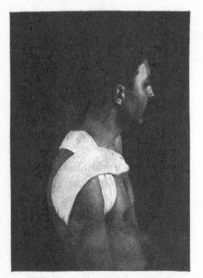

FIGURE 37.—Bis-axillary cravat.

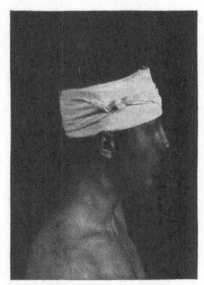

FIGURE 38.—Cravat of head or ear.

(*b*) *Bis-axillary cravat.*—After making a triangle into a cravat of the proper width, place the middle of the cravat in the axilla, carry the ends upward to the top of the shoulder, crossing them there and continuing across the back and chest, respectively, to the opposite axilla, where they are tied in a square knot. It is used to retain dressings in the axilla or on the shoulder (fig. 37).

(*c*) *Cravat of head or ear.*—After making a triangle into a cravat of the proper width, place the middle of the cravat over the point desired, carry the ends to the opposite side of the head, cross them, and bring them back to the starting point and tie with a square knot. Use: To apply pressure to control serious hemorrhage from wounds (fig. 38).

**129. Dressings.**—*a. Types.*—A dressing consists of everything used to cover or dress a wound. The pad put directly over the wound is called a "compress." In ordinary emergency treatment, a wound dressing consists of a compress with bandage to hold it on. A dressing may be either dry or wet, asceptic or antiseptic.

(1) An *asceptic dressing* is one which is sterile, that is, with no bacteria on it.

(2) An *antiseptic dressing* is one which, in addition to being sterile, contains some substance for killing bacteria.

(3) A *wet dressing* generally is an antiseptic dressing and is used in wounds where infective inflammation is going on. Wet antiseptic dressings generally are made up of a layer of sterile gauze saturated with the antiseptic solution. A layer of sterile cotton is then applied, with some impervious material such as oiled silk put over the dressing to retain the moisture, and a bandage over all. The dressing must be kept wet with the antiseptic solution, either by frequent changing or by having perforated rubber tubes between the gauze and cotton through which the dressing can be periodically moistened with the antiseptic solution.

(4) A *dry dressing* is used to cover a recent wound which is considered to be free from infection.

*b. Purpose.*—The purpose of a wound dressing is to stop hemorrhage, to prevent introduction of bacteria, and to prevent further injury to the wound.

*c. Types in first-aid packet.*—The Army supplies two first-aid packets, one small and one large, which are hermetically sealed tin cans containing dry sterile dressings. (See figs. 39 to 42, incl.). All these dressings consist of a sterile gauze compress with bandages attached.

*d. Preparation of wound for dressing.*—(1) *General.*—Any piece of cloth, such as gauze, cotton, linen, muslin, or a handkerchief, provided it is rendered sterile, is suitable for a compress in case of emer-

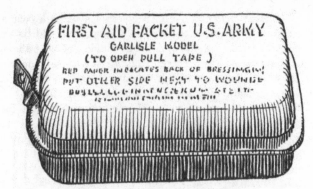

FIGURE 39.—First-aid packet, U. S. Army.

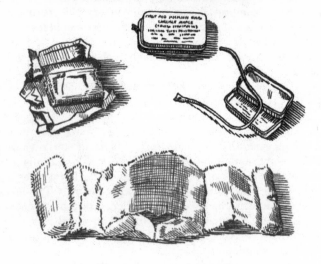

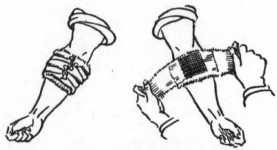

FIGURE 40.—Application of dressing, first-aid packet, small.

gency. The most vital point about material used as a compress of a wound is that, before it is applied to a wound, it should be rendered sterile. The part of the dressing which is to come in contact with the wound must not be touched with any part of the body or anything else except sterile instruments before its application to the wound. In an emergency, material to be used in a wound dressing may be sterilized by boiling it for 10 minutes.

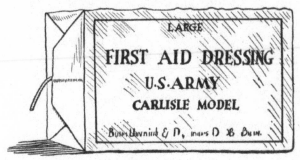

FIGURE 41.—First-aid dressing, large.

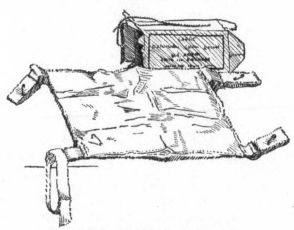

FIGURE 42.—First-aid dressing, large, open.

(2) *Procedures.*—When a patient can be brought under the care of a medical officer in the near future, the procedure necessary in the first-aid treatment in the case of ordinary wounds is to stop the hemorrhage, treat the shock, and apply a sterile dressing to the wound. If a medical officer is not available, the wound must be further treated as described below.

(*a*) In treating a freshly made wound, the following procedure is recommended :

1. Cleanse the hands as thoroughly as possible by a thorough scrubbing with soap and hot water, followed, if possible, by immersion in hot 1–2,000 bichloride of mercury solution and then 70 percent alcohol.

2. Sterilize all instruments to be used in removing foreign bodies such as dirt, glass, splinters, or for shoving the skin about the wounds.

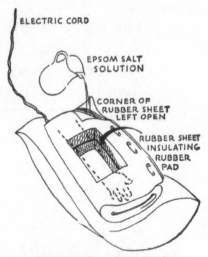

ELECTRIC CORD

EPSOM SALT SOLUTION

CORNER OF RUBBER SHEET LEFT OPEN

RUBBER SHEET INSULATING RUBBER PAD

Figure 43.—Type of wet dressing.

3. If there is bleeding, arrest the hemorrhage.

4. If there is grease in or about the wound, remove it with turpentine or gasoline.

5. Remove all foreign particles with sterile forceps.

6. Apply tincture of iodine to all parts of wound and the skin about the wound for a distance of about one-half inch beyond the wound edges. After the skin has been well dried, the wound edges are brought together and a dry dressing applied.

7. There is no substance which should be used by the first-aid man to wash a wound; more dirt is washed in than out, and ordinary water is dangerous since it is not sterile. Strong antiseptics, such as bichloride of mercury or phenol, will destroy the cells of the body which dispose of

the pus bacteria before they kill the latter.  Peroxide of hydrogen is not strong enough to kill all bacteria and in large or deep wounds it washes some of these bacteria to uninfected parts which then become infected.  *Tincture of iodine is the only substance to be used in an ordinary fresh wound by the first-aid man, aside from benzine and gasoline to cut grease, if present.*

(*b*) The manner in which a wound showing evidence of infective inflammation is treated is as follows:

*1.* Elevate the part.

*2.* Put it at rest.

*3.* Remove foreign bodies, if present.

*4.* Remove sufficient sutures, if present, to obtain good drainage.

*5.* Insert drain.

*6.* Apply a wet antiseptic dressing (fig. 43).

*7.* Treat the constitutional symptoms.

## Section III

## SPLINTS AND THEIR APPLICATION

130. **General.**—*a.* Splints are devices used for the fixation of broken bones.  They are used in the emergency treatment, as well as in the final treatment, of a fracture.  It is most important to fix a broken bone as soon as possible after injury.  In fractures of large bones, especially of the thigh bone (femur), the injured person within a short time often enters into a state of shock or collapse which may cause death.  Fixation of the fractured part with adequate splints as soon as the injured person is seen prevents the development of more shock, or if shock has not already set in, it may not occur. It should be remembered that in addition to splinting the fracture, the patient should be covered with blankets and given hot drinks, if possible, to aid in the prevention or decrease of shock.

*b.* Fixing the fragments of a broken bone prevents the rough and jagged edges of the bone ends from injuring and tearing nearby blood vessels and nerves, thus serious bleeding and paralysis is avoided. In simple fractures (one in which the bone has not punctured the skin) proper application of a splint will prevent penetration of the skin by fragments of bone and introduction of infection into deeper tissues. If the fracture is compound (one in which the skin has been punctured by a fragment of bone) splinting will prevent the bone from sliding in and out of the wound and the introduction of more infection. In addition, proper splinting greatly relieves the pain associated with the fracture. The patient is made much more comfortable and the amount of shock is reduced.

*c.* Thus, proper splinting of a fracture prevents the occurrence of, or increase of, the following:

(1) Shock.

(2) Local tissue damage (to nerves and blood vessels).

(3) Infection.

*d.* Always remember that every fracture of a long bone should be *splinted where they lie.*

Figure 44.—Army hinged half-ring thigh and leg splint.

**131. Army hinged half-ring thigh and leg splint.**—*a.* The Army leg splint is the most valuable of all splints when the saving of life is considered. It is used in nearly all fractures of the femur and can be used in fractures of the leg as far down as the ankle. The mortality rate for compound fractures of the femur was reduced from 50 percent to 15 percent in one army during the World War due to proper splinting of this bone.

*b.* For the purposes of training, application of the Army leg splint is done in 10 steps with a team of four men consisting of the following:

　　No. 1. Operator.
　　No. 2. First assistant.
　　No. 3. Second assistant.
　　No. 4. Patient.

NOTE.—The procedure here described appears in the pamphlet *The Demonstration and Application of the Army Leg Splint* (1940, Revised), published by the Medical Field Service School, Carlisle Barracks, Pennsylvania.

*c.* The equipment required for each team is as follows:

(1) One litter, standard wooden pole or aluminum.
(2) One Army leg splint, half-ring, hinged.
(3) Two footrest and splint supports.
(4) One traction strap.
(5) Two rolls of muslin bandage, 5 inches by 5 yards, and one gauze bandage.
(6) Three blankets.
(7) Six safetypins.
(8) One first-aid packet.

*d.* The 10 steps are as follows:

(1) Dress litter.
(2) Extension.
(3) Dress wound.
(4) Apply splint.
(5) Support leg.
(6) Traction strap.
(7) Footrest.
(8) Foot splint support.
(9) Fix splint.
(10) Cover patient.

*e.* The procedure is as follows:

(1) *Step No. 1, dress litter.*—The litter is "dressed" by Nos. 2 and 3. A litter is said to be dressed when blankets have been arranged upon it as follows: Place the first blanket on the litter lengthwise so that one edge corresponds to the outside pole of the litter and its upper edge is even with the head of the canvas. Then fold it back upon itself once, leaving the folded edge even with the inside pole of the litter. Place the second blanket folded lengthwise on the first so that one edge corresponds to the inside pole of the litter, and its upper edge is even with the head of the canvas. Then fold it back upon itself once in the same manner as the first. The free edges

of each of these blankets hang over opposite sides of the litter. The No. 4 man now lies on the litter and acts as patient. The third blanket is placed under the patient's head until the tenth step.

(2) *Step No. 2, extension.*—The No. 2 man of the team stands at the foot of the litter facing the patient. Grasping the heel of the shoe with his right hand and the toe with his left, keeping the arm straight, he exerts a steady pull to produce the necessary traction. The litter sling may be placed across the patient's chest, under the arms, and attached to the litter stirrup to provide countertraction. Traction should be continued until the traction strap has been fixed.

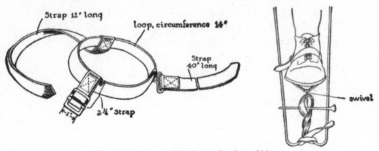

① Strap made of 1-inch nonelastic webbing.

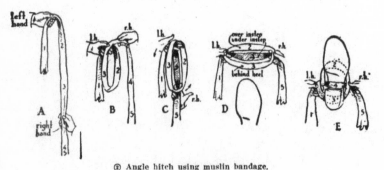

② Angle hitch using muslin bandage.

FIGURE 45.—Adjustable traction splint strap.

(3) *Step No. 3, dress wound.*—While extension is continued by No. 2, the No. 1 and No. 3 men dress the wound designated by the instructor.

(4) *Step No. 4, apply splint.*—The splint is applied by rolling it from the outside inward, the short rod to the inner side of the leg and the half ring well up under the buttock. The splint must be horizontal. It is held in place by buckling the upper strap.

(5) *Step No. 5, support leg.*—The leg is supported on the splint by arranging the muslin bandages in the following manner:

(*a*) The first bandage is placed across the upper part of the splint under the thigh.  The ends of the bandages are then reversed by crossing them under the splint and tying above and to the side.

(*b*) The second bandage is applied above the ankle in the same manner as the first.

(*c*) The third bandage is placed just above the knee.  The ends are drawn downward between the two side rods of the splint and knee, are folded upward, then around the leg, and are tied on the upper outer surface.

NOTE.—The positions of the bandages may vary, depending on the location of the fracture.  A fourth muslin bandage may be placed under the calf of the leg for additional support.  (See fig. 44.)

(6) *Step No. 6, traction strap.*—The traction strap is applied to the foot by the No. 1 man.  The loop of the strap is first placed behind the heel and under the foot, and the short buckling strap is brought over the top of the instep and buckled on the inside of the foot.  The long strap is then brought over and under the end of the splint, is folded back upon itself, and is inserted through the metal ring.  Traction is then maintained by pulling on the free end of the strap.  The free end is now secured by tying with the ordinary cinch knot.

(7) *Step No. 7, footrest.*—The footrest is attached to the splint with the lower hooks downward and inside the splint rods.  The footrest is pushed against the shoe to prevent foot drop.  Spread the footrest, if necessary, for a more secure fit.  Secure with bandage to prevent lateral movement of the foot.

(8) *Step No. 8, foot splint support.*—The Army leg splint is applied with the splint support fastened to the side rods of the splint in such position that it will rest on the litter end about 1½ inches from the end of the canvas.  The splint support will normally rest not on the canvas of the litter but upon the blankets of the dressed litter.  (See fig 46 ④.)

(9) *Step No. 9, fix splint.*—(*a*) Take a roll of the bias muslin bandage and stretch it to its greatest length.

(*b*) Tie one end of the bandage to the litter stirrup on the side of the fracture, placing the knot near the pole.

NOTE.—The knot is placed on the stirrup near the pole and the bandage wound around the bevel of the handle near the edge of the canvas to keep the bandage from slipping and becoming loose.

(*c*) Keeping a constant tension on the bandage, carry it to the bevel of the handle close to the canvas and wind it around the handle twice.  (Fig. 46 ①.)

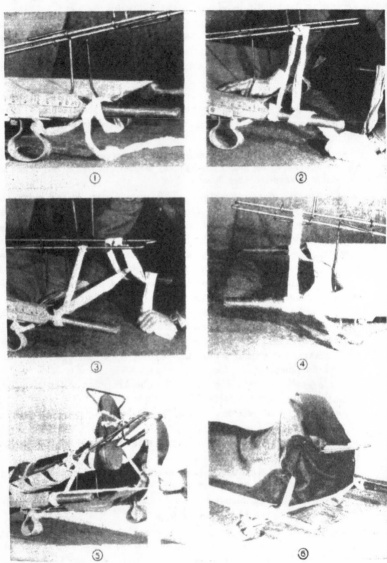

FIGURE 46.—Use of bandage for fixation of Army hinged half-ring leg splint for transportation.

(*d*) Carry the bandage to the near side of the rod of the leg splint, keeping it at a 90° angle (perpendicular) to the splint. Wind the bandage around the side rod twice and carry it back and around the same handle. Then press the splint firmly down on the litter and continue the constant pull on the bandage so that all the slack in the bandage going from the litter to the splint and from the splint back to the litter will be taken up. (Fig. 46②.)

Note.—The bandage is kept under constant tension as it is applied in order to overcome the elasticity. The small amount of elasticity remaining is considered beneficial. In an emergency, wire, rope, or other material can be used for fastening the splint to the handles of the litter.

(*e*) Then carry the bandage across the litter to the bevel of the opposite handle and wind it around twice.

(*f*) Next secure the side rod of the splint on that side in the same manner as was done on the near side, ending by tying the bandage to the stirrup. (Fig. 46③.)

Note.—When the muslin bandage is properly applied and tied, the splinted leg and end of the litter can be lifted clear of the ground without loosening the muslin bandage. The position of the splint rest on the blanket and canvas remains unaffected and the bandage is still taut when the end of the litter is again lowered to the ground. (Fig. 46⑤.)

(10) *Step No. 10, cover patient.*—Fold the third blanket once lengthwise and place it over patient, the upper edge under the chin. Next, fold the free edges of the first two blankets over the third and hold them in place with safetypins. Inclose the feet of the patient by folding the lower ends of the blankets. (Fig. 46⑥.) This gives *four thicknesses of blanket over* and *four under* the patient, thus assisting in the prevention of shock.

(11) *Alternate step No. 6.*—In the absence of the traction strap, the following may be substituted for step No. 6:

(*a*) An ankle hitch (fig. 45②) is applied by the No. 1 man, assisted by No. 3.

Note.—A piece of muslin bandage about 1 yard long is held in the left hand, one-third falling to the left. Pick up the long end with the right hand and form a loop. Drop the long end over the loop as if to tie a single knot, but do not bring it through the loop. The hitch is now ready to apply to the foot. Hold the hitch as shown in figure 45②, place it around the ankle, and apply the Spanish windlass.

(*b*) To apply the Spanish windlass, cross the two free ends of the bandage under the instep of the shoe; pass one free end over and one free end under the end of the splint. Bring the two ends together and securely tie to the notch at the end of the splint. Now insert a 6-inch stick or nail between the two ends of the bandage just above the tie. Fix the stick or nail between the two rods of the splint.

*f.* In actual practice three persons to apply the splint will often not be available, and in emergencies or on the battlefield variations of the preceding will, of course, be necessary. However, if possible, two men should apply the splint, as it is important that one maintain a pull on the injured leg until traction is started within the splint.

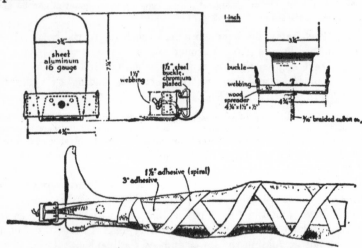

FIGURE 47.—Skin traction with zinc oxide adhesive and spreader.

*g.* (1) Instead of using a traction strap or ankle hitch, skin traction may be applied, using adhesive tape. This is done when it is necessary to transport the patient for a long distance and also for final hospital treatment when it is necessary to maintain traction for long periods. Before the adhesive tape is applied, the leg is shaved and cleansed with ether. A long strip of 3-inch adhesive tape is then prepared by folding one end back on itself so that two nonsticky surfaces are obtained. This doubled portion is made long enough to extend from 1 or 2 inches above the ankle to the end of the splint. A second strip is made in the same way and both are cut to the desired length. The straps thus formed are then heated over a flame and one is applied to each side of the leg extending up to thigh, slightly below the line of fracture. In fractures of the lower leg the straps are placed below the knee and extend up to within about an inch of the fracture line. The ends of straps are then tied to the end of the splint, or to a spreader which in turn is attached to the end of the splint, and a Spanish windlass applied. Two narrow strips, 1½-inch, are then spiraled about the leg and a snug gauze or bias muslin bandage is applied about the leg to increase adhesion of the straps.

(2) An improved type of skin traction, using an adhesive solution and flannel bandage straps may be used if such is available. A satisfactory solution is Ace Adherent, which is painted on each side of the leg and on which the flannel bandage straps are applied. They are applied in the same manner as the adhesive tape straps, except that the leg is not shaved.

**132. Thomas arm splint.**—*a.* The Thomas arm splint is used in fractures of the arm from the shoulder down to and including the upper third of the forearm. As with the Army leg splint, it may be applied in steps for purposes of training and the following is from a pamphlet, *Demonstration and Application of the Army Arm Splint* (1939), published by the Medical Field Service School, Carlisle Barracks, Pennsylvania.

*b.* A three-man team is necessary:

No. 1. Operator.

No. 2. Assistant.

No. 3. Patient.

*c.* The equipment required for each team is as follows:

(1) Two rolls of 2-inch adhesive plaster.

(2) One Thomas arm splint with full ring.

(3) Three wooden tongue blades.

(4) Three rolls 2-inch roller gauze bandage.

(5) Three 1-yard strips of 2-inch muslin bandage for each three students.

*d.* The procedure is as follows:

(1) *Step No. 1, extension.*—The operator holds the full ring splint while No. 2, his assistant, inserts his right hand through the full ring. Then the No. 2 man, with his right hand, grasps the patient's injured arm firmly at the wrist and makes steady extension, placing his left hand in the armpit of the patient. The operator then puts the splint in place on the patient well up under the arm, and the end of the splint well up against the thigh of the No. 2 man. The No. 2 man then removes his left hand from under the armpit and grasps the wrist of the patient with his left hand, assisting the right hand.

(2) *Step No. 2, dress wound.*—This is done by the operator or No. 1 man. It should be done neatly and quickly.

(3) *Step No. 3, applying adhesive strips.*—Use two strips, one over the arm and one under the arm, starting about 2 inches above the elbow, down the entire length of the forearm, and about 8 inches over the hand. The two strips should be the same length.

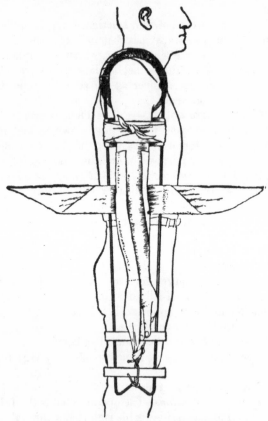

FIGURE 48.—Thomas splint, arm-hinged, for right or left arm.

(4) *Step No. 4, anchor adhesive with bandages.*—Support the adhesive strips by applying bandage. Start the bandage at the wrist and use a spiral reverse all the way up the forearm to the elbow. This anchors the adhesive strips to the arm. Do not make bandage too tight because it will affect seriously the circulation of the blood.

(5) *Step No. 5, completing fixation and traction.*—Tie the ends of adhesive together and over the end of the splint. Then with the use

of a short object, such as a stick or wooden tongue depressor, make a Spanish windlass, pulling the arm until proper extension is secured.

(6) *Step No. 6, support arm.*—Using the muslin triangular bandage, make a narrow cravat, bringing it up between the rods of the Army arm splint and over the side of the rods. Then reverse the two ends and bring them around the outside of the rods, tying on the outside of the splint. One to three of these supports may be used, one at the wrist, one just below the elbow, and one on the upper arm. The splint may then be secured to the patient's thigh to insure greater immobility of the injured limb while he is being transported.

(7) A hitch around the wrist should never be used and it should be remembered that the adhesive straps for traction extend up to a level slightly below the fracture and not above it.

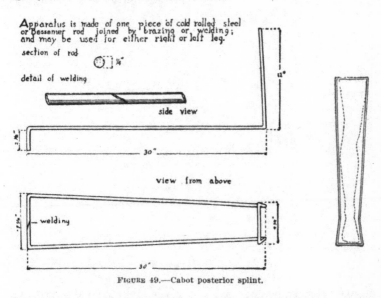

FIGURE 49.—Cabot posterior splint.

**133. Cabot posterior splint.**—*a.* The Cabot posterior splint is used for fixation of the leg without traction. It is used for fractures of the patella (kneecap), for sprains and other injuries in the region of the knee, for fractures of the ankle, for fractures in the lower leg when only one bone is broken (tibia or fibula), and for injuries to soft parts of the leg or foot which require fixation for transportation.

*b.* The splint is a frame of rolled steel rod which is bent at a right angle at one end so as to form a support for the foot, and it is long enough to extend up to the middle third of the thigh. A supporting hammock is then made by wrapping bias muslin or gauze bandage around the lateral bars of the splint. Additional gauze and cotton padding is added as necessary to prevent pressure on the leg. The splint is then applied to the back of the leg and secured with a bandage which passes around both the leg and the splint.

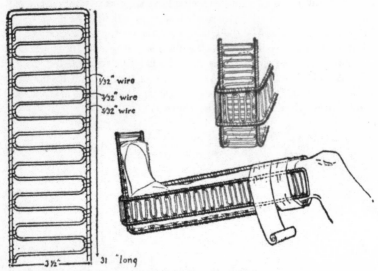

FIGURE 50.—Wire ladder splint.

**134. Wire ladder splint.**—*a.* The wire ladder splint is used for fractures and injuries of the foot and ankle, and to maintain a fixed position of the shoulder, elbow, or wrist when a position other than extension is desired. It is occasionally used for side splinting, in combination with a Cabot posterior splint.

*b.* It is made up of sheets of malleable wire in the shape of a ladder and may be molded into any desired shape and then cut into desired lengths. The splints are padded for comfort and applied with bias muslin or gauze bandage.

**135. Aeroplane or abduction splint.**—*a.* This splint is used for fractures of the upper end of the humerus, for fractures of the scapula (shoulder blade), for nerve injuries which cause a paralysis of the shoulder and upper arm, and for bursitis of the shoulder. It is not used in dislocations of the shoulder.

*b.* It is a frame of rolled steel rod which is bent at a right angle to fit under the armpit, so that the lower portion lies along the side of the chest and abdomen down to the hip. The upper portion forms a shelf for the arm to rest upon. This is also bent at a right angle so that the elbow is flexed when the arm is resting upon it. Canvas or similar material is sewed around the frame to form a supporting hammock and the entire splint is held in place with three straps. Sufficient gauze and cotton pads are added for comfort. The arm is secured by wrapping bandage around both the arm and the splint.

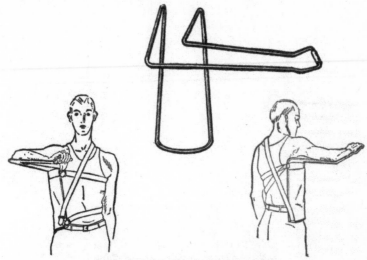

FIGURE 51.—Aeroplane or abduction splint.

**136. Clavicular or T-splint.**—This splint is used for fractures of the clavicle (collar bone), and resembles the letter T as its name implies. The cross bar of the T is placed behind the shoulders with the longitudinal bar extending downward along the spinal column. Straps from the ends of the cross bar are passed around the shoulders so as to pull the shoulders upward, outward, and backward. A strap passing around the abdomen is attached to the lower end of the splint to allow for a snug fit.

**137. Wooden splints.**—Wooden splints are usually made of ½-inch by 4-inch basswood, but boards from discarded fruit crates are also satisfactory. They are mainly used for fractures and other severe injuries of the forearm and hand. The splints are cut into the desired shape and are well padded. Usually two splints are applied, one on the back of the forearm and hand and the other on the inner or palm side. They are held in place with adhesive tape and bandage which should be applied snugly but not too tightly. The forearm can then be suspended in a sling.

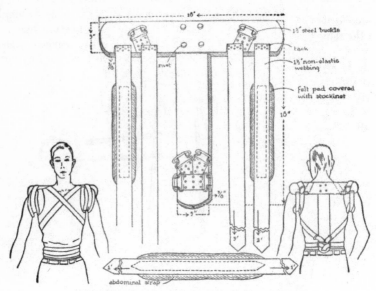

FIGURE 52.—T-splint with straps for fractured clavicle.

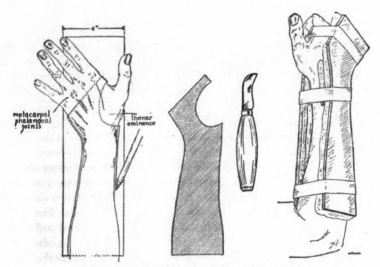

FIGURE 53.—Splinting of lower forearm fractures.

**138. Other splints.**—*a*. Aluminum splints are more satisfactory than wooden splints but they are not always available. They are used in the same manner as wooden splints and may be molded and cut to any desired size and shape.

*b*. It should be remembered that to obtain adequate fixation of a fracture one does not always need a special splint which has been made for a certain type of fracture. When nothing else is available any handy article may be used. Examples of these are rifles, swords, scabbards, tent pins, wire, umbrellas, canes, mop or broom handles, sticks, small pieces of board, etc. These may not be quite as satisfactory as a finished appliance, but if care is taken in applying them, enough support can be obtained to prevent further injury to the patient. Thus, in fractures of the thigh, if a Thomas splint is not available, a long splint extending from well above the hip to beyond the foot on the outside, and a shorter splint extending from the crotch to beyond the foot on the inside will afford a good support when carefully applied.

SECTION IV

EMERGENCY MEDICAL TREATMENT

**139. First aid.**—*a*. First aid is the temporary emergency treatment given a case of sudden illness or accident before the services of a medical officer can be obtained. This period of temporary care, if intelligently given, will often save a life. In all cases, first aid, properly administered, will reduce the mental and physical suffering and thereby place the patient in the medical officer's hands in a better condition to receive further treatment. Very often the only first aid practicable is the prevention of further injury to the patient by well-meaning but poorly informed onlookers.

*b.* In rendering first aid there are certain things to be done in all cases of injury or illness. These procedures are—

(1) Send immediately for a medical officer.

(2) Keep bystanders far enough away to permit work without hinderance.

(3) Do not move the patient until the extent of injury is determined. Keep the patient lying in a comfortable position with the head level with the body.

(4) Loosen the patient's clothing about the head, neck, and abdomen.

(5) Examine the patient to determine the nature of the injury or illness, paying particular attention to evidence of hemorrhage, shock, asphyxia, poisonings, fractures, dislocations, burns, and wounds.

(6) Proceed with the first-aid treatment at once, treating serious hemorrhage first, asphyxia next, then shock, and other conditions in the order of their seriousness. Remember never to give an unconscious person any liquids as they may enter the windpipe and strangle him. Keep the patient warm.

*c.* A soldier giving first aid should do so with evident display of self-assurance and authority born of knowledge, with calmness, and with decision, thereby obtaining the confidence of the patient and of the bystanders.

**140. Wounds.**—*a.* A wound is a break in the skin or in the mucous membrane of one of the body cavities.

*b.* The principal kinds of wounds are clean or aseptic wounds, infected or septic wounds, and poisoned wounds.

(1) An *aseptic* wound is one in which no germs have gained access, the best example being a wound made by the surgeon's sterile knife.

(2) A *septic* wound is one in which there has been introduced pus-producing organisms or such organisms as produce tetanus, gas gangrene, or hydrophobia.

(3) *A poisoned* wound is one in which some nonliving poison, as distinguished from bacteria or microorganisms, has been introduced by the agent causing the wound, as for example the stings of insects or the fangs of snakes.

*c.* Classified as to causative agent or appearance, wounds are—

(1) *Incised* wounds, made by sharp cutting instruments such as knives, razors, and broken glass, the class of wounds commonly known as "cuts."

(2) *Lacerated* wounds, often irregular and torn. They are caused by contact with angular surfaces, by shell fragments, and machinery. These wounds present ragged edges which do not retract much and

which, as a rule, consist of masses of torn tissue, frequently with dirt ground into the tissue.

(3) *Contused* wounds, wounds in which the division of tissue is accompanied by more or less severe crushing. Crushed wounds are more serious than they may appear at first, due to the fact that the dead tissues are an excellent media for the growth of bacteria. This may result, in an infection causing the loss of a part or general blood poisoning.

(4) *Puncture* wounds or *stab* wounds, caused by such penetrating objects as nails, wires, or bullets. They are usually deep and narrow and may be very dangerous if they penetrate deeply enough to seriously injure important organs or cause internal hemorrhage.

*d.* Infection, severe bleeding, and shock are the principal dangers from any type of wound. Rapid bleeding requires immediate attention. In most cases bleeding is readily controlled. Infection can occur whenever the skin surface is broken, the size or location of the wound not being related to the possibility of infection. A skin puncture with an ordinary pin may cause a serious infection. A wound should never be touched with anything except sterile dressings or instruments; unclean hands, bandages, or instruments may infect a wound that is relatively clean.

**141. Treatment of wounds.**—*a. Wound in which bleeding is not severe.*—(1) In these cases the chief duty is to keep the wound clean and prevent infection. If an antiseptic is available, apply this gently to the wound and to the skin for an inch around the wound. Allow this to dry well, then apply a clean dressing. If neither antiseptics or dressings are at hand, do not apply a substitute but allow the wound to remain open; bleeding will usually stop in a few minutes.

(2) Do not touch the wound with the hands, mouth, clothing, or any unclean object.

(3) Do not wash the wound with any solutions such as soap or water, as this may carry germs into the wound.

(4) Do not massage or squeeze any wound; you may start severe bleeding or injure the tissue.

(5) Do not attempt to explore the wound with any object or remove blood clots.

(6) Do not reapply antiseptics such as iodine. Never use iodine in the eye or in any body cavity.

*b. Wound in which bleeding is severe.*—Pressure is the only first-aid method for the control of bleeding. If sterile gauze or bandage material is available, this can be used by direct pressure on the wound and held in place until a dressing is applied or a tourniquet adjusted.

When direct pressure to a wound is not possible, or when the direct pressure does not control the bleeding, apply pressure with the fingers or with a tourniquet between the wound and the heart. At certain places in the body large arteries lie near bones and may be compressed so as to decrease the flow of blood through them. (See par. 143.) Shock is always present with severe bleeding. Do not give any stimulants until the bleeding is controlled. Wounds, especially puncture wounds caused by gun powder or dirty objects, are subject to additional danger from infection by tetanus organisms. Wounds contaminated by soil or street dirt are frequently infected by the organisms of gas gangrene. Serum containing antitoxin is always available against tetanus or gas infection.

142. **Miscellaneous wounds.**—*a. Snake bites.*—(1) All snake bites are not poisonous. By inspection of the wound one can sometimes tell if a person was bitten by a poisonous or nonpoisonous snake. In poisonous snakes the teeth are arranged in two rows, with a fang on each side, outside of the teeth near the point of the jaw. In nonpoisonous snakes there are four rows of teeth without fangs. The venom of poisonous snakes differs in its action. The poisonous constituents of the venom are neurotoxin, a nerve poison; hemorrhagin, which injures the lining of the blood vessels so that an escape of blood occurs into the surrounding tissue; and hemolysin, which destroys red blood cells. Poisonous snakes are classified as viperine and colubrine. The viperine snakes are those whose venom is made up principally of hemorrhagin and to this group belong the rattlesnake, copperhead, water moccasin, and viper. The colubrine snakes are those whose venom is made up principally of neurotoxin, and to this group belong the cobra and coral snake.

(2) The symptoms of colubrine poisoning are not marked; there may be severe pain and some tenderness, swelling, and discoloration at the site of the bite. In 1 to 2 hours, however, the patient begins to feel tired and drowsy and has some nausea and vomiting. Paralysis generally follows, affecting first the extremities and then becoming generalized, finally affecting respiration and producing death.

(3) The symptoms of viperine poisoning are pain at the seat of the bite with excruciating pain, rapid swelling, and discoloration, some nausea and faintness, rapid, feeble pulse, labored breathing, and in fatal cases death follows within 24 to 48 hours.

(4) The treatment of snake bite should start immediately. A tourniquet should be placed around the limb and just above the bite to increase bleeding and to reduce the amount of absorption of the

venom into the general circulation. A necktie, handkerchief, or bandage may be used as a tourniquet and should be tight enough to prevent the flow of blood back through the veins but not tight enough to prevent the flow of blood in the arteries. A cross incision should then be made over each fang mark, and preferably one to connect the two fang punctures, about a quarter to one-half inch deep to insure free bleeding. Suction should then be applied for at least one-half hour, either by glass breast pump or by heating a bottle and applying its mouth tightly over the wound. The cooling bottle will produce considerable suction. The patient should be kept quiet. Antivenom is now available which neutralizes neurotoxin and hemorrhagin. These are injected hypodermically or intravenously and are very effective, but the application of the tourniquet, free bleeding, and suction are of far greater value if applied immediately.

*b. Insect bites and stings.*—(1) The bites or stings produced by mosquitoes, fleas, and bees usually require little treatment. The application of Calomine lotion is soothing and 2 percent phenol may be added to this lotion in cases of extreme irritation. If the sting of the insect is left in the skin, it should be removed by a pair of small forceps. The poison from these insects is chiefly acid, and the local application of some alkali such as baking soda, solution of ammonia, or washing soda affords relief.

(2) The bites or stings of the more poisonous spiders, centipedes, tarantulas, or scorpions require prompt treatment. The general treatment is similar to snake bites, that is, the application of a tourniquet, cross incision with free bleeding, suction, and treatment of shock if present. Local treatment of the bite with fuming nitric acid or cautery is recommended.

*c. Bites of rabid animals or those suspected of being rabid.*—It is very important to catch the animal uninjured and place it in quarantine. Under no circumstances should it be killed as it is only after a period of observation that one can determine if the animal is rabid. The wound should be cauterized with fuming nitric acid and neutralized with sodium hydrate solution 1 percent or sodium bicarbonate solution 10 percent. If fuming nitric acid is not available, sterilize the wound by cautery with a red-hot needle. Do not use silver nitrate or phenol as this will precipitate by coagulation the albumin in the tissues, producing anaerobic conditions necessary for the growth of infective organisms. Apply a dry dressing.

*d. Human bites.*—Human bites are always more or less poisonous from the presence of bacteria constantly found on the teeth and other parts of the mouth. A human bite is potentially a very serious bite and fatal infection can result. These wounds should be thoroughly disinfected and wet antiseptic dressing applied.

**143. Hemorrhage.**—*a. General.*—Hemorrhage or bleeding is the escape of blood from the blood vessel due to a break in the walls. Hemorrhage is spoken of as arterial, venous, or capillary, depending upon whether the escape of blood is from arteries, veins, or capillaries.

*b. Arrest.*—Nature attempts to arrest hemorrhage by the clotting of blood forming a plug at the point of bleeding. In the average healthy person it takes from 3 to 5 minutes for the blood to clot. This clot of blood which arrests the hemorrhage eventually contracts and permanently plugs the break in the vessel wall if allowed to remain undisturbed. We can assist nature in arresting hemorrhage by elevation of the bleeding part, thus decreasing the pressure of the blood at the point of hemorrhage; by keeping the patient at complete rest so that the blood clot at the point of bleeding will not be disturbed; by the application of heat or cold, which tends to cause the blood vessel wall to contract, and by the use of pressure to close the bleeding vessel. In no case give stimulants in hemorrhage, as they increase the blood pressure and tend to cause the dislodgement of the clot at the bleeding point.

*c. Types.*—(1) *Capillary hemorrhage.*—In this condition there is a steady oozing of blood from all over the wounded surface. Capillary hemorrhage is treated by the elevation of the part, the application of either very hot or very cold water and the application of uniform pressure by means of a gauze compress and bandage to the part involved. Nosebleed is an example of capillary hemorrhage. The treatment of nosebleed consists of placing the patient in a sitting position, the removal of any constricting clothing about the neck and the application of cold to the back of the neck which causes a reflex contraction of the blood vessels of the nose. If these measures fail place a roll of paper under the upper lip between it and the gum and in severe bleeding pack the nostril with some sort of soft material such as cotton, linen, or lint, gently forcing this well back into the nose.

(2) *Venous hemorrhage.*—In this condition there is a rapid flow of dark blood, a welling up as it were, without any spurting. Venous hemorrhage is treated by the elevation of the part, and the application of direct pressure over the wound with a sterile compress or bandage. This is usually sufficient. If venous hemorrhage should occur from an extremity, the limb should be bandaged from toes or

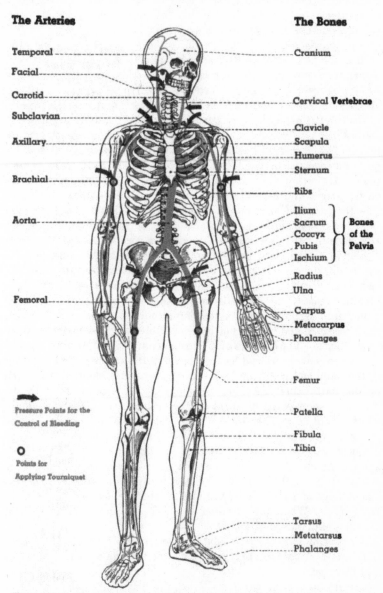

**The Arteries**

Temporal
Facial
Carotid
Subclavian
Axillary
Brachial
Aorta
Femoral

**The Bones**

Cranium
Cervical **Vertebrae**
Clavicle
Scapula
Humerus
Sternum
Ribs
Ilium
Sacrum
Coccyx
Pubis
Ischium
} **Bones of the Pelvis**
Radius
Ulna
Carpus
Metacarpus
Phalanges
Femur
Patella
Fibula
Tibia
Tarsus
Metatarsus
Phalanges

Pressure Points for the Control of Bleeding

Points for Applying Tourniquet

FIGURE 54.—American Red Cross first-aid chart, showing skeleton, large arteries, and points of digital pressure.

fingers up to the bleeding point in addition to pressure over the point of hemorrhage. A common location for severe venous hemorrhage is from varicose veins of the legs.

(3) *Arterial hemorrhage.*—In this condition there is a rapid flow of bright red blood which escapes in spurts. Arterial hemorrhage demands prompt measures, especially if the bleeding is from a large artery. Pressure to control arterial hemorrhage always must be applied at some point between the bleeding point and the heart, preferably, at a point where the bleeding artery may be compressed against bone. Pressure may be applied by means of the finger, by means of compress, or by the application of a tourniquet. A tourniquet is a constricting band, and there are various kinds. The principle of all tourniquets is a pad over the artery to bring the pressure on the artery and take it off the veins, a band around the limb and over the pad, and some means of tightening the band. The common improvised tourniquet is the so-called Spanish windlass, in which any smooth, hard object, such as a stone, a cork, or a roller bandage is used as a compress; for the band, a handkerchief, a suspender, a waist belt, or a bandage may be used. To tighten the band a stick, bayonet, or scabbard is passed under the band and twisted until the bleeding ceases, and the ends tied to the limb to prevent the band from becoming untwisted. Applying a tourniquet may be a dangerous procedure and should not be used if bleeding can be stopped by other means. The dangers of a tourniquet are that if applied tightly enough to control arterial hemorrhage it will cause pain and swelling of the limb, and if left on long enough may cause gangrene or death of the part below the constricting band. It should therefore be watched and released at about half-hour intervals. The tourniquet itself should be at least an inch wide, for if it is too narrow, it will cut off the entire blood supply to the injured part and require very frequent removal. If on loosening the tourniquet, bleeding starts again, tighten it up. Never cover a tourniquet with a bandage or splint, as it may be forgotten. Shock is always present with severe hemorrhage and immediately after the arrest of hemorrhage it must be treated. When the bleeding has stopped, and not until then, should stimulants be given.

*d. Pressure points in treatment of arterial hemorrhage.*—(1) *Bleeding from the scalp.*—Apply pressure over the wound with compress and bandage.

(2) *Bleeding from the lips.*—Grasp lips between thumb and fingers on each side of the wound, as the arteries to the lips come from both sides.

(3) *Bleeding from other parts of the face.*—Apply digital pressure on the facial artery against the lower jaw midway between the ear and chin where its pulsations can be felt.

(4) *Bleeding from the neck.*—Apply digital pressure with the thumb on the carotid artery against the vertebrae.

(5) *Bleeding from the armpit.*—Place a compress in the armpit and bind the arm tightly to the side. If this fails compress the subclavian artery behind the clavicle between the thumb and first rib, or compress it with a key, the handle of which has been padded.

(6) *Bleeding from an arm, forearm, or hand.*—Apply pressure on the brachial artery on the inner side of the biceps and then apply a tourniquet a little higher up. In case of hemorrhage in the forearm a pad may be placed in the bend of the elbow and the forearm forcibly flexed on the arm. In case of hemorrhage from the palm, either of these two methods may be used, or a large firm compress may be placed in the hand with the fingers very tightly closed over it and bandaged in place.

(7) *Bleeding from the thigh, leg, or foot.*—Apply pressure on the femoral artery against the head of the femur just below the middle of the groin with both thumbs, then apply a tourniquet to replace the thumbs. In case the hemorrhage is in the leg or foot, place a pad behind the knee, flex the leg forcibly and tie it in that position. In the foot when bleeding is from the dorsal surface apply pressure on the anterior tibial artery at the instep. In the foot when the bleeding is from the plantar surface apply pressure on the posterior tibial artery behind the internal malleolus.

(8) *Hemorrhage from the stomach.*—The vomited blood is usually dark in color and may be mixed with food. It always should be remembered that vomited blood does not necessarily indicate hemorrhage from the stomach; blood coming from the back of the nose and throat may have been swallowed, and inquiry should be made to find out if there has been any nosebleed. The treatment consists of keeping the patient quiet and applying an ice bag over the stomach.

(9) *Hemorrhage from the lungs.*—May result from wounds of the lungs, but more often is due to disease of these organs. The patient is usually seized by a fit of coughing and spits up bright red, frothy blood. The treatment consists in keeping the patient perfectly quiet and applying an ice bag over the chest.

(10) *Hemorrhage from the bowels.*—This is bright red if the hemorrhage is recent and if old the stools will be black and tarry in color. Cancer and hemorrhoids are the most common causes of blood in the

stools. If recent hemorrhage, keep the patient quiet and apply an ice bag over the abdomen.

**144. Shock.**—*a.* Shock is a profound depression of all physical and mental processes usually resulting from injury or severe bleeding, but may be caused by exposure, fatigue, hunger, or extreme emotion. Some degree of shock follows all injuries; it may be slight, lasting only a few minutes, or it may be prolonged and end fatally. If an injury of any type is severe, it can safely be assumed that a corresponding degree of shock will be present. Even if evidence of shock has not appeared after severe injury, it is well to anticipate it and prevent it by instituting shock treatment.

*b.* A person suffering from severe shock lies in a drowsy condition, with the limbs limp, but generally is not totally unconscious. The skin is pale and cold; the temperature subnormal; the pulse feeble, fluttering and rapid, and may be irregular and barely perceptible; the respirations are shallow and sighing; and the pupils are generally dilated. The sensibility of a patient in shock is lowered and pain is not felt as acutely as in a normal condition. If shock does not result in immediate death a condition known as reaction sets in. At first there is usually vomiting, then a gradual return of the color of the skin, with a rise in body temperature, stronger pulse and improved respiration. The patient then often falls into a sound sleep.

*c.* Concealed hemorrhage resembles shock very closely and must be kept in mind in all cases of severe shock.

*d.* The treatment of shock requires heat, correction of position of the body, and stimulants. The arrest of hemorrhage, if severe, is of prime importance.

*e.* Heat applied to the body of an injured person is most important both in preventing and in treating shock. All types of additional clothing may be used; external heat with hot water bottles, hot bricks, or pads may be used freely, keeping in mind that it is easy to burn a person who is in shock. Rubbing of the limbs is of doubtful value. In examining the person remove no more of the clothing than is necessary and replace it immediately when through.

*f.* The position of the patient will greatly affect the blood supply to the vital organs. Lay the patient on his back with the head low. This can best be done by raising the body so that the head is lower than the rest of the body. If a fracture is present, immobilization of the fractured part where the patient lies is of paramount importance.

*g.* Stimulants should be used only with conscious patients in the absence of bleeding, skull fracture, apoplexy, or sunstroke. Warmth may be applied internally by hot drinks such as coffee or hot beef tea in small amounts given frequently, and hot enemas, such as 2 pints of hot saline solution or hot water. Stimulants may be used by mouth as a teaspoonful of aromatic spirits of ammonia in a glass of hot water, hot coffee, hot tea, hot beef broth, or plain hot water. If a patient is unconscious, inhalation of smelling salts or ordinary water of ammonia is of value.

*h.* The most important treatment in electrical shock is artificial respiration, which should be continued for at least 4 hours in all cases. Shocked patients who have resumed breathing, often later stop breathing and they should be watched closely for hours after the treatment.

**145. Asphyxia.**—*a. General.*—Asphyxia is the condition where respiration or breathing has ceased. This condition occurs most frequently in drowning, electrical shock, or gas poisoning. The treatment is to first remove the cause or remove the patient from the cause; then give artificial respiration; later, treat for shock.

*b. Artificial respiration.*—The prone pressure, or Schafer method, is the safest and most effective method of artificial respiration. As soon as the person is rescued, the mouth should be forced open and any foreign substances such as gum, false teeth, or food removed. As every minute is valuable, begin actual resuscitation without delay. The standard technique is as follows:

(1) Lay the patient on his stomach so that his face is free for breathing. One of his arms should be extended over his head, the other bent at the elbow so that his face can be turned outward and rested upon his hand.

(2) Kneel astride the patient's thighs, knees placed at such distance from the hips as will allow exertion of pressure on lower ribs as described below. Place palms of hands on the small of the back with fingers on the lower ribs, little finger just touching the lowest rib, thumbs and fingers in natural position and tips of fingers out of sight just around the sides of the chest wall.

(3) With arms held straight, swing forward slowly so that the weight of the body is gradually brought to bear upon the patient. Do not bend the elbows. This operation should take about 2 seconds.

(4) Now immediately swing backward so as to remove all pressure completely and suddenly.

(5) After about 2 seconds repeat the operation. The movement of compression and release should take about 4 or 5 seconds; this should be done at the rate of about 12 to 15 respirations per minute.

(6) Continue the operation without interruption until natural breathing is restored or until a medical officer declares the patient

dead. Remember, many patients have died because artificial respiration has been stopped too soon. Always continue the operation for 4 hours or longer.

(7) Aside from resuscitation, the most valuable aid that can be rendered is keeping the patient warm. After artificial respiration has been started, have an assistant loosen the clothing and wrap the patient in any clothing that is available. Use hot bricks, heaters, or similar means, but be sure the patient is not burned.

(8) When the patient revives, he should be kept lying down and not allowed to stand or sit up; thus preventing undue strain on the heart. Stimulants such as hot coffee or tea can be given provided the patient is conscious.

(9) At times, a patient, after temporary recovery of respiration, stops breathing again; artificial respiration should be resumed at once.

(10) Due to the length of time this operation may be kept up, one or more operators may be necessary. A change of operators can be made without loss of rhythm of respiration. The great danger is stopping artificial respiration prematurely. In many cases breathing has been established after 3 or 4 hours of artificial respiration, and there are instances where normal breathing has been reestablished after 8 hours.

*c. Treatment for a person apparently drowned.*—Begin immediately to loosen the clothing about the neck, chest, and abdomen. With a handkerchief or towel, gently swab out the mouth and throat to remove mud or mucus. Turn the patient over, face downward, place the hands under the abdomen, one on either side, and lift the patient in order to drain the lungs and stomach; then with a large roll of clothing under the abdomen, and by making firm pressure upon the loins, continue the effort to expel the water from the lungs and stomach. If the individual then does not breathe, proceed immediately with artificial respiration.

*d. Treatment for a person in electrical shock.*—The rescue of a person from a live wire is always dangerous. If the switch is near, turn the current off, but lose no time in looking for the switch. Use a dry stick, dry clothing, dry rope, or other dry nonconductor in removing the victim from the wire. Start artificial respiration immediately. Do not regard early stiffening as a sign of death; keep up the artificial respiration for several hours.

*e. Treatment for asphyxiation from poisonous gases.*—Illuminating gas and the exhaust gases from gasoline engines are the most common causes of gas poisoning. Here again, the rescue is dangerous.

The first thing after the rescue is to get the patient into the fresh air. This does not mean cold air. The fresh air of a warm room is desirable. If breathing has stopped or is weak or irregular, start artificial respiration. Oxygen is an aid to these patients, but does not take the place of artificial respiration.

*f. Treatment of other causes of asphyxia.*—Asphyxia from hanging, choking, blows on the head and abdomen, or burial in a cave-in are handled in a similar manner.

**146. Unconsciousness.**—*a. General.*—(1) To treat a case of unconsciousness is one of the most difficult things that may fall to the lot of the first-aid man. There are numerous causes for unconsciousness and in order to properly treat an unconscious person, the cause must be discovered. Frequently it is impossible to determine the cause, and treatment must be general. Lay the patient on his back with the head and shoulders slightly raised; apply cold cloths or an ice pack to the head; insist on absolute quiet; do not move the patient unless urgent and then do so very carefully; have sufficient cover to keep patient warm; and use no stimulants until the patient's condition permits.

(2) In all cases of unconsciousness send for the medical officer immediately. In examining an unconscious patient, look carefully for the cessation of breathing and for symptoms of poisoning, bleeding, or sunstroke, as special treatment for these conditions must be given at once.

*b. Fainting.*—Is due to too little blood in the brain and is caused by mental impressions, exhaustion, heat, bleeding, overcrowded rooms, etc. There is sudden unconsciousness, pallor, cool moist skin, weak pulse, shallow breathing, and dilated pupils. The treatment is to lay the patient flat on his back with head low and legs raised, sprinkle cold water on the face and hold ammonia or smelling salts near the nostril. Get patient out of a crowded area and into fresh air.

*c. Epilepsy or fits.*—In this condition there may be fits with insensibility, or a mere momentary unconsciousness with slight muscular twitching, but in which the patient does not fall. In severe forms the patient cries out in a pecular manner and falls in a fit; at first the entire body is rigid, then there are general convulsions with jerking of the limbs, contortion of the face and foaming at the mouth. These convulsions are followed by deep stupor which passes off into a deep sleep. Often there is involuntary evacuation of the bowel and bladder and the patient bites his tongue. There is no treatment which will stop the fit or control it; all that can be done is to prevent the patient from hurting himself and to make him as comfortable as possible. Do not attempt to hold the patient but twist a handkerchief, passing it between his jaws, and tie it over the back of his neck until after the fit to prevent the tongue being bitten. After the fit is over let the patient sleep as long as he will. In the military service one must be on the lookout for men feigning epileptic fits in order to obtain a discharge. These feigned attacks usually occur at night, the man does not fall so that he hurts himself, he does not bite his tongue, he flinches when his eyeball is touched and the pupils are not dilated. The opposite is true of the epileptic and in addition there may be involuntary evacuation of the bowels and bladder.

*d. Concussion.*—Concussion of the brain is a condition present when we say a man has been "knocked senseless" or "stunned." It is a jarring and shaking of the brain due to blows or falls. The symptoms are unconsciousness, pallor of the face, breathing so quiet and shallow that it can hardly be detected. Fluttering pulse, pupils equal and usually contracted. The treatment consists of rest in a dark, quiet room; warmth externally, aromatic spirits of ammonia internally, or by inhalation if there is depression.

*e. Compression of the brain and apoplexy.*—Pressure on the brain is usualy due either to a piece of bone broken from the skull or to blood from a torn vessel which has escaped inside the cranium and, as it cannot get out, must compress the brain. This compression prevents certain parts of the brain from working. When the bleeding is the result of injury, the condition is called simply compression of the brain; when it is the result of the bursting of a diseased vessel without any violence, it is called apoplexy. The result and the symptoms are the same. The symptoms of compression are profound unconsciousness; loud, snoring breathing; slow pulse; pupils usually unequal and not reacting to light, and paralysis on one side of the body. If the symptoms are due to a piece of broken bone, the symptoms come on immediately after the injury, while if it is due to bleeding they may come on later and gradually. The treatment of both conditions consists of keeping the patient quiet, at rest in a comfortable position, and applying cold compresses to the head during the acute stage. Do not administer any stimulants.

*f. Hysterical unconsciousness.*—Hysteria is a disease of the nervous system accompanied by loss of control over the emotions and is manifested in a great variety of ways. It may be accompanied by convulsions. The patient usually has an attack of laughing or crying and gradually "works himself up" to such an extent that he has a convulsion. He appears to be unconscious but in falling always picks out some soft chair or spot to fall upon, being careful not to injure himself. The patient is to be treated with firmness. He usually craves sympathy and this is the worse form of treatment that can be given. Leave him alone, being sure to watch that no harm comes to him.

*g. Uremia or the insensibility of Bright's disease.*—The insensibility of Bright's disease is really an acute poisoning from the retention of the waste products which the diseased kidneys are not able to eliminate. The unconsciousness is often attended with delirium and convulsions. The pupils are contracted, the pulse is slow, there is a peculiar odor to the breath, and the breathing is loud and snoring. The distinguishing features are the history of Bright's disease, the waxy color of the skin, sometimes dropsy, abnormal urine (albumen, casts, etc.) and ordinarily the absence of paralysis. Emergency treatment consists in applying cold cloths to the head and hot packs or mustard poultice to the back.

*h. Unconsciousness caused by acute alcoholism.*—The use of alcohol, if carried to excess, produces a condition of unconsciousness which is very likely to be confounded with other similar conditions. Too great care cannot be taken in examining these cases thoroughly, as mistakes are of frequent occurrence, and cases of fractured skull or apoplexy often are pronounced as alcoholism. The patient may have been drinking and had a stroke of apoplexy, or may, in falling, have fractured his skull. If there is the least doubt, it is better to give the patient the benefit of the doubt than to run any risks. A person suffering from alcoholic coma lies in a stupor but usually may be partially aroused and made to answer questions. The face is flushed, the pulse is first full and rapid, then feeble and slow, and respirations are deep. The pupils are usually dilated and the breath has the heavy odor of alcohol. Ordinary intoxication rarely requires any treatment but rest and sleep. If the patient is in an exhausted state, it is well to wash out the stomach and cover him warmly and apply heat to the extremities. If the pulse is weak, stimulants should be given. The use of strong coffee by rectum is often of great value if the patient will not take anything by mouth. One can determine by the Bogan's test the amount of alcohol in the circulating blood or urine if the patient is in the hospital, and the urine should be saved for examination.

**147. Injuries due to heat.**—Injuries due to heat are classified as *general,* which embraces heat cramps, sunstroke, and heat exhaustion, and *local,* which includes burns and scalds.

*a. Heat cramps.*—Heat cramps are painful, spasmodic contractions of muscles, usually of the abdomen and extremities and are caused by exposure to heat and conditions causing muscular fatigue. The condition is brought about by the excessive loss of body fluids and salts. This is the mildest form of generalized body injury from heat, and the treatment is essentially the same as that for heat exhaustion.

*b. Sunstroke and heat exhaustion.*—Both conditions are caused by excessive heat, but they differ in their symptoms and treatment.

(1) *Sunstroke.*—(*a*) This is a very dangerous condition and is caused by the direct exposure to the rays of the sun, especially when the air is moist. Exhaustion and improper clothing are contributing factors, as they prevent the proper elimination of heat from the body surface. This condition is apt to occur most frequently on forced marches with the men in close formation, on a hot, sultry day.

(*b*) The symptoms are headache, dizziness, irritability, frequent desire to urinate, and seeing things red or purple. Examination reveals an intensely hot and dry skin; a rapid, full pulse; high temperature, often ranging from 107° to 110°. Unconsciousness usually results and the body becomes relaxed. Convulsions sometimes occur.

(*c*) Treatment has for its object the rapid reduction in temperature and the restablishment of water balance and of the salts in the body. The patient should be brought to the coolest accessible spot in the shade. The clothing should be removed and cold applied to the head by means of wet cloths, ice bags, or ice. At the same time the body should be cooled by rubbing with ice, and if a tub is available, the body should be immersed in cold water. Wrapping a patient in a sheet and pouring on cold water every few minutes is a good method of treatment. If the body is immersed in a cool bath, massage the limbs and trunk briskly. Observe the patient and do not overtreat. Observe the body temperature every few minutes, and if the skin is hot, repeat the treatment. Continue the treatment until the body temperature is reduced. If a patient is able to swallow, cold, but not iced, water to which table salt has been added in the proportion of one-half teaspoonful to each glass should be given freely. If the patient is unconscious, give copious and frequent enemas of 1,000 cubic centimeters of cool salt water (1 teaspoonful of table salt to each pint of solution). Give enemas every 30 minutes or hourly, depending upon the condition of the patient.

(*d*) Serious results may follow a sunstroke, even when death does not occur. The most common after effects are permanent headaches, paralysis, mental confusion, or even insanity. Moreover, one who has had a sunstroke is more susceptible to the action of the sun.

(2) *Heat exhaustion.*—(*a*) Heat exhaustion is due to the same causes that produce heat cramps and sunstroke. It results from ex-

posure to high temperatures, especially boiler rooms, foundries, bakeries, and similar places. This condition often occurs on the march and while soldiers are standing at attention on a hot day.

(*b*) The warning symptoms are dizziness, often nausea and vomiting, cramping in the muscles, and an uncertain gait. Frequently certain muscles or muscle groups are thrown into violent contraction, which causes excruciating pain. The patient usually falls, the face is pale, the skin is cool and covered with profuse perspiration, breathing is shallow, pulse is weak, and one or several muscles may be in painful contraction. The patient is not unconscious and may be aroused.

(*c*) The treatment of heat exhaustion is to move the patient to the shade, loosen the clothing, keep the head low, and give cool salt water. Coffee or hot tea to which salt has been added is excellent. If severe muscle contractions are present, this condition can be relieved by the immersion of the part in a hot bath, or by the administration of morphine sulfate by hypodermic. On removal to the hospital the patient should be kept quiet in bed, with heat around him if necessary.

(3) *Prophylaxis.*—The prophylaxis of heat cramps, sunstroke, and heat exhaustion is the replacement of loss of salt by taking table salt in drinking water whenever exposed to excessive heat.

*c. Burns and scalds.*—(1) *General.*—Burns are produced by flame, hot solids, hot fluids, caustics such as strong acids and strong alkalies, wires charged with heavy electric current, sun's rays, and X-ray. Scalds are produced by hot liquids. Burns differ from scalds in that in the former the hairs are removed. The treatment is the same.

(2) *Classification.*—They are classified in degree according to the depth to which the tissues are injured.

(*a*) *First degree.*—The skin is reddened, as in sunburn.

(*b*) *Second degree.*—The skin is blistered, as from contact with boiling water.

(*c*) *Third degree.*—The skin is destroyed or charred, as from contact with flames.

(3) *Symptoms.*—The symptoms of burns are shock, which may be profound, chilly sensation, and pain. The pain may be slight or agonizing.

(4) *Results.*—The results of burns depend more upon the extent of surface affected than upon the depth, a burn of first degree being fatal if two-thirds of the body be affected, and one of second degree if one-third of the body is burned. The chances of recovery are much less in children and elderly people. The danger in the first 24 hours is from shock; after this period, from internal congestion and inflam-

mation, suppression of urine, ulceration of the duodenum, intestinal hemorrhage, and finally from exhaustion, infection, blood poisoning, or tetanus. If entire thicknesses of skin are destroyed, marked deformity from contraction during healing may occur.

(5) *Treatment.*—In all burns the treatment of the patient's general condition is of prime importance. The general principles are always the same, that is, the prevention of shock, the protection of the lesion, relief of pain, and the minimizing of infection.

(a) *First degree burns.*—Here the treatment is directed toward the relief of pain, since the skin is unbroken and there is no danger from infection. Pain is relieved by covering the burned surface so that air is excluded. This may be done by the application of tannic acid jelly dressings or by the use of fresh bland oil such as cold cream, vaseline, liquid petrolatum, castor oil, olive oil, or butter. The application of cold water or soda water if immediately applied, is soothing. If the burn is at all serious, oily substances are not to be applied.

(b) *Second and third degree burns.*—The most important treatment is the detection and prompt treatment of shock. This takes precedence over all other treatment. The patient should be kept quiet and protected against chilling and any further trauma. Pain should be controlled by the administration of opiates, such as morphine. Elevation of the patient's feet may be necessary. External heat should be supplemented by the administration of hot drinks. Care in removal of clothing, particularly that which is adherent to the burned area, should be employed. The patient should not be transported while in shock.

After recovery from shock, and not until then, attention to the local treatment of the burn can be given. This consists of removal of the clothing about the burned area and of material adherent to the skin by immersing the part in warm water or applying sterile gauze soaked in a solution of epsom salts in the proportion of 2 tablespoonfuls to 1 pint of boiling water. The dressings should be kept moist and warm until further aid is obtained. The wound must be regarded as open, and only sterile dressings applied. Blisters should be left undisturbed.

On arrival of the patient at a hospital, if the burned area is clean a freshly prepared 5 percent aqueous solution of tannic acid should be sprayed on with an atomizer or spray gun every 30 to 60 minutes until a good "tanning has occurred." After a light tan has occurred, the area may be sprayed a few times with an aqueous 10 percent silver nitrate solution. Following this, a 5 percent tannic acid aqueous solution combined with a 10 percent silver nitrate aqueous solution may be applied until a good crust is formed. A heat cradle applied over the burned area will hasten the drying process. The tannic acid and silver nitrate spray has many advantages over previous treatments. It keeps the burned area aseptic, lessens the possibility of pain and suffering, prevents loss of water from injured tissue and loss of body heat, and serves as a protective covering for the new tissue forming and growing to replace that which has been destroyed. Do not apply iodine or like substances to a burn and do not apply absorbent cotton next to a burn.

(6) *Burns of the eye.*—Emergency treatment consists in flushing the eye with boric acid solution in an attempt to remove any foreign particles. If not available, water will do. Instillation of liberal amounts of liquid albolene or any bland oil such as olive oil, mineral oil, etc., helps protect the eye. The eyelid should then be closed and a bandage applied over the eye. If there is extreme pain, cold compresses on the eyelid will relieve the pain.

(7) *Chemical burns.*—Burns caused by acid or alkalies should be washed with large quantities of water, preferably not too cold, until the chemicals are thoroughly removed. Burns caused by acids should be neutralized with a solution of bicarbonate of soda or ordinary baking soda, and the alkali burns by a weak solution of acetic acid or ordinary vinegar. Phenol and carbolic acid burns should first be washed with alcohol if available. The usual treatment for burns, depending upon the degree, should then be followed.

*d. First aid at a fire.*—In rendering first aid at a fire the points to be kept in mind are—

(1) Prevent draft from fanning the fire.

(2) Shut all doors and windows.

(3) Have patient lie down and cover all but head with coat, blanket, rug, or the like in an endeavor to smother the fire.

(4) Tie moist cloth of any kind over the mouth to minimize the danger of suffocation.

(5) Remember that air 6 inches from the floor is free from smoke, so when unable to breathe, a rescuer should crawl along the floor with head low, dragging anyone he has rescued behind him.

**148. Injuries due to cold.**—The effects of cold, like those of heat, may be classified as *general*, as in chilling, or *local*, as in frostbite or chilblain.

*a. Cold or chilling.*—Prolonged exposure to extreme cold results in a general depression or lowering of the vitality, a gradual chilling of the body, and a congestion of the internal organs. The body and limbs first feel numb and heavy and then become stiff; drowsiness and irresistible desire to sleep take hold of the individual if left alone; unconsciousness readily follows. When found as above, if alive, the victim should be taken into a cold room, clothing removed, and the body rubbed briskly with sheets or towels wet with cold water. As soon as the stiffness is removed, artificial respiration should be performed; and when the patient is able to swallow, warm drinks should be given. When there are signs of returning consciousness and circulation, the body may be enveloped in blankets and the temperature of the room gradually raised. A frozen person must not be removed to a warm room, as sudden restoration of the circulation gives rise to violent congestions and often to sudden death from the formation of a clot in the blood vessels.

*b. Frostbite.*—This often occurs in intense cold without one's knowing it, but usually the ears or fingers become painful and cold, and then suddenly numb. The color of the frozen part is white or grayish white. Treatment consists in bringing the frozen part gradually to its normal temperature. The danger of sudden thawing is the congestion and bursting of the capillary walls which have been weakened by freezing. This may result in gangrene or death of the part; therefore the patient should not go into a warm room or near a fire. Rub the part vigorously with wet snow or ice water; never with dry snow, as the temperature of the dry snow may be much below freezing and rubbing with it would aggravate the condition. Do not rub too briskly as it may tear the frozen tissue. When the pain and redness return, use warm water gradually.

*c. Chilblain.*—Chilblain is a condition of acute or chronic congestion occurring especially in the feet and due to bringing cold feet near the fire too suddenly or merely following exposure to cold, in persons with poor circulation. On the part affected are red spots, more or less swollen, which burn and itch intensely. The treatment consists in stimulating applications such as liniments. Susceptible persons should wear woolen socks as a preventive against chilblain.

**149. Fractures.**—See section III.

*a. Signs.*—They are pain and tenderness at the point of the break; partial or complete loss of motion; the broken part is deformed; swelling, and later, discolorations occur; crepitus or grating may be felt, but no attempt should ever be made to elicit this grating; shock is usually present. Remember, all symptoms are not present in every fracture.

*b. Treatment of simple.*—(1) Splint the patient where he lies. Do not transport or move him about until after some type of splint is placed in position. Improper handling may cause the sharp ends of the bones to injure nerves, cut through vessels, or even pierce the skin, and thus produce a compound fracture. In splinting a simple fracture of an extremity, place the limb in as near the natural position as possible by taking hold of the lower part of the limb and pulling gently and steadily. At the same time, an assistant should support the part of the limb on either side of the break in order to steady the bone. Then hold the limb in this nearly normal position until some type of splint can be applied. If a traction splint is not available, improvised splints can be made of any type of rigid or semirigid material. They should be as wide as the limb, always well padded with clothing, and long enough to immobilize the next joint in either direction from the fracture. Pillows, blankets, or even newspapers can be used for padding. Pieces of tin or mesh wire make excellent splints. After the splint is in place it should be tied on rather loosely, as a fractured limb usually swells considerably within 1 or 2 hours. For this reason the limb and the splint must be examined every 20 minutes to be sure that the circulation is not obstructed. Also, if much pain develops, the splints and bandages should be examined.

(2) Following the adjustment of the splint the patient should be placed in a comfortable position and treated for shock. Keep him warm and give him stimulants, such as hot coffee, tea, or beef tea.

*c. Treatment of compound.*—(1) If severe bleeding is found, check this with pressure between the wound and the heart, then apply a tourniquet. Even where bleeding is not present, it is safe precaution to place a tourniquet loosely around the part, so that if bleeding should start it can be stopped immediately. A tourniquet should never be bound in with the bandages or splint; it may be forgotten and not released when necessary.

(2) Traction splints should be applied to compound fractures of the extremities before the patient is transported.

(3) If the bone is protruding, do not attempt to push it back in place with hands or instruments. Apply iodine, first to the exposed bone, next to the parts of the wound about the bone, and finally to the skin over a wide area about the wound. Place a sterile dressing over the wound.

(4) After the bleeding has been controlled and the wound dressed, a traction splint should be applied.

*d. Treatment of skull.*—Any person receiving a severe blow on the head or who has been rendered unconscious even for a very short period of time should be kept quiet until examined by a medical officer if at all possible. Head injuries should never be regarded lightly, as frequently the serious symptoms following such an injury do not appear for some hours. Move the patient only in a recumbent position and handle very carefully. Apply cold cloths or an ice bag to the head. Keep the patient lying down with the head slightly raised. Do not give stimulants. Keep the patient warm.

*e. Treatment of spinal.*—A patient who has sustained a spinal injury should be placed on his back immediately. A folded coat under the small of the back provides greater comfort for the patient. In transporting a patient with a spinal cord injury, the chief object is to prevent any movement of the patient which will increase the deformity of the vertebral column. The patient should be lifted from the ground like a log. To accomplish this, three persons are necessary, and possibly a fourth to prevent movement of the head, especially in cervical spine injuries. The patient should be placed flat on his back on a rigid support. A stretcher does not supply this rigid support. Flat boards bound together will serve the purpose. Whatever is used, it should be well padded. Another method of moving a patient with spinal injury is to apply splints on both sides, from his armpits to his feet, so as to make the body as rigid as possible, then to work a blanket under him, and, drawing it as tightly as possible, to lift him to the litter on it.

*f. Treatment of pelvic.*—The pelvis is so strong that bones are broken only by the most severe direct violence. If a severe fracture, the bone spicules may penetrate the bladder. If there is an injury to the bladder the urine will usually contain blood. Fractures of the pelvis should be supported by a swathe pinned tightly about it to afford support. Splints may be applied also on both sides from the axillae to the feet for added support.

*g. Treatment of fractured rib.*—In this type of fracture the sharp ends of the fractured bones are apt to stick into the lung every time the patient breathes; hence in these cases the patient will often complain of a sharp pain on breathing and there may be a cough, with the spitting of frothy blood. The treatment consists in confining the movement of the fractured chest as much as possible in order to give the broken bone an opportunity to rest and knit. This is done either by strapping the affected side with adhesive tape, or by a circular bandaging of the whole chest.

**150. Dislocations and sprains.**—*a.* When a bone gets out of place at a joint the condition is called a dislocation. A sprain is an injury or bruise to a joint. In these conditions the pain is usually severe, marked swelling occurs rapidly, and shock is present.

*b.* Treatment consists in elevation of the part. If an upper extremity, elevate by means of a sling; if the lower extremity, have the patient lie with pillows, coats, or other support under the leg. Apply cold applications to the site of the injury to retard the swelling and reduce the pain. If shock is severe, apply heat to the body and call a medical officer at once. When in doubt, treat the case as a fracture and apply splints, especially if the patient must be transported. Never attempt to reduce or correct a dislocation, as permanent damage may be done to the joint.

**151. Common emergencies.**—*a. Foreign bodies in the ear.*—The only safe method is to syringe the ear canal with lukewarm water. In syringing the ear be sure to direct the force of the flow of water along the side of the ear canal and not in the direction of the drum. If the object does not come out, leave the ear alone until it is seen by a medical officer. Never use pins or wire to dislodge these objects, as there is great danger of seriously injuring the ear. Insects in the ear can usually be killed by dropping in a little oil and then washing out the ear.

*b. Foreign bodies in the nose.*—These usually present no immediate danger. Gentle blowing of the nose may be tried; if unsuccessful, drop in a little olive or mineral oil and consult a medical officer. Any attempt to remove the object with forceps or wire usually causes more swelling and lodges the foreign body more securely. The object can often be dislodged by stoppage of the unaffected nostril and forceful blowing of the nose.

*c. Foreign bodies in the eye.*—(1) They are of frequent occurrence and are attended by considerable danger. Do not attempt to remove the foreign object with the fingers or to rub the eye. Close the eye for a few minutes until the worst of the irritation is over, then grasp the upper lid lashes and elevate the lid; repeat this process a few times. In many cases the object will be washed out by the tears.

(2) Where the above method fails, a search must be made under the upper lid. To examine under the lid, have the patient look down, place the thumb near the edge of the lid, and then with the other hand raise the lashes. Wipe the object with the corner of sterile gauze or irrigate the eye with water that has been boiled and cooled, using a small rubber ear syringe to direct the stream of water directly into the eye. This is a safe and easy procedure.

(3) If the object is embedded in the eye or lid, or if there is difficulty in attempting to remove the substance, close the eye and apply a small bandage, just sufficient to keep the eye closed, and consult a medical officer as soon as possible. Do not use a knife, toothpick, pin, or any similar object to remove an object from the eye. The eye is easily injured and may be damaged by ill-chosen procedures.

*d. Pain in the abdomen.*—This may be due to a variety of causes, many of which may be serious. In any case where pain occurs over any part of the abdomen, with nausea and vomiting, and accompanied or followed by pain and tenderness in the lower right part of the abdomen, appendicitis must be suspected. Put these cases to bed at once and call a medical officer. Do not give a cathartic or laxative. Do not give any food, water, or anything by mouth.

**152. Poisons.**—*a.* The principal point to be remembered in the treatment of poisoning is that poisons, when diluted, are not absorbed as rapidly as when they are in a concentrated form. Clean out the stomach by causing vomiting, or washing; continue the washing until the returned fluid is clear. The following fluids are useful in producing vomiting: Soap suds, salt water, soda water, lukewarm water, or milk, the last especially for corrosive poisons. Give four to seven glassfuls, preferably lukewarm. Tickling the throat with the finger, after drinking of the fluid, will usually induce vomiting. A large dose of Epsom salts may safely be given after the stomach is cleaned out.

*b.* For carbolic acid (phenol) poisoning, give soap suds with Epsom salts. For the corrosive poisons such as bichloride of mercury, give milk or the whites of eggs.

*c.* For sleep-inducing drugs, the patient must be kept awake by physical exercise; strong coffee may also be used.

*d.* For strychnine poisoning, do not give stimulants; keep the patient as quiet as possible; wash the stomach with weak potassium permanganate solution.

*e.* Most cases of poisoning show signs of shock. Heat is beneficial and artificial respiration may become necessary.

## Section V

## EMERGENCY DENTAL TREATMENT

**153. General.**—*a.* In the absence of a dental officer, enlisted men of the medical department, particularly those who have had practical experience with the dental service, are frequently called upon to treat some of the more common emergencies of a dental character. Such emergency treatment as the medical soldier may be able to render will often diminish pain so that the sufferer may continue on his duties, or, if at night, be assured of rest. Such treatment is necessarily of a temporary nature and usually intended only to keep the patient comfortable, until the services of a dental officer become available. While performing such a service the medical soldier should inspect carefully the appearance of the mucous membrane of the entire mouth. Patients desiring treatment for a particular condition are often unaware of the presence of other existing lesions which may be of grave importance. Any unusual or suspicious condition should be reported as soon as possible to a dental or medical officer for the proper observation, diagnosis, and treatment.

*b.* Below is a brief description of the principal dental conditions which frequently give rise to pain, and the usual methods employed to cope with such emergencies. These dental diseases or injuries are dental caries, pulpitis, abscesses, gingivitis, vincent's infection, osteitis, and pericoronitis.

**154. Dental caries.**—*a.* Dental caries, commonly called tooth decay, is a disease of the hard structures of the tooth characterized by the destruction of tooth substance to form localized cavities. The initial stage of dental caries consists of decalcification of the enamel or of the cementum by acids which are confined to particular tooth surfaces. These particular areas are the pits and fissures, and those smooth surfaces of a tooth which are habitually unclean. The acids of dental decay are produced by the action of certain acid-forming bacteria upon food sugars. While heredity, general disease, certain dietary deficiencies (minerals-vitamins), and faulty tooth structure may influence the carious process, the most important factors in the production of dental caries are poor oral hygiene, food impaction and general mouth uncleanliness. Allowing food to remain on the teeth results in the retention of carbohydrate material and the localization of the products of fermentation on the surfaces of a tooth. Once the enamel or the cementum is broken through, additional food is retained in the cavity, the dentin is quickly involved, and if allowed to continue, the cavity will progressively involve the whole tooth. Caries of the enamel is painless, pain not being elicited until the dentin becomes affected. The first symptoms of serious tooth involvement may be only a slight discomfort to thermal changes (usually cold), sweets, acids, or to pressure from the packing of food into the cavity while chewing. When the decayed area starts between the teeth the cavity may go unnoticed and without pain until the enamel breaks while chewing. When this occurs, it indicates that the enamel has been seriously undermined, and a toothache will soon develop if the condition is not treated within a short period of time. An offending cavity may be found upon inspection in most instances by the aid of an explorer and mouth mirror. When the cavity is not exposed to view, it may frequently be detected by changes in the transparency of the enamel. Occasionally a cavity may be detected only by aid of transillumination or the X-ray.

*b.* To treat carefully remove all debris and soft decay from the cavity with suitable instruments, and wash with warm water. Isolate the affected tooth with a roll of cotton or gauze, and dry the cavity with small pellets of cotton. Sterilize the cavity with a small pellet of cotton moistened in phenol (excess should be removed by touching against a cotton roll), followed by another pellet of cotton to remove the excess phenol and to dry the cavity. Fill the cavity with a paste made by mixing zinc oxide and eugenol to a fairly thick consistency. This paste hardens within a few hours upon contact with the saliva, and will serve as a temporary filling for several weeks. The patient is instructed not to use the tooth for several hours, and to brush his teeth thoroughly after each meal to remove all adhering food debris. If zinc oxide paste is not available, a small pellet of cotton moistened in eugenol may be placed in the cavity and the remaining portion of the cavity filled with temporary stopping (after softening by heat), or with another pellet of cotton saturated with sandarac varnish, cavity lining, or compound tincture of benzoin. Phenol may be used in place of eugenol as a sedative, but care must be exercised to avoid a burn. Should any phenol come in contact with the surrounding tissues, wipe the area immediately with cotton dipped in alcohol.

155. **Pulpitis (toothache).**—*a.* The pulp (nerve) is an extremely sensitive organ which reacts readily to any irritation or injury. An inflammation of the dental pulp (pulpitis) gives rise to a characteristic pain, sharp and stabbing. A prominent feature of the condition is that it is intermittent, the patient being entirely free from pain in the periods of remission. At times the pain may be somewhat obscure, the offending tooth being difficult for the patient to locate, as a tooth which is the seat of an inflamed pulp is not sensitive to biting or tapping. It is, however, markedly sensitive to thermal changes, especially cold, and this latter feature may be utilized in efforts to locate the disturbance. This sensitiveness is of a temporary character, occuring only upon the stimulation of cold water,

cold air, ice cream, etc. and subsiding as soon as the irritation is removed. The pain in pulpitis is the result of a hyperemia (increase quantity of blood) in the pulp chamber, which compresses the terminal nerve fibres of the dental pulp against the hard unyielding walls of dentine. Pulpitis is most commonly caused by an invasion of the pulp tissue by bacteria from a carious cavity. A search should be made for the offending tooth, the cavity carefully cleaned of all soft debris and decay, and treatment instituted as outlined above for dental caries.

*b.* In addition to caries, there are other possible causes of pulpitis. Pain of pulpal origin may arise as the result of a newly inserted filling which is too high, to a loose filling, to an ill-fitting clasp, or to marked food empaction between teeth with loose contacts. When a patient complains of toothache in the absence of caries an effort should be directed toward other possible causes and the condition corrected, if possible.

**156. Periapical (alveolar) abscess.**—*a. General.*—Deep caries, trauma, or other injury to a tooth may set up a severe irritation, and eventually cause the death of the dental pulp. Sooner or later this mass of dead tissue is subject to attack by suppurative and putrefactive bacteria resulting in the formation of pus and gas. Pressure within the tooth from these enclosed gases forces toxic products through the apical foramina into the surrounding periapical tissues and alveolus, causing irritation and the subsequent infection of these tissues. Periapical abscesses may be acute or chronic in nature, depending upon the infectiveness of the invading organisms and the resistance of the individual.

*b. Acute.*—(1) An acute alveolar abscess due to the internal pressure from accumulated pus and irritation of the periapical tissues causes most excruciating pain. This pain is of a boring or throbbing character, and increases with movement of the jaw, muscular exertion, or when assuming a recumbent position. The offending tooth is readily located. It appears to be loose, slightly raised in its socket, and extremely sensitive to pressure or to touch. Due to the marked inflammation, adjoining teeth may be somewhat sensitive to pressure. The application of cold water or small chips of ice to the affected tooth will relieve the pain temporarily, while hot water increases the symptoms. In the early stages of an acute alveolar abscess there is no apparent swelling. Later, 24 to 72 hours, the overlying soft tissues are markedly swollen, the edema often involving the tissues of the face. When the pus has found an exit by boring its way through the bone into the soft tissues, the internal pressure is relieved, and the pain ceases.

(2) To relieve the pain caused by an acute alveolar abscess in its early stages, it is essential to establish free drainage through the root canal to allow escape of the accumulated exudate. Generally, the offending tooth will contain a large cavity. All decay and soft debris should be carefully removed and the pulp chamber opened. In these cases the pulp is usually nonvital and an offensive odor and a free flow of pus will be noticed. If it is necessary to use a bur to open the cavity or pulp chamber, the tooth should be held firmly to counteract the pressure of the drill, because of its excessive tenderness. After free access and drainage is established, the cavity is washed with warm water, and packed lightly with a pellet of cotton to prevent the lodgement of food from further blocking the pulp canal. When pus has accumulated in the surrounding tissues, the swollen area within the mouth is palpated with the finger to determine the place of pointing of the abscess. At the point of softening an incision is made with a sharp pointed lancet directly toward the bone in the direction of the apex of the tooth for the evacuation of pus. Pending the development or pointing of an abscess the patient should be kept quiet and at rest. Instructed to frequently use hot saline mouth washes, to drink freely of water, and to apply an ice pack to the face over the affected area. Sedatives may be administered for the relief of pain.

(3) In certain cases all attempts to relieve the pain is futile, and an extraction is the only possible remedy. During the absence of a dental or medical officer such procedure should be undertaken only in extreme emergencies and as a last resort. (See par. 162.)

*c. Chronic.*—After an acute alveolar abscess has run its course and the acute symptoms have subsided, the condition is known as a chronic alveolar abscess. An abscess of this type usually has a fistulous tract opening onto the surface of the gum tissue (gumboil). However, in certain cases, where the pulp (nerve) has died and the resulting infection is mild in character, nature throws up a wall or sac of granulation tissue at the root apex and the condition is then commonly designated a dental granuloma or blind abscess. A chronic alveolar abscess is as a rule painless and rarely causes sufficient trouble to require emergency treatment. Occasionally they become reinfected, developing acute symptoms, in which case the treatment is the same as just outlined for an acute alveolar abscess.

**157. Parietal abscess.**—A parietal (lateral) abscess is caused by an infection of the tissues around a tooth whose products of inflammation fail to find an exit to the surface through the gingival crevice.

They may occur on the lateral surfaces of the roots of the teeth in which the pulps and periapical tissues are normal. Infection in these cases arise as a result of some form of irritation at the gingival margin, such as impacted food particles, calculus, broken toothpicks, toothbrush bristles, or other foreign objects. In most instances they appear on the roots of the teeth involved with pyorrhea, particularly at the bifurcation of the roots of molars. The symptoms are similar to that of an acute alveolar abscess. However, the pain is less severe, the swelling less extensive, and definitely localized at the site of the lesion. In treatment, remove the calculus or other foreign body, and probe the gingival crevice with a small blunt instrument until the opening to the pocket is found in order to establish adequate drainage. Gently apply pressure to the overlying gum tissues to aid in the evacuation of the pus, and paint the involved area with $3\frac{1}{2}$ percent iodine in glycerine. Patient is instructed to use a mouth wash, and to keep the affected area free of adherent food debris.

**158. Gingivitis.**—Gingivitis is a local inflammation of the soft tissues surrounding the necks of the teeth. The gum tissues are swollen, dark red in color, tender to pressure, bleed easily, and the tissue from between the teeth may be lifted readily from their interdental spaces. Dental calculus (tartar) is usually the main source of gingival irritation. Lack of proper oral hygiene, food debris, food impaction, gingival caries, foreign bodies, and faulty dental appliances may also be contributing factors. To reduce the irritation the calculus is carefully removed, and other possible causes corrected. The gingival crevice is thoroughly irrigated with warm saline or antiseptic solution, and the affected parts painted with $3\frac{1}{2}$ percent iodine in glycerine. The patient is advised relative to the importance of oral hygiene and instructed to frequently brush and massage the gums in order to restore their normal tone and resistance.

**159. Vincent's infection (trench mouth).**—*a.* This disease is an acute, infectious, destructive inflammation of the gingival tissues caused by certain specific anaerobic organisms. It usually begins with a sudden onset, accompanied by fever, malaise, salivation (profuse flow of saliva), mental depression, headache, loss of appetite, and constipation.

*b.* The gingival margins, particularly between the teeth, present a dirty, grayish, ragged, ulcerative appearance, are extremely painful to touch, and bleed easily. The patient has a characteristic offensive fetid breath, and complains of a constant pain about the teeth and gums which may be so intense as to interfere with sleep or eating. Ulcerations may not be confined to the gingival tissues alone, but may extend to the mucosa of the lips, cheek, palate, or throat. Most cases of Vincent's infection occur in mouths in which a low standard of hygiene prevails. To improve this condition is an effective means of reducing the infection and raising local tissue resistance. Treatment consists in thoroughly spraying or irrigating the mouth and inaccessible areas with an antiseptic solution, preferably a week peroxide solution, to remove soft deposits and toxic bacterial products from about the teeth and gums margins. Remaining adherent debris and necrossed tissue should be carefully removed by small cotton applicators dipped in peroxide solution. Copious spraying or irrigating of the mouth at this stage aids materially in reducing the infection. If peroxide is used, after this preliminary clean-up or toilet of the oral cavity is accomplished, the excess is removed by spraying with a saline or an alkaline wash. The affected areas are then dried, protected by cotton rolls, and 5 percent chromic acid in distilled water, 1 percent solution of acriviolet (0.5 gm. neutral acriflavine and 0.5 gm. gentian violet in 100 cc. of distilled water), or 10 percent arsphenamin in glycerine is applied directly to the necrossed areas.

*c.* Home or ward care consists in the constant and frequent use of a mouth wash and gargle. The following mouth washes are applicable:

(1) Equal parts of peroxide of hydrogen and water.

(2) Equal parts of peroxide of hydrogen and 1–1,000 bichloride of mercury. (This should be labeled poisonous and the patient instructed not to swallow the medicament.)

(3) One teaspoonful of sodium perborate dissolved in a glass of hot water. This latter should not be used over long periods of time, as it may cause additional inflammation to the oral mucosa.

(4) Potassium permanganate 1–2,000 solution.

*d.* Severe cases of Vincent's infection with constitutional symptoms should be hospitalized. The patient should be given a cathartic and placed on a soft diet containing an abundance of fresh fruit juices and vegetables. After the acute symptoms subside, a thorough prophylaxis is indicated, the patient is instructed in the use of the toothbrush, and the treatments continued until the local tissues have regained their normal color, free from irritation and infection.

*e.* Since Vincent's infection is a communicable disease, the patient is instructed to use his own mess utensils, towels, and toilet articles to prevent spread of the infection. The mess sergeant is informed of the patient's condition in order that proper measures may be instituted to sterilize all eating utensils following use. All Vincent's cases while undergoing treatment should mess at a separate table.

**160. Osteitis (painful socket).**—This is an extremely painful condition which occasionally follows tooth extraction. It seldom arises until a day or more after an extraction, and it indicates that a normal blood clot has failed to form, leaving the tooth socket empty or partially filled with debris. The socket should be gently irrigated with warm saline or antiseptic solution, and a small piece of plain, Bipp's, or iodoform gauze slightly moistened in eugenol placed lightly into the socket, using care not to exert pressure. The dressing should be changed once or twice daily until relief from the symptoms is obtained.

**161. Pericoronitis.**—This is an inflammation of the gum tissue around the crown of a partially erupted tooth. It is most commonly associated with the lower third molars (wisdom teeth). The tissue covering the crown is inflamed, swollen, painful, and extremely sensitive to pressure, with associated swelling at the angle of the jaw and lymph node involvement. Frequently the patient complains of a sore throat on the affected side, with difficulty in opening the jaw. Suppuration may or may not be present. Treatment is mainly palliative in character. Thoroughly spray or irrigate the affected area with an antiseptic solution. Gently probe the area beneath the flap and around the crown to evacuate the presence of any free pus should the inflammation be purulent in character, indicating a pericoronal abscess. Spray the area again, and then isolate with cotton rolls or gauze. Dry with air or with large loose pellets of cotton, and carefully insert tincture of iodine under the infected flap by aid of a small probe wrapped tightly with cotton or a Rheims file number 31 or 32. The beaks of cotton pliers may be used to advantage in carrying the medicament to the involved area. Paint the involved tissues with half strength tincture of iodine in glycerine. Patient is instructed to hold hot salt water in the mouth at frequent intervals forcing it back and forth over the affected area, to apply an ice cap to the affected side of the face (if the condition is severe), to keep the mouth clean, and to return daily for treatment until the acute symptoms subside. After preliminary therapy, complete relief may not be obtained until the overlying tissue is removed either by surgery, the electric knife, or cauterization. At times pericoronitis is aggravated by the opposing upper third molar. In these instances an imprint of the tooth may be seen on the inflamed tissue. Grinding the cusps of the offending tooth will help to temporarily relieve the condition.

**162. Extraction of teeth.**—*a*. In the absence of a dental or medical officer, an extraction should be attempted only in extreme emergencies and as a last resort to alleviate pain, after all other emergency measures have proven unsuccessful. Teeth that are firmly set in the jaw, badly decayed teeth, or broken down roots are difficult to remove, and attempts to remove such teeth will often prove disastrous and aggravate the patient's symptoms. The various teeth have definite extraction movements for their removal which must be rigidly adhered to in order to prevent their breaking or damage to the supporting bony structures. Only those teeth that are extremely painful and definitely loose, indicating no difficulty in removal, should be undertaken by the medical soldier. An extraction is a form of surgery, and all instruments and the hands must be scrupulously clean, or serious infection may result.

*b*. The procedure is as follows:

(1) Thoroughly spray the patient's mouth with salt water.

(2) Examine carefully to be definitely sure of the offending tooth.

(3) Remove all deposits, that is, food debris and calculus, from the involved tooth and those adjacent.

(4) Wash with water and paint the gum margins and overlying tissues with $3\frac{1}{2}$ percent iodine.

(5) Detach the soft tissues from the neck of the tooth to be removed with a suitable instrument (Woodson No. 1) so that they will not be lacerated, and paint again with iodine.

(6) Select suitable forceps.

(7) In applying the forceps to any tooth, one beak is first placed on the lingual side. The tooth is then grasped by slightly closing the forceps, and the instrument is pushed as far as possible under the gum, thereby gaining a firm grasp on the root of the tooth. Care should be exercised not to grasp the gum tissue or the alveolar process with the forceps, as damage to these tissues is a frequent cause of after pain and delay in healing. Do not grasp the crown, as the force of the instrument is liable to cause it to crush, but use only as a guide for placing the beaks on the root of the tooth.

(8) Secure a firm grip on the forceps handles.

(9) Rotate the tooth slightly, or slight lateral movement is applied, according to the shape and number of roots. Rotation of single conical rooted teeth is usually successfully accomplished, while those whose roots are not conical and multirooted teeth require a definite lateral motion, first inward, which is followed by an outward movement. Care should be exercised in not applying too much force laterally, as the tooth may readily break.

(10) **After the** tooth is loose, apply a pulling force to dislodge from the socket. The extraction of teeth is not a matter of crude force, but governed by exacting, definite movements.

(11) Isolate the area to protect from saliva and allow a normal blood clot to form.

(12) Paint with iodine.

(13) Instruct the patient not to rinse the mouth and to remain quiet for several hours.

*c.* For postoperative hemorrhage, see paragraph 236*c.*

## Section VI

## EMERGENCY VETERINARY TREATMENT

**163. General.**—Emergency veterinary treatment implies the initiation of measures for the restoration of animal health. Such measures may be very simple, and may or may not include the use of so-called medicines, but of such importance as to save a life or prevent permanent disability.

**164. Recognition of emergency.**—The ability to recognize the abnormal condition existing is necessary for probable success in treatment. This entails a thorough knowledge of the normal habits and actions of the horse (see par. 238) and the development of one's powers of observation in order to detect the abnormal condition early.

**165. Agents available for simple treatment.**—Ropes, slings, and similar devices are used for the movement, restraint, and support of disabled animals. Other agents used in treatment include hot and cold water, ice, soap, protective clothing, bandages, and simple drugs largely of a stimulating or antiseptic nature.

**166. Bandages.**—*a. Roller.*—Roller bandages consist of long strips of various lengths and widths and may be obtained in an assortment of materials. For convenience of application, they are wound into snug rolls. Roller bandages are used particularly on the legs from the knee and hock down to and including the foot. The greatest danger in applying a roller bandage to the leg above the foot lies in getting it so tight all over, or at one or more points, that the underlying blood vessels are compressed, and circulation of the blood is interfered with. This is particularly true when horses are worked in bandages, or the inelastic type of material is used. The following general rules are applicable for all roller bandages:

(1) Use one hand to hold and direct the roll; the other to keep each lap smooth and to hold the turn when changing direction or taking up slack.

(2) Wrap snugly enough to exert the desired amount of pressure and prevent slipping, but be careful not to shut off circulation by too much pressure.

(3) Secure the end with the same pressure used in wrapping.

(4) Always fasten the bandage on the outside of the leg.

(5) Bandages may be secured as follows:

(*a*) Pass the tapes on the end around the last wrap in opposite directions and tie in a bowknot.

(*b*) Slit the last 12 or 14 inches of the gauze or muslin with the scissors. Tie the two slits with a straight knot and proceed as with the tapes.

(*c*) Double back the last 20 inches of the gauze or muslin bandage around the last wrap and tie that end with the folded end.

(*d*) Secure the bandage with safety pins by pinning the end to the wrap underneath.

(*e*) Leave a bight protruding at the start and tie the end to this bight.

(6) Roller bandages are made of gauze, muslin, flannel, and knitted elastic material. Aside from the bias cut muslin and canton flannel bandages in the stable sergeant's veterinary set, the most commonly used bandage is the derby bandage. The latter is not an article of issue but is often purchased for polo and horse show use.

*b. Foot.*—The foot is bandaged as follows: The 5-inch muslin bandage cut on the bias is most suitable for bandaging the foot. Hold the foot in the same manner that a horseshoer holds it when shoeing. Hold out a bight 12 inches long, make one complete turn around the foot one-half inch below the coronet, and take a half turn around the bight, holding the end of the bight in the left hand and the roll in the right. After drawing up snugly, take another turn around the foot in the opposite direction to the first. Complete by another half turn and pull around the bight. Make these half turns around the bight come over the quarter. Continue the turns around the foot by working down toward the toe and back so as to cover the whole foot. Take a half turn around the bight each time and draw the bandage tight before starting a new wrap. Secure by tying the end to the bight.

*c. Eye.*—In certain traumatic injuries to the eye it is necessary to apply wet antiseptic compresses. This form of treatment also produces very good results by virtue of excluding light. This bandage may be made from a burlap sack. Hold the material up to the head and mark the place to cut openings for the ears and the sound eye. Lay it on a flat surface and cut out elliptical holes large enough for the base of each ear. Cut a circular hole for the sound eye about 6 inches in diameter. Then cut four strips, each about 8 inches long on each lower border. Sew a gauze compress on the inside so that it comes over the injured eye. Apply the bandage by laying it on the face and forehead, placing the ears in their proper holes, and adjusting it so that the sound eye is in the center of the hole cut for that purpose. Tie the four pairs of strips underneath the jaws. (See fig. 55.)

*d. Many-tailed.*—The many-tailed type of bandage is used principally on the knee and hock. It acts only as a protection and support for a compress held in place by a loosely applied roller bandage. (See fig. 55.)

*e. Maltese cross.*—The maltese cross bandage is an accessory foot bandage used as a protection for a compress which has first been secured by a roller bandage. (See fig. 55.)

*f. Foot pouch.*—The foot pouch is an accessory bandage cut from the corner of a burlap sack and has the same function as the maltese cross. (See fig. 55.)

(1) Lay a gunnysack down on the floor with the open end toward the operator. Starting at the open end and 2 inches inside the left hand seam, cut straight down toward the bottom and parallel to the seam until about 8 or 10 inches from the bottom of the sack. Repeat this cut 2 inches inside the right hand seam. Join these two by cutting across the sack parallel to and 8 to 10 inches above the bottom edge. This leaves the bottom 8 to 10 inches of the sack intact with long strips, one on each side. Grasp the bottom left hand corner with the left hand and the bottom right hand corner with the right hand and invert the sack by pushing the right corner into the left corner. This

leaves the sack shaped similar to a bonnet with both strings together on the left side.    Cut a hole 1 inch in diameter in the corner diagonally across from the corner to which the strips are attached.    Tie the strips together with a simple knot and pass through the hole just cut, in opposite directions.    This serves as a puckering string for the pouch.

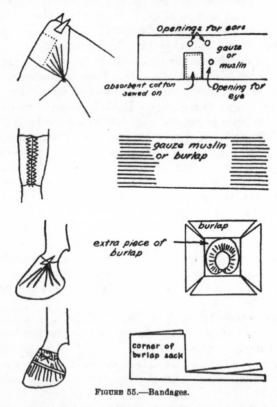

FIGURE 55.—Bandages.

(2) Place on the foot by inserting the toe into the corner opposite the one in which a hole was cut for the strips to pass through.    Pull up snugly around the foot, wrap the loose ends around the coronet and pastern.    Secure by passing the strips in opposite directions around the coronet and tieing over the wall below the coronet.

**167. Wounds.**—*a. General.*—(1) *Classification.*—Wounds may, for the purpose of description, be divided into—

Incised wounds, or cuts.

Lacerated wounds, or tears.

Punctured wounds, or holes.

(2) *Cleanliness.*—The great fundamental in the successful treatment of wounds may be summed up in the word cleanliness. Cleanliness of the wound itself, of the dressing, and the dresser are of the greatest importance.

(3) *Bleeding.*—Stoppage of bleeding is the first point to be attended to if it is serious. The most ready means of stopping bleeding is pressure, which may be carried out by tight bandaging above and below the wound or by placing a pad on the wound and bandaging over it. For ordinary wounds a simple pad and bandgage is usually sufficient to control the flow. If there happens to be a large vessel cut and the end exposed it should be tied around with clean thread which has been soaked in an antiseptic.

(4) *Cleaning.*—When the bleeding has stopped cut the hair from the edges of the wound and remove all dirt, clots of blood, splinters, and foreign bodies of every kind. This may be done by carefully syringing the parts with clean warm water or a warm antiseptic solution. Foreign bodies may be removed with forceps or by pressing small pieces of cotton soaked in an antiseptic solution gently over the surface of the wound. Punctured wounds (except those around joints) should be probed to ascertain if any foreign bodies are in the channel.

(5) *Closing.*—(*a*) Sutures and bandages are used for this purpose, but no wound that has been dirty must ever be entirely closed. Sutures and instruments must be aseptically clean.

(*b*) Sutures as a rule may be dispensed with entirely. They may be occasionally used in parts where there is little flesh, such as around the forehead, eyelids, and nose. They are less useful in the fleshy parts, because the movements of the muscles and the swelling resulting from the inflammation of the injured tissues cause them to pull out. Again, sutures must not be used when the edges of the wound are badly torn.

(*c*) In applying sutures the borders of the wound must be brought together in their natural position, care being taken not to allow the edges of the skin to curl inward. The thread, with the aid of a needle, is passed through the skin at one side of the wound and out at the other. The sutures should be from one-fourth to one-half inch from the edge, about three-fourths of an inch apart, and their depth should be about equal to their distance from the edge of the wound. They should be drawn just tight enough to bring the edges of the skin together. As a rule, they should be removed in about 8 days.

(6) *Drainage.*—In all infected wounds drainage is necessary for the removal of pus that would otherwise accumulate in them. The escape of such material must be provided for at the lowest part of the wound. If the wound be a vertical (upright) one this may be accomplished by leaving out a stitch at the bottom. In horizontal wounds (those running lengthwise of the body) a small vertical openings must be made below the line of the stitches.

(7) *Dressings.*—(*a*) Wounds that have been sutured and also wounds that are to be treated without suturing should be dried carefully with dry gauze or cotton, and a bandage applied. Or cotton soaked in an antiseptic may be put on and held in position by a bandage, care being taken to avoid undue pressure.

(*b*) If the location will not permit bandaging, the injured parts may be treated with an antiseptic and covered with a clean piece of cloth or gunny sack, the inside of which may be lined with a piece of gauze large enough to cover the wound.

(*c*) After a wound has begun to granulate (fill in with repair tissue), it will often heal much better if no dressing or bandage is placed in contact with the wound, provided it is not irritated by flies. Bandaging too long may prevent the area from covering itself with skin and result in proud flesh.

(8) *Rest and restraint.*—This will depend entirely upon the nature and extent of the wound. If the injury is slight the animal may continue at work; otherwise he may be kept in a box stall, cross-tied, or subjected to some other form of restraint.

(9) *Aftercare.*—All wounds should be kept dry and dressings should be changed only often enough to keep the wounds clean. As little washing as possible should be done, and the parts should be sopped instead of rubbed. After cleaning and drying a new dressing should be applied if it seems advisable.

(10) *Flies.*—The healing of wounds that cannot be covered is sometimes retarded by the presence of flies. The edges of such wounds, and also the surface if not too moist, may be covered lightly with pine tar.

(11) *Maggots and screw worms.*—(*a*) Wounds sometimes get fly-blown and maggots appear. Their presence is recognized by a thin bloody discharge from the wound and the red, angry appearance of its edges. If the bottom of the wound is carefully examined, movement of the worm may be seen.

(*b*) With the forceps pick out all the worms that are visible and wipe out the cavity with a swab of cotton that has been saturated with tincture of iodine.

(12) *Excessive granulations,* (*proud flesh*).—In sluggish, slow-healing wounds small rounded fleshy masses which protrude beyond the edges of the wound are often formed. These fleshy masses are called proud flesh. The growth may be kept down by removing with scissors to the level of the skin and treating with boric acid or tincture of iodine or by searing to the level of the skin with a heated iron, care being taken to see that the surrounding skin is not burned.

*b. Penetrating foot wounds* (*nail pricks, etc.*).—(1) *Causes.*—Most penetrating wounds of the foot are caused by the animal stepping on nails or screws. At times the sensitive tissue of the foot may accidently be penetrated by a misdirected shoeing nail.

(2) *Prevention.*—Police corrals and roads for loose nails and screws. Exercise care in riding animals in the vicinity of wrecked buildings or new construction. In the field many nails and screws are picked up in horses' feet near ammunition dumps or warehouses. When packing cases are burned in rolling kitchens, nails from burned cases are often strewn along the roads.

(3) *Symptoms*—Most nail wounds occur in the frog at the juncture of the frog and bar. Noticeable lameness may not be immediate unless the nail remains in the foot, but will appear in a day or so and if not treated properly pus will form under the horn and break out at the heel. In such cases the foot is hot, the animal is in great pain, and lameness is very pronounced.

(4) *Nursing and first-aid treatment.*—If the nail is still imbedded in the horn, before removing it thoroughly clean all dirt from the bottom of the foot by washing and then wash with cresolis solution. Remove the nail or other object and with a knife, thin the horn over a fair-sized area surrounding the penetration and make a final opening about one-eighth to one-fourth inch in diameter through the horn to the sensitive tissue. A complete opening through the horn for drainage of wound secretions is essential. Saturate a rather small piece of gauze with tincture of iodine and place it *on* the wound. Over this place a pad of oakum covering part or all of the bottom of the hoof and held in place with strips of tin or light sheet metal of such length and width that their ends can be engaged between the hoof and the shoe on the inside at both sides of the shoe. Do not probe the wound in the sensitive tissue and do not compress the dressing so tightly that the secretions are dammed back into the wound. Dress daily with a mild antiseptic until the wound appears to be dry and healing and then apply a tar dressing under an oakum pack about every 3 days until no further dressing is necessary.

**168. Eye injuries.**—*a. Causes.*—Eye injuries are usually due to blows, scratches, or punctures from brush, forage, etc., and small objects lodging on the front of the eyeball or under the lids.

*b. Symptoms.*—Watery eye, flow of tears from the eye, reddened membranes, and partial or complete closing of the eye are symptoms of all forms of eye injury. If the cornea or clear part of the eyeball itself is injured, the cut or wound may be visible and surrounding it the eye will become milky white in color. Ordinarily, foreign matter merely lodged behind the lids does not cause the eyeball to become milky in color. The former is always more serious.

*c. Nursing and first-aid treatment.*—If there is a foreign body under the lids, flood it out with clean water, using the dose syringe or remove by the careful use of a tightly rolled swab of cotton or gauze. Then flood the eye several times daily with boric acid solution prepared by dissolving two level mess-kit spoonfuls of boric acid in a mess-kit cupful of warm water. Use the eye dropper for this purpose. Cover the eye with a pad of cotton about 8 inches square covered with gauze and held in position with strings tied about the head and to the halter or sew the pad on the inside of an improvised head bandage made from a grain sack. In bad cases soak the pad in boric acid solution before applying. Keep the animal in as dark a place as possible.

**169. Fractures.**—A fracture is a broken bone or other hard tissue such as hoof or cartilage.

*a. Causes.*—Most fractures result from kicks inflicted by other animals. Fractures of the bones of the legs are sometimes caused by sudden turn, stepping in holes, etc. The tibia, the long bone just under the skin on the inside of the hind leg between the hock and stifle joints, is the most frequently fractured bone in the body. This is accounted for by the fact that it has no muscular protection on the inside of the leg and a kick delivered from one side of the animal may pass under the belly and strike the inside of the opposite hind leg. The bone forming the point of the hip may be fractured by falling on the side or by an animal's striking it against the side of a door.

*b. Symptoms.*—When any long supporting bone of the leg is completely fractured, the leg dangles helplessly and will bear no weight. The skin over the fractured bone may or may not be broken either by the blow or by the ends of the bone. When the bone forming the point of the hip is fractured the animal may show but few symptoms other than lameness, difficulty in advancing the hind leg on that side, tenderness, and swelling over the seat of injury and a noticeable lowering of the point of the hip on that side.

*o. Nursing and first-aid treatment.*—Complete fractures of any of the supporting bones of the legs of horses or mules are considered incurable and the destruction of the animal is authorized without delay. The animal may recover from a fracture of the bone forming the point of the hip provided the animal is given complete rest for a month or 6 weeks.

**170. Sprains and strains.**—*a. Cause.*—Violent effort in work or play or sudden checks, as in jumping or galloping over rough ground. Falls and similar accidents frequently result in injury to a joint or tendon.

*b. Symptoms.*—Lameness; heat and swelling in the affected leg; sensitiveness to pressure. The tendons of the forelegs are far more frequently affected than are those of the hind legs. The entire length of the tendons in the cannon region may be affected or only in a part of their length. The lameness and swelling may not be noticeable until the day following the actual injury.

*c. Nursing and first-aid treatment.*—Hot water applied several times daily is beneficial. If the joints below the knee or hock are affected the injured part can be immersed in a bucket of hot water. The parts are usually bandaged during the acute stage of the injury.

**171. Contusions.**—*a. Causes.*—Pressure from poorly adjusted or improperly cared for equipment and incorrect riding posture are the greatest causes of contusions to military animals. This is of particular importance in riding and pack animals, as an injured back results in an otherwise sound horse being lost from duty, frequently for long periods of time.

*b. Prevention.*—(1) Prevention of equipment injury entails training and discipline in which all concerned must realize the extraordinary damage which may be inflicted in a very short time by an ill-fitting saddle or collar. The individual rider must be held strictly responsible that the adjustment of his saddle, arms, and pack is correct; that his blanket is clean, and accurately folded; and that he reports at once to his immediate superior the slightest injury of any kind discovered on the back of his animal. Officers and non-commissioned officers must be unremitting in their efforts to prevent men from slouching in the saddle. Riders must sit erect in the saddle at all times. Riding on the cantle or standing in one stirrup is sure to bring saddle sores.

(2) The requirements for carrying weight successfully on a horse's back are briefly as follows:

(*a*) The back must be well muscled and conditioned to withstand this type of work.

(*b*) The pressure must be evenly distributed and borne only on the weight-carrying part of the back. (This requires more or less constant adjustment.)

(*c*) No pressure can be borne on the withers or the tops of the spine.

(*d*) Pressure must be partially removed from time to time (usually by dismounting each hour during a march) and entirely removed at least once during each 24 hours. Correct riding posture must be constantly maintained.

(*e*) The back and equipment must be kept clean.

*c. Symptoms.*—The symptoms are obvious. Abrasions, swelling, or tenderness on some part of the back. The condition most amenable to emergency treatment is a circumscribed swelling which appears soon after the weight has been removed. These are commonly known as "bunches" and unless properly treated will develop into serious wounds.

*d. Treatment.*—The treatment should be started as soon as it is apparent that a bunch is forming, usually 30 minutes to 1 hour after unsaddling. Apply cold irrigations or baths with gentle hand rubbing. This should be followed by the application of packs saturated and kept wet with cold water and held in position by means of a surcingle or bandage. The pad may be of oakum or it may be made by folding a gunny sack three or four times. Injuries to the withers and ridge of the spine should be irrigated or bathed with cold water but without pressure and without massage. Slight galls, chafes, or abrasions are treated with white lotion or powdered boric acid. Every effort should be made to ascertain and remove the cause with a view to preventing further injury.

**172. Thumps (spasms of diaphragm).**—*a. Causes.*—Overwork or fast work during hot weather, especially among animals not properly conditioned.

*b. Symptoms.*—General appearance of fatigue with spasmodic jerking noticeable in the belly and flanks. Frequently a distinct thumping sound will be heard.

*c. Treatment.*—If marching, halt the animal and if the temperature is found elevated reduce it by sponging the body with cold water. Then have the animal ridden or led into camp at the walk. The condition will usually disappear in 2 or 3 hours if the animal is given complete rest.

**173. Heat exhaustion (overheating; sunstroke).**—A condition resulting in disturbances of the nervous system due to heat.

*a. Causes.*—Long-continued hard or fast work during hot or very humid weather, especially among animals not in good condition or having heavy coats.

*b. Prevention.*—Keep animals in good condition to perform work required. Do not overtax the strength of the animal. Fit the marching rate and frequency of halts to the condition of the animal. Watch animals for early symptoms. Clip animals that have heavy coats. Water frequently on hot days.

*c. Symptoms.*—Thumps, a condition previously described, often precedes overheating. The animal that has been sweating freely will cease to sweat, or sweating is diminished, and the animal will be dull and require urging. The gait is staggering or wobbly, especially in the hind quarters. If halted, the animal stands with the legs spraddled; breathing very rapid and shallow; nostrils dilated; expression drawn and anxious; nasal membranes bluish red in color; and trembling of body muscles. The body feels hot to the hand and the temperature will be from 103° to 109° F. If in this stage the animal is forced to continue on the march, he will soon fall and likely die later, or drop dead.

*d. Nursing and first-aid treatment.*—Prompt first-aid treatment is of utmost importance. Stop the animal at once and in the shade if any is nearby. Remove the equipment and apply large quantities of cold water to all parts of the body but especially to the head, sides of the neck, groins and flanks. Inject cold water into the rectum with a syringe. Wash out the mouth and nostrils with cold water. Give the animal three or four swallows of water every few minutes. Under this treatment the temperature will drop quite rapidly, and as improvement is noted move the animal about very slowly and rub the body to prevent chilling. As soon as the temperature is near normal the animal may be moved slowly into camp. If possible the animal should be excused from work the following day but may continue the march as a led animal.

**174. Exhaustion.**—*a. Causes.*—Overexertion, excessive or prolonged heavy work, and lack of condition.

*b. Symptoms.*—After the animal arrives in camp, he may lie down and refuse his feed, especially his grain, yet drink considerable quantities of water. The temperature may be slightly elevated and the pulse may be weak and thready. Sweating may be quite noticeable and possibly patchy, yet the body may feel cold and clammy.

*c. Nursing and first-aid treatment.*—Make a comfortable place for the animal to lie. Cover the body with a blanket to prevent chilling. Hand rub the legs. Give small amounts of water frequently. Do not annoy the animal by too much attention. A period of rest is all that is needed for recuperation from this excessive fatigue. When rested, the animal will resume eating. Refusal of animals to eat for some little time after the termination of a hard day's march is not uncommon.

**175. Colic.**—A general term applied to abdominal pain caused by some form of digestive disturbance. For practical purposes, it is often classified as spasmodic and flatulent (or gas) colic.

*a. Causes.*—The causes of both forms of colic are very similar, but flatulent colic is more frequently caused by foods likely to ferment in the digestive tract, such as green clover or alfalfa, especially when wet or after being frosted. General causes are indigestible or spoiled foods, sudden changes in food, overeating while fatigued, working too soon after feeding, watering while exhausted or hot, bolting the feed, overeating of green feed, and watering too soon after feeding. Windsucking is frequently a cause of flatulent colic. Parasites, tumors, and abnormalities of any of the digestive organs may be a cause. Collections of sand in the bowel resulting from an animal eating from a sandy picket line may result in repeated attacks of colic.

*b. Prevention.*—Feeding suitable feed of good quality and attention to the principles of feeding and watering will prevent most cases of colic not due to internal causes.

*c. Symptoms.*—Pain as indicated by restlessness, pawing, stamping of the feet, looking around at the flanks, kicking at the abdomen, lying down, rolling, sweating, and frequent attempts to defecate usually resulting in the passage of but a few pellets of dung or a discharge of gas. In the so-called spasmodic form the attacks of pain are often intermittent with short periods of a few minutes of apparent freedom from pain. In the flatulent (gas) type of colic, the digestive tract is filled with gas and so the belly is often greatly distended. Breathing is often difficult because of pressure on the lungs caused by the bloat. The temperature is normal or but slightly elevated in the beginning of all forms of colic. If the sickness continues for a day or so the temperature may rise considerably.

*d. Nursing and first-aid treatment.*—Rational treatment includes relief of pain and elimination of the irritating bowel contents. Place the animal in a well bedded box stall, or if in camp bed down a section of the picket line and have an attendant hold the animal's tie rope. Do not force an animal with colic to move about at a trot, as it never can do the animal any good and often does great harm or may cause death if the animal is bloated. Do not attempt to keep the animal from rolling, etc., unless he is throwing himself to the ground so violently that it is evident he may rupture some organ. Give frequent rectal injections of 2 or 3 gallons of warm, soapy water. Wring blankets out of hot water and wrap around the belly and flanks as hot as can be borne without burning the hands or animal. Do not allow any food, but water may be given in small amounts. Do not attempt to drench the animal with various concoctions, as may be suggested. Improper or excessive medication has resulted in the death of many animals that would have otherwise recovered. Withhold all food for at least 12 hours after all pain has disappeared and feed light for 2 or 3 days.

176. **Diarrhea.**—*a. Causes.*—Spoiled food; overfeeding of "washy" foods such as alfalfa, clover, bran, etc.; nervousness; sudden changes of diet; and errors of feeding.

*b. Prevention.*—Careful attention to kind, quality, and quantity of feed and methods of feeding. Exclude "washy" feeds from diet of animals which tend to scour.

*c. Symptoms.*—The droppings are frequent and of semifluid nature. They may be of a normal color and odor or of a gray color and fetid odor. If the condition continues long, the animal loses flesh and appetite is wanting.

*d. Nursing and first-aid treatment.*—Correction of diet in mild cases will be sufficient. Give the animal absolute rest while withholding all food and limiting the amount of water for a period of 24 to 48 hours. After this period feed lightly and do not allow excessive amounts of water. Rest the animal until the droppings have returned to their normal consistency.

177. **Azoturia.**—*a. Causes.*—More or less violent exercise following enforced idleness of animals in good condition when appropriate reduction has not been made in the ration during the period of idleness.

*b. Prevention.*—When conditioned animals accustomed to regular work are given a period of complete rest for longer than a day, reduce the grain ration by at least one-half or cut it to one-fourth of the usual allowance and give more hay. When animals are first exercised after a period of rest they should be first walked for a period of at least 20 minutes after leaving the stables and not called upon to do more than a very small amount of fast work the first day.

*c. Symptoms.*—The disease usually appears within the first 20 minutes after leaving the stable if the animal is restive or in high spirits and exerts himself accordingly, but may not appear until much later. Increased excitability, profuse sweating and rapid breathing are the first symptoms. Very soon the animal begins to stiffen in his hind quarters, drag the hind legs and knuckle over in the hind fetlocks. The muscles over the croup and loins become swollen and dense but not sensitive to pressure. There is no marked increase in temperature but because of exercise and excitement the temperature may be as high as 102° F. If continued in work the animal will become completely incapable of supporting weight on the hind legs and fall to the ground and in such cases the chances of recovery are remote. The urine is scanty and red or coffee-colored.

*d. Nursing and first-aid treatment.*—Stop the animal immediately when the first symptoms are observed. Remove the saddle or harness at once, and cover with three or four blankets. Keep the animal standing, if possible; if not, provide a good bed. Heat some oats or common salt, place in a sack, and spread over the loins to relieve the pain. If hot water is available, a hot blanket wrung out, placed over the back and loins, and covered with dry blankets is very beneficial. This should be changed often. After a few hours the average case can be moved slowly to the stable, provided the distance is not too great. At this time the animal should be given a purgative and be fed on bran mashes, grass, and hay for a few days.

**178. Thrush.**—*a. Causes.*—Lack of proper grooming of the feet, particularly failure to clean out thoroughly the depths of the commissures and cleft of the frog. Lack of frog pressure, filthy standings, dryness of the feet, and cuts or tears in the horny frog are all contributing causes.

*b. Prevention.*—A thorough washing of the under surface of the hoof once a week will materially assist in prevention of this disease. Correct shoeing and regular exercise are also important preventive measures.

*c. Symptoms.*—Cracks, depressions, or fissures in the horn of the frog in which is found a thick, dark colored discharge with a very offensive odor. The cleft of the frog and the sides of the frog at the depths of the commissures are the parts usually diseased. The destruction of horn is progressive and the horn may be under-run and loosened some distance back from the edges of the external opening. Lameness is usually absent except in advanced cases where the destruction of horn has extended to the sensitive tissues.

*d. Nursing and first-aid treatment.*—Clean and wash the hoof. With a sharp hoof knife, trim away all diseased and under-run horn and all ragged pieces. This is very important. With cresolis solution (1½ mess-kit spoonfuls to mess cup full of water) and a stiff brush thoroughly scrub the horn. After it has dried, paint the area with iodine. Repeat the washing and iodine treatment daily until the horn begins to appear dry and then apply pine tar. If hoof is contracted, shoe to correct. Ordinary cases of thrush can be readily cured, but cases in which the horn in the cleft has been completely destroyed and a deep fissure extends up between the bulbs of the heels are more difficult, and if not carefully watched will recur.

**179. Communicable diseases.**—*a. General.*—Communicable diseases are diseases that are transmitted or spread from animal to animal either by direct contact between the sick and well or indirectly through the medium of infected stables, water troughs, corrals, stock cars, food, etc. The diseased animal throws off in the discharge from his nose, mouth, digestive system, urinary system, or from the skin the poison or material which will cause disease in the susceptible animal. These diseases deserve more attention than noncommunicable diseases among military animals because they are most likely to appear where animals are congregated in considerable numbers. Some of these diseases are incurable, some may be transmitted to man, and all may cause great losses, especially during campaign, if not held in check. They are one of the chief causes of animal losses during active service in campaign. Communicable diseases are always marked by a period of incubation, which is the time interval that elapses between the infection and the appearance of symptoms. This period may vary from a few hours to several weeks.

*b. Predisposing causes.*—Certain causes or conditions that lower the vitality and natural resistance of animals to disease, thereby rendering them more susceptible to infection are termed predisposing causes. The chief of these are—

(1) Exposure.
(2) Working animals hard before they are in good condition.
(3) Lack of sufficient food.
(4) Improper grooming.
(5) Change of environment.
(6) Long shipment by rail or sea.
(7) Other diseases.
(8) General debility.

*c. Prevention.*—(1) *General.*—The most economical and logical way, to prevent the entrance of a communicable disease is to correct the faulty conditions that predispose the animal. Proper conditioning and seasoning, plenty of wholesome food, good grooming, and protection from undue exposure to the elements and mud keep the animals strong and in such state of health that they can resist a great amount of infection. When a disease once gains entrance to a group of animals, there are certain rules of procedure that have been found absolutely necessary in checking the spread to healthy animals and in stamping out the disease. These measures may be listed as follows:

(a) Daily inspection of all animals in order to detect new cases. This insures the prompt removal of the sick as a source of infection and the initiation of the proper treatment or destruction.

(b) Quarantine of exposed animals.

(c) Isolation of the sick animals.

(d) Disinfection of infected premises, equipment, and utensils.

(2) *Daily inspections.*—It is the duty of the veterinary officer to make daily inspections. Constant vigilance on the part of the officers in charge of animals materially assists in the prompt detection of new cases.

(3) *Quarantine.*—(a) Quarantine is the separation of the apparently healthy that have been exposed to the risk of infection from those that are healthy and have not been so exposed.

(b) The object of a quarantine is to afford to a disease that may be latent a sufficient time for it to become both active and obvious. In other words, to give exposed animals time to develop a disease before allowing them to associate with those that have not been exposed.

(c) A uniform quarantine period of 21 days has been adopted by the Army. This is the average time after exposure to infection required by most communicable diseases to develop the first symptoms. The discovery of a new case in a quarantine group is cause for beginning a new 21-day period of quarantine. The quarantine of exposed animals during an outbreak is both mandatory and necessary. Paragraphs 23 and 24, AR 40-2035, prescribe that all animals newly arrived from any place whatever must be quarantined 21 days before being allowed to mingle with other animals in the command. This is a very necessary measure for preventing the introduction of a disease into a healthy command.

(d) The place selected to use for quarantine purposes should be located so that it is impossible for other animals either to enter or come in contact through the corral fences. The ideal corral is surrounded by two fences 10 to 12 feet apart and has separate watering facilities. The attendants should not have to handle other animals. The severity of the quarantine rules depends largely upon the nature of the disease. The seriousness of such diseases as glanders and anthrax calls for carrying out the most stringent rules of quarantine in order to be effective. The following general rules should be observed in conduting a quarantine stable or corral:

1. Post "Quarantine" signs at the gate and doors and allow no unauthorized persons or animals to enter.

2. Clean the watering troughs or buckets daily.

3. The attendants should not be allowed to handle other animals.

4. Inspect all animals daily for the early symptoms of disease.

5. Remove new cases immediately.

6. Burn the manure, bedding, and soiled forage or remove same to a dump and burn.

6. Disinfect the feed boxes, mangers, water buckets, troughs, and woodwork frequently.

8. Prevent animals drawing police wagons from coming in direct contact with quarantine animals.

9. Clean and disinfect the premises; also all equipment and utensils at the conclusion of the quarantine.

(4) *Isolation.*—The absolute segregation from all other animals of an animal affected with a communicable disease or one suspected of being infected is termed isolation. It differs from a quarantine in that it is a segregation of animals that are actually sick. It must be complete in every detail in order to be of any value. The degree of isolation necessarily varies with different diseases.

(5) *Disinfection.*—The application of agents called disinfectants for the purpose of destroying disease-producing material is called disinfection.

(a) *Cleanliness.*—Germs find temporary resting places to propagate and are hidden by dust and dirt. It is essential that a thorough cleaning always precede disinfection. It is time wasted to disinfect a stable, grooming kit, stockcar or anything else unless it has been previously prepared by cleaning.

(b) *Disinfectants.*—Fresh air, wind, and sunlight are powerful disinfectants, for which reason a stable with plenty of windows and well ventilated is more sanitary than one that is dark, damp, and evil-smelling. The chemical disinfectant used almost entirely in the Army is a 3 to 5 percent compound solution of creosol in water. This solution should be sprayed on all surfaces with a fine spray under pressure. Stable utensils and equipment may be immersed in the solution for 2 to 4 hours.

**180. Cast and falls.**—*a.* Occasionally an animal will fall in the stable or become cast in the stall in such a manner that it is unable to rise. In such a case the following procedure should be followed:

(1) See that the animal has plenty of room. If it is in a single stall pull it out into the aisle.

(2) Turn it over, by attaching ropes to the lower hind feet and forefeet. Then see that the feet are on the same level with or lower than the back.

(3) Assist the animal to roll up on its breast, and allow it to remain quiet for a few minutes.

(4) Pull the front feet out in the position naturally assumed by a horse when it is about to rise.

(5) Stand close against the buttocks and grasp the tail. Be prepared to exert a pull upward and forward. Leave the head alone.

(6) Now speak sharply to the animal or slap it lightly with a strap and lift the tail as directed.

*b.* In case it is impossible to raise the animal by this means, it may be necessary to use a sling. The articles required are a block and tackle of sufficient strength and 30 feet or more of rope. The block may be fastened above the animal in the stable, or in the field a tripod may be improvised from strong poles. The rope is placed around the animal as follows:

(1) Double it, put the head through the loop, and carry the loop back to the collar seat. Pass the free ends of the rope between the front legs, crossing the ropes just before they go between the legs. Pass the lower rope under the body so that it emerges just back of the withers.

(2) Lay the upper rope over the chest so that it crosses the lower rope at this point.

(3) Bring the lower rope over the body and between the hind legs.

(4) Pass the upper rope under the body in a position corresponding to the other rope, crossing the two ropes as they emerge from between the hind legs.

(5) Bring both ropes up over the buttocks, one on each side of the tail, and pass them forward along the back, under the crossed ropes, and tie to the loop which lies at the top of the neck. Draw the ropes as tightly as possible before the knot is tied. Now attach the hook of the block under all the ropes at the point on the back where they intersect, namely, the single strands crossing to go between the hind legs and the double strand coming forward from the tail, and the animal is ready to be raised.

SECTION VII

## X-RAY SERVICE

**181. General description.**—The X-ray department serves three general purposes in a hospital: fluoroscopy, roentgenography, and roentgenotherapy.

*a.* For fluoroscopy, the patient is placed in front of the X-ray tube (at a distance of 12 to 14 inches) and between the tube and a "fluoroscopic screen." The fluoroscopic screen is simply a cardboard, usually measuring about 12 by 16 inches and having a coating of tungstate or zinc crystals, this coating being covered by a lead-impregnated glass facing the medical officer. When the X-ray switch is closed, many of the X-rays which are produced pass through the patient and those which hit the fluoroscopic screen produce a "fluorescence," or a lighting effect. The fluoroscence on the screen is variable, depending upon the quantity of X-rays which play upon the crystals of the chemical contained on the screen. The result is that where densities such as the heart, liver, or bones interfere with the passage of the X-rays, less fluorescence is produced and therefore the image on the fluoroscopic screen is that which we might imagine seeing if we were to look right through the less dense tissues of the individual. When studied in a darkened room the more dense tissues appear dark, while the less dense tissues appear lighter; for instance, the lungs, which contain much air, appear as large spaces in the chest. The contrast of the fluorescent densities is controlled by adjustments on the X-ray machine. In the case of very thin individuals, relatively low "settings" are made whereby the electrons which hit the target of the X-ray tube are driven with a relatively low force or voltage. In the case of very large individuals, more penetrating X-rays must be produced and in order to produce more penetrating X-rays, a greater force (voltage) must be developed in the X-ray machine and therefore a higher "setting" is made.

*b.* For roentgenography (X-ray pictures), the part of the patient to be studied is usually placed beneath or in front of the X-ray tube and instead of using a fluoroscopic screen, a film, enclosed in either a lightproof cardboard envelope or a metal "cassette", is placed under the part to be studied. Depending upon the density of the part and thickness of it, one or another quality of X-ray is selected by the X-ray technician on the basis of low or high "settings." The quantity of X-rays showered through the part is also varied. A good technician will know exactly how much X-radiation and what quality of X-ray should be applied for any particular part. If the exposure technique be sufficiently scientific, it will then merely be necessary to take the X-ray film into the darkroom and immerse it for a definite number of minutes in a "developing" solution and then after washing it, immerse it into a "fixing" solution (again, for a definitely set time). The developing solution produces a chemical change, blackening those silver salts of the emulsion which have been affected by the X-rays, but not affecting the silver salts which were not affected by the X-rays. The "fixing" solution removes all of the silver salts and other chemicals which have not been affected by the X-rays. It also hardens the emulsion on the film so that it cannot be easily scratched off. After "fixing", it is necessary to completely wash the film; otherwise, the fixing solution will dry on it and the film will appear as if it were covered by a coating of salt. Then the film is dried. This procedure of handling the film through the chemicals and wash waters is called "processing."

*c.* For roentgenotherapy (X-ray therapy), the part of the patient to be treated is usually placed under the X-ray tube. For this purpose, considerable quantities of X-rays are applied and therefore all parts of the patient other than those to be treated are covered with lead or they are protected in some other way. The medical officer selects a certain quality of X-rays by means of changing the voltages of the electrical currents and by inserting filters into the stream of the X-rays. He varies the quality and the quantity of the X-rays, depending upon the type of lesion and its location, (that is, whether it be located on the surface, a few centimeters beneath, or very deep). During X-ray treatments, the whole room becomes filled, more or less, with X-rays, because "secondary X-rays" are given off from the patient due to the effects of the "primary X-rays" which come from the tube itself. Therefore, neither the medical officer nor anyone else, except the patient, should be in the room while a treatment is being given.

**182. Component parts of an X-ray machine.**—There are certain component parts which are common to all X-ray machines— a main switch, an auto-transformer, an X-ray switch, a high tension transformer, a low tension transformer, a filament regulator, and an X-ray tube.

*a.* The main switch may be of a double pole, throw switch design or it may be of a plunger type. By closing it, provided the line cable be connected, usually the circuit to the auto-transformer as well as the circuit to the low tension transformer are closed. Because of the later effect the filament of the X-ray tube is lighted.

*b.* The auto-transformer is an instrument which serves to vary the voltage which is to be applied to the high tension transformer. The various "settings" are made on it.

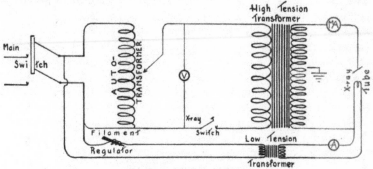

FIGURE 56.—X-ray machine.

*c.* The X-ray switch closes a circuit between the auto-transformer and the high tension transformer. Thereby another circuit is induced wherein the electrons flow through the X-ray tube. This latter circuit is the "secondary circuit" from the high tension transformer.

*d.* The high tension transformer is an instrument which "steps up" (increases) any voltage which is applied to its primary windings so that there is developed in its secondary windings a much greater voltage, as much as ten thousand times or more the voltage applied to the primary winding.

*e.* The low tension transformer is an instrument which "steps down" (decreases) any voltage which is applied to its primary windings. It is designed to supply quantity of electrons rather than voltage (or pressure) and in the case of X-ray equipment it is found in a filament circuit.

*f.* The filament regulator is an instrument (usually a "rheostat" or a "choke coil") which is used to change the volume of current which flows through the filament of the X-ray tube.

*g.* The X-ray tube is a tube which is energized by at least two circuits: the filament circuit and the high tension circuit. Within the X-ray tube, there is an almost perfect vacuum. The high tension circuit is incomplete to the extent that there is a gap in it, between the filament and the target of the X-ray tube. Ordinarily, electrons cannot flow across a gap, in a vacuum, regardless of how great the voltage might be and regardless of how short the gap might be. However, when a metal which is acting as a conductor of electrons, is heated, the electrons are set free and thereby the resistance of a gap is lessened. By means of a filament current, one terminal (cathode end) of the potential high tension circuit is heated; electrons are thereby freed and move outside of the conductor, and with the voltage of the high tension circuit itself they are forced to "jump" across the gap and to hit the target, which is the other terminal of this high tension circuit. The electrons move on to complete the circuit back to the high tension transformer. X-rays are produced at the site on the target receiving the impact of the electrons. The resistance between the filament and the target can be varied by controlling the heat of the filament with the use of the filament regulator. Depending upon the amount of this heat, more or less electrons get across to the target, and thereby more or less X-rays are produced. Depending upon the voltage which is selected by variable settings on the auto-transformer, the effective high tension voltage of the secondary winding of the high tension transformer can be controlled and thereby the force of impact of the electrons upon the target of the X-ray tube can be controlled. The greater the impact of the electrons within the X-ray tube, the shorter the wave-length of the X-rays produced; and the shorter the wave-length of the X-rays produced the greater is their penetrating power (through tissues and objects) and vice versa.

*h.* Many other component parts might be mentioned: fuses, circuit breakers, valve tubes, meters, line voltage compensators, relays, condensers, etc., but all of these are simply auxiliary to the more important parts described above.

**183. Hazards.**—*a.* X-ray equipment should be manipulated only by those who have received special training and who understand how the equipment functions. X-rays are invisible and they are developed by means of very high voltages of electricity. Actually, X-rays are produced by the impact of electrons. Electrons are the most minute particles of matter; they are the units of electricity. X-rays are produced during thunderstorms when at the time of the "lightning" a torrent of electrons are flowing like water in a powerful waterfall, and because of the tremendous voltage (having force) which causes them to flow, they hit a tree or a building or the ground with a terrific impact. We seldom think of X-rays being produced at such occasions because we cannot see the X-rays. We see the lightning; in other words, we see the effect of a torrent of electrons but if camera or X-ray films were left in the vicinity where lightning were to strike, even though these films be protected against light, it would be found that the emulsions would become sensitized by X-rays produced at the time of the lightning striking some object— the impact of electrons. All of us respect and fear lightning bolts. We should have the same degree of respect toward the equipment which is used to develop X-rays, and we should have the same degree of fear as regards the possibilities of what might happen in case of doing the wrong thing, for within X-ray apparatus harnessed lightning bolts are put to use. This means that unless we have a thorough understanding of what will happen when inserting a plug into an electrical receptacle or when closing a switch or turning a dial, unless we fully understand the consequences of all such handlings, we should never risk a "tryout" with any part of an X-ray machine.

*b.* So far, mention has been made only as to the danger concerned with the electricity aspect of X-ray apparatus. There are at least three types of danger concerned with the handling of X-ray equipment—electrical, X-radiation, and fire.

(1) *Electrical dangers.*—(*a*) Electrocutions are conducted with voltages varying from 1,800 to 3,600 volts. X-ray activities are conducted with voltages varying from 30,000 to 1,000,000 (and more, year by year). It is true that voltage by itself is not a killing factor, but by means of voltage (that is, electrical force) electrons are able to jump very great distances and thereby make "contact." Death is dependent upon the volume (that is, the numbers) of electrons which make this jump and which flow through the body. The duration of the flow of electrons is also a factor concerned with the likelihood of killing or burning. Moreover, the direction of flow of the electrons through the human body is important. Whether a part of the body might be burned or whether death of the individual actually results depends upon the quantity of electrons going through the heart. For instance, if the electrons flow from one hand through the chest and out by way of the other hand or by way of one hand and out by way of the opposite foot, the heart is likely to be affected by a large proportion of the electrons and death is most likely to result. This type of death would be an electrocution, and since it is not always instantaneous, it is important that every soldier know what to do in attempting to rescue anyone who is so afflicted and then to know how to proceed in the way of treatment.

(*b*) Usually, the victim is unable to detach himself from the electric current because the stimulation of electricity causes his muscles to contract and to hold on to the electrical contacts. Nevertheless, his friends or rescuers should never actually grip him, for in so doing they themselves may also be electrocuted before they can detach this victim from the electrical supply. So, instead of forging ahead and grasping a victim of an electrical contact, the first thought should be to detach the wall connection or to open the main switch having to do with the supply of the electricity. If such connections or switches are not in ready reach, a sheet or a rope might be thrown over the victim and in that way he should be quickly pulled away. After once detaching him from the electricity, treatment can be given. The victim should immediately be placed flat on his abdomen; his face turned to one side to promote the greatest ease of breathing and then the Schafer method of resuscitation should be instituted.

(2) *X-radiation dangers.*—(*a*) With any single large quantity of X-radiation, considerable damage to the skin and blood cells might result. Even with small quantities, if the exposures be repeated, very serious damage might occur. In the first instance, there might result a so-called "X-ray burn." This would not be realized for a week or more after the exposure. In the beginning, its appearance is similar to that of an ordinary sunburn. We are all familiar with the fact that a sunburn becomes manifest 12 to 24 hours following the actual exposure to the sun rays. With an X-ray burn, there is even greater delay in the appearance of the effects; as mentioned, the redness and irritation might not appear for as long as 10 days after the exposure to the X-rays. After it once appears, it is much more stubborn than are the effects of sunburn. The redness may progress to blistering, to the exudation of a watery secretion, to crust formations, and even to the development of actual ulcers. These effects usually persist for a long time—weeks, months, and even years. Even mild dosages of X-rays are sufficient to cause hairs to fall out. These effects, too, are delayed; the hairs usually begin to fall out about 1 week following the exposure and by the end of 10 days to 2 weeks the area exposed may be entirely smooth and free of hairs. With much smaller dosages, there may be no evidences of damage to the body until months later. As mentioned, if repeated small dosages of X-radiation be received, the effects may be as serious as if a single large dosage were received. Usually, though, when smaller dosages are received repeatedly over a relatively long period of time, the effects are not concerned with the skin but with the blood cells. There may be no redness nor irritation. The individual may simply develop a feeling of tiredness and general

weakness. He may appear pale and if a blood count is made it is likely that there will be found a very low white cell count and particularly a low count of lymphocytes. There might be a low red cell count, as well. All of these effects are very serious, because if they continue very long the tissues which ordinarily produce the blood cells will become exhausted and there may result a real "aplastic anemia." On the other hand, in trying to restore the needed number of blood cells which have been destroyed, these restorative tissues may become overstimulated and produce too many cells. This is especially to be considered with regard to the excessive manufacture of white blood cells, in which case a "leukemia" may result.

(b) These possibilities must be considered as far as protection to one's self is concerned and also as far as protection to patients who are being X-rayed is concerned. Attendants working in an X-ray department understand these dangers and they know what to handle and what not to handle; moreover, they know where to stand where not to stand. It is best that the stranger keep well away from equipment, whether it is being operated or not. As far as possible, it is well to wait in a hallway or in another room whereby there will be a wall as protection against the X-ray apparatus. If it is absolutely necessary to be in the room with the machine, it is always well to be to one side of the X-ray tube and away from the "X-ray beam," at a distance of 6 feet or more.

(c) X-ray effects are also destructive of all types of films. Very little X-radiation exposure will completely fog or blacken hundreds of films. Therefore, it is important that all films be removed from the X-ray room unless they be stored in lead-lined boxes. Moreover, films should not be stored in an adjoining room without protection by 1 or 2 millimeters' thickness of lead, for X-rays are able to get through most walls, floors, and ceilings. This fact should be known to all soldiers of the Medical Department and Quartermaster Department, for X-ray technicians may not be handy to give or advise the necessary care of these films and it is likely that films will be handled at some time or another by any soldier even if only to carry them from a supply depot to the hospital.

(3) *Fire hazards.*—A number of very disastrous fires have occurred because of carelessness about X-ray films. Formerly X-ray films were composed of a highly combustible base. More recently, these films have been improved somewhat so that now a less combustible base is used. But this base will burn. It burns more slowly and at about the rate that paper would burn, but there still remains considerable fire hazard. Therefore, it is still important to avoid smok-

ing in an X-ray department and "No smoking" signs should be posted and heeded. It is important to remove all patients from the vicinity where films are smoking or burning.

**184. Attending patients in the X-ray department.**—Practically every member of the Medical Department will at some time of his service be required to escort patients to the X-ray department. When doing so, it is important to realize that most of these patients are really sick. Sometimes they may not appear to be so, just because they may want to appear brave. A very large percentage of people are afraid of physical examinations, but they seldom care to admit it. These people are usually particularly afraid of an X-ray examination. Their fears are increased when they have to go into the darkroom for fluoroscopic studies. Attendants of such patients should be kind and polite. When escorting women patients, it is always important to see that there is a nurse or a relative present.

The best plan is simply to take the patient to the waiting room until called for by the doctor.

**185. General care.**—Even the smallest designs of X-ray machines cost as much as an automobile. The larger designs cost as much as an armored tank. Of course, X-ray equipment is much lighter than either, and sometimes it has to be moved around. When handling it, every soldier should realize its worth and exercise great care to avoid breakage of it. In addition to the value of the machines themselves, most of the other equipment about the X-ray department is likewise expensive. For instance, the film holders (cassettes) cost approximately $100 and yet one can be ruined simply by leaving it open and allowing a very small quantity of water to collect on it.

# Nursing and Ward Management

## SECTION I

## GENERAL

**186. Introduction.**—*a.* The fact that Army nurses are on duty at all of the larger hospitals of the Army does not relieve medical soldiers of the responsibility of acquiring a practical knowledge of the principles of nursing. Even where graduate nurses are assigned, enlisted men work side by side with them in ministering to the sick and wounded.

*b.* Army nurses are not assigned to many of the smaller hospitals or to clearing stations in the field. All of the nursing required in those establishments and units must be rendered solely by enlisted men. The conditions most essential to the recovery of the sick are rest, absolute cleanliness, an abundance of fresh air, and the timely administration of the treatment prescribed by the medical officer. These the nurse should always seek to assure. Not all medical soldiers are fit to become nurses. They must, however, receive training in this subject in order to show whether or not they possess aptitude along those lines. Study and experience are necessary, and the two must go together.

*c.* There are certain attributes or qualifications which are essential for those upon whom falls the nursing care of the sick or wounded. Certain physical qualifications are necessary and these include good health, strength, endurance, and strict obedience to the laws of personal hygiene. This necessitates daily bathing, frequent brushing of the teeth, keeping the hair properly cut and clean, regular habits of eating and sleeping, and plenty of exercise in the open air. Mental qualifications include intelligence, good judgment, a sense of order, good memory, truthfulness, obedience, tactfulness, sympathy, and a sense of professional ethics.

**187. Wards.**—*a.* Wards of all hospitals are as a rule arranged on the same general plan. The number of beds in each ward varies from 12 to 50, each ward having toilet facilities including latrines, washbowls and baths, and tub or shower or both. Wards usually have one or several private rooms for special or seriously ill cases, and in addition, a ward surgeon's office, a nurses' room, a utility room, and a linen room.

*b.* In peacetime hospitals the beds are usually arranged in pairs between adjacent windows, with a space of 3 to 4 feet between beds. About 100 square feet of floor space and 1,200 cubic feet of air space is allowed to each bed, a minimum of 72 square feet of floor space being allowed under certain circumstances. In the tropics the space allowed should be increased to 150 square feet of floor space and 3,000 cubic feet of air space.

*c.* Adjoining each bed is a bedside table and a chair, while behind each bed, in some military hospitals, is a wall locker. Folding screens or cubicle curtains are available so that at least some of the beds on the ward can be inclosed, forming private cubicles for bathing, examining, or isolating patients. Many of the wards in our military hospitals have solaria or recreation rooms where ambulant and convalescent patients can congregate. In the nurses' office is a desk, medicine cabinet, sterilizer, washbowl, and frequently a refrigerator.

**188. Heating and ventilation.**—The average ward temperature should be 70° F. during the day and 65° F. at night. A thermometer should hang in a central place in the ward and the temperature checked from time to time so as to keep this temperature as constant as possible.

**189. Duties of personnel.—***a.* Each ward is under the care of a nurse or wardmaster who under the ward surgeon is responsible for the comfort, diet, and medication of the patients, the performance of their duty by the attendants, the guarding of government property, the regulation of the heat, lights, and ventilation, and the cleanliness of the bed linen, clothing, lavatories, baths, washbowls, and floors.

*b.* The nurse or wardmaster accompanies the medical officer on his rounds. Cultivating the habits of observation, neatness, and system is essential. In passing about the ward, they should observe the condition of the patients, the beds, chairs, and tables, and should at once correct anything that is out of order. There should be a place for everything and everything should be in its place. It is the duty of the nurse or, if a nurse is not available, of the wardmaster to see that all orders written by the ward surgeon in the ward order book are carried out.

*c.* Ward attendants must be in proper uniform at all times; the uniform should be clean, the brass shined, and shoes polished. The uniform prescribed for ward attendants in the Army hospitals is the white uniform. The fatigue uniform can be worn when doing police work that would soil the white uniform. Ward attendants are required to wear a blouse when waiting on patients. Smoking should be done while absent from ward, while on errands, or at meal times. The hair should be kept neatly trimmed, and the hands and nails kept scrupulously clean. Clothing should be neat and clean. Attendants should not have financial dealings and should not engage in games with the patients. Gentleness, kindness, and tolerance should be exercised at all times when dealing with patients.

*d.* A ward attendant, if seated, should immediately arise and come to attention when an officer enters the room. When strangers or visitors enter the ward, the nurse should ascertain their business and show them proper courtesies; they should not be allowed to wander through the ward unescorted. The nurse or wardmaster should not leave the ward without informing the next nurse or attendant in charge where they are going, and for how long. The latter should be placed in charge formally before leaving.

*e.* Ward attendants should assist the medical officer in charge and the nurse in the proper control and supervision of the patients. Any disregard or disobedience of the rules and regulations of the hospital by any of the patients should immediately be reported to the nurse or, in her absence, to the ward surgeon. Ambulant patients are required to keep their hair brushed and trimmed, their nails clean, to wear socks, to keep their shoes laced, and to exercise good personal hygiene. Convalescent suits, if worn, should be clean and kept buttoned, and bathrobes, if worn, should be kept belted and tied. Ambulant patients are often assigned by the ward surgeon to assist the ward attendant in the various duties in the ward. It helps to keep the patients' minds occupied and has a good psychological effect in hastening their recovery.

**190. Fundamentals of ward management.**—Responsibility for the proper management of the ward rests upon the ward surgeon. This management, however, can be successfully carried out only with the wholehearted cooperation and assistance of the nurses and ward attendants. The professional attention, care, and treatment of patients is of primary importance, but such care and treatment cannot be properly accomplished unless efficient administrative methods are maintained. Absolute cleanliness, orderliness, and quietness are the first essentials of ward administration and can be obtained only through the constant vigilance and effort of the ward personnel.

**191. Ward cleaning.**—*a.* Going on duty in the morning, the nurse or wardmaster must begin at once to get things in order for the morning rounds, usually at 9 o'clock. All ward attendants must report promptly and assist in this work. Chairs should be put in their places, beside tables cleared of superfluous articles, and beds made up. Bed patients should have their hands, faces, and teeth washed and hair brushed.

*b.* Everything in the ward should be dusted daily. This includes the beds, bedsprings, chairs, lockers, bedside tables, windows, radiators, electric light fixtures, woodwork, doors, and desks. Particular attention should be taken to insure the removal of all dust in the corners, behind radiators, and in cracks and crevices.

*c.* The cleaning of the floors will depend upon the composition of the floor. Linoleum and hardwood floors should be kept polished. Composition floors should be mopped daily with warm, soapy water. In mopping floors the water should be changed frequently. After mops are used, they should be cleaned well and dried in the sun. Floors should be swept at least three time daily, care being taken so that no dust is raised in this procedure. Slippers, shoes, baggage, and other such articles should be kept off the floor.

*d.* Copper, brass, and nickel should be polished frequently with metal polish. Porcelain utensils, sinks, and tubs are best cleaned by warm water and soap, using the necessary amount of muscular effort. Sand soap should not be used, since this will scratch the surface.

*e.* After the ward is made ready the lavatory should be attended to; all urinals, bedpans, and bottles should be thoroughly cleaned, shelves wiped off, closet bowls and seats washed, and bathtubs scrubbed.

*f.* Whenever a bed is vacated, mattress and bedding should be thoroughly aired and sunned and disinfected if necessary. The same bed linen should never be used for two consecutive patients without washing.

*g.* To prevent pollution and avoid unpleasant odors, all discharges such as urine, feces, sputum, and vomited matter, soiled dressings and linens, and dirty vessels should be promptly removed. The vessels containing discharges should be covered at once, a bedpan or urinal cover being used, and should never be carried through the ward uncovered.

*h.* Soiled dressings should be placed in a special covered pan or a paper bag.

*i.* Sputum cups, if of the metal type, must be frequently disinfected by boiling, and bed pans and urinals scalded with hot water after use. All should be kept scrupulously clean.

*j.* All articles of clothing and toilet articles used by the patients should be neatly arranged on the bedside table or in the locker. Window sills and radiators should not be used as shelves.

*k.* All mops and brooms, when not in use, should be kept on a rack provided for that purpose. All scrub and waste buckets should be kept clean and free of deposits. *Phenol preparations are not necessary nor indicated for cleaning purposes.* Upon entering a properly maintained ward one should not be met with the odor of disinfectants. The liberal use of soap, water, and muscular effort are all that are needed to keep a ward clean.

*l.* The ward should be kept in such state of cleanliness at all times that, regardless of the time the commanding officer may appear, it will be ready for inspection.

*m.* Cleaning procedures should be carried out in such manner that they will disturb the comfort of the patient as little as possible and will not interfere with the treatment and care of the patient.

**192. Care of property.**—*a.* The utmost care must be taken in keeping the ward property in good condition and guarding it against loss. Any permanent installation in the ward broken or out of order should immediately be reported so that all utilities function perfectly at all times. Items of issue needing repair should be exchanged, through the medical supply, so that the property in the ward is serviceable at all times. Expendable items are obtainable through requisition, usually once a week on a specified day, from the medical supply and should not be requisitioned in excessive amounts. Only the amount of each item necessary for 1 week should be asked for and then every effort should be made to prevent loss or breakage of these items. This particularly pertains to thermometers, which are often broken through carelessness and requisitioned in excessive amount.

*b.* A list of the nonexpendable property charged to the ward is furnished on a memorandum receipt. Constant vigilance and effort are required by the entire ward personnel to prevent loss of this property. A property inventory is taken once a month and any loss is reported at once.

*c.* Linen should receive special attention. Soiled linen is exchanged for clean linen daily and is counted both before it is sent to, and after it is returned from, the laundry. The wards in most of our military hospitals have a linen room in which the linen is stored and this room should be kept locked at all times. Soiled linen is kept in linen hampers, which are also kept in the linen room.

*d.* Bed patients should have their bed linen changed as often as necessary to give them comfort and a sense of cleanliness, while ambulant patients should have their bed linen, pajamas, and bath towels changed twice a week. Clean hand towels should be given to the patients at least every second day.

*e.* Stains on linen should be removed before sending to the laundry. Blood stains, when fresh, can be removed by soaking in cold water, followed by washing in warm, soapy water. Meat and egg stains can be removed in the same manner. Vomitus and feces can be removed by holding under cold running water and brushing and then washing in warm, soapy water. Iodine stains can be removed by soaking in a solution of sodium hyposulfite. Silver nitrate stains can be removed by applying ammonia and then washing. Ink stains can be removed by applying salt and lemon juice, laying in the sun, and then washing. Mercurochrome stains are removed by soaking in 20 percent chlorinated soda solution (Labarraque's solution) for 2 minutes, then adding 5 percent solution of acetic acid in an amount equal to one-fifth the volume of the soda solution.

**193. Ward rules.—***a.* The head nurse or, in wards in which Army nurses are not assigned, the wardmaster of each ward is directly responsible to the ward officer, and will be in charge of the ward and the enlisted assistants and patients therein, and will be obeyed and respected accordingly.

*b.* The head nurse or, in wards in which Army nurses are not assigned, the wardmaster is responsible for the cleanliness and order of the ward and is responsible for the prompt delivery of prescriptions to the pharmacy, of medicines to the ward, and of the diet cards to the mess office.

*c.* In wards to which Army nurses are not assigned, the wardmaster is responsible for the administration of medicines and other treatment prescribed, the keeping of records, and all other duties that may be assigned to him by the ward officer. No enlisted men, except those authorized to do so in writing by the responsible medical officer, will administer medicine to a patient in a hospital, and then only as directed by the responsible medical officer and under such limitations as his written authorization shall prescribe.

*d.* Alcohol, alcoholic liquors, and narcotics, when necessarily on hand in the ward, will be kept under lock and key and every precaution taken to prevent their improper use. Disinfectants such as formalin, cresol, etc., and medicines for external use only, will not be kept on the same shelf or in the same medicine cabinet as medicines for internal administration.

*e.* On the death of a patient the wardmaster will notify the ward officer, or in his absence the medical officer of the day. He will not remove the body from the ward until after it has been examined by a medical officer.

*f.* The wardmaster will see that patients are acquainted with ward rules.

*g.* Before leaving the ward at the end of his daily tour of duty, the wardmaster will turn over to his relief all orders of the ward officer, accompanied by such explanation and instructions as may be necessary.

*h.* Upon reaching the ward patients will be promptly bathed, clothed in clean hospital clothing, and put to bed, unless their condition indicates otherwise or a specific order forbids.

*i.* Money and valuables found on patients will be disposed of in the prescribed manner. The commanding officer will not be responsible for money or valuables of patients not turned over for deposit in the hospital safe.

*j.* A clinical record will be carefully kept for each patient. Upon final disposition of the case this record will be completed and signed by the ward officer and turned in to the record office.

*k.* No information regarding the diseases or condition of patients under treatment will be given to anyone except those authorized under the regulations to receive it.

*l.* Visitors will be allowed to see friends in the ward at a specified time, when their presence will in no way disturb other patients.

*m.* Bed linen will be changed on occupied beds at least twice weekly, and oftener if necessary to insure cleanliness. Whenever a bed is to be occupied by a new patient, clean linen will be furnished. All bedding and clothing used by infectious cases will be promptly disinfected when removed from the beds. Patients will not occupy their beds when dressed in other than hospital clothing.

*n.* Loud noises, boisterous actions, the use of profane language, and gambling are forbidden in the wards, and no food, intoxicants, or other articles of food or drink, except as prescribed or authorized, will be brought into the wards.

*o.* Patients are forbidden to use towels, basins, toilet articles, eating utensils, or articles of clothing pertaining to another patient.

**194. Admission and discharge of patients.**—*a.* Patients are admitted to Army hospitals at the receiving office, where the necessary data for the initial form of the clinical record (W. D., M. D. Form No. 55a (Clinical Record Brief)) is obtained and recorded. This form is forwarded to the ward with the patient. In some of the larger hospitals, patients, if not too ill, are given a bath and furnished hospital clothing before being sent to the ward.

*b.* After arrival at the ward, the patient should be promptly attended by the nurse or ward attendant and should be treated with consideration and courtesy. He should be given a seat next to the nurse's or ward attendant's desk and made comfortable while the routine slips are made out and the temperature, pulse rate, and respirations are taken and recorded. If his condition permits, and in those hospitals where a shower is not given at the receiving office, he should be conducted to the bathroom where he should be instructed to take a tub or shower bath. During this procedure he should be furnished pajamas, bathrobe, bath towel, face towel, and slippers. Then he should be conducted to his bed.

*c.* Those patients who are too ill to take a bath, as shown by increased temperature over 100° F., by being brought to the ward on a stretcher or in a wheeled chair, or showing evidence of acute illness, pain, distress, discomfort, or injury, should not be sent to the bathroom until authority is obtained from a medical officer. These patients should be put to bed immediately, being disrobed by the nurse with the assistance of the ward attendant. The patients should be given a bed bath as soon as practicable. During the bathing process, the body should be inspected for the presence of skin lesions or vermin and evidence of contagious or infectious disease.

Anything unusual about the patient's body, or symptoms should be recorded and reported to the ward officer or the medical officer of the day.

*d.* In accordance with Army Regulations, a clinical record of every patient will be kept by fixed hospitals in time of peace or war, excepting those serving in a theater of operations. W. D., M. D. Form No. 55a and W. D., M. D. Form No. 55j (Clinical Record Treatment) will be used in every case; the other lettered blanks of the 55–series will be used as the nature or importance of the case may warrant. In most Army hospitals a complete record is kept, including forms 55a to 55j, inclusive, and the other Medical Department or local hospital forms, depending upon what laboratory or other diagnostic procedures have been requested and received.

*e.* On admission of a patient to the ward, the nurses or ward attendant will initiate such laboratory examinations as are required by standing orders of the ward officer. All other laboratory requests or diagnostic procedures must be ordered and signed by the medical officer. The nurse's bedside notes (W. D., M. D. Form No. 68) are usually of a temporary nature. They are not filed with the clinical record and may be destroyed or retained at the discretion of the commanding officer of the hospital.

*f.* At each ward is an Admission and Discharge Book in which the register number, name, status, and date of admission of each patient is entered. A bed card and two roster cards are also made out for each patient. The bed card, upon which is typed the register number, name, status, and date of admission, is kept at the foot of the bed by a bed card holder. The roster cards, upon which is typed the same data as upon the bed cards, are kept on ward directory boards upon which are the locations of the beds in the ward. These ward directory boards are kept in the ward surgeon's and the nurses' offices and should be kept up to date.

*g.* Any infectious case admitted should be isolated immediately and his clothes sent to the proper place for sterilization.

*h.* Valuables in most Army hospitals are taken up by the receiving officer and turned over to the custodian of the patients' fund, the necessary local form for receipt for valuables having been made out. If a patient is admitted to a ward with valuables, these should be taken up by the ward surgeon and turned over with the proper form to the custodian of the patients' fund for safekeeping.

*i.* Whether or not a patient is allowed to keep his clothing depends upon the rules and regulations formulated by the commanding officer of the hospital concerned. In most Army hospitals the patients are required to turn in their clothing at the baggage room which is connected with the receiving office and they are furnished hospital clothing in return.   They are allowed to retain two suits of underwear, two pairs of socks, a pair of shoes or slippers, and the necessary toilet articles.

*j.* Patients are discharged from the hospital when they have recovered from the disease for which they were hospitalized, when they are discharged on a certificate of disability, and when they are transferred to another hospital. They can be temporarily discharged in case of furlough or leave, at the expiration of which furlough or leave they return to the hospital. A case might also be terminated in case of death or in case of absence without leave or desertion.   In case of discharge from the hospital, the clinical record should be brought up to date, all notations entered, all forms attached in the proper sequence, and the record sent forward 24 hours prior to the contemplated time of discharge of the patient.   The main diagnosis and the date of discharge is entered opposite the patient's name in the ward Admission and Discharge Book.

**195. Serving food.**—*a.* One of the most important duties in the hospital and perhaps one that is frequently neglected is the serving of diets.   Treating disease by diet therapy is just as important as treating by means of medication and in certain types of disease such as diabetes and peptic ulcer diet is probably more effective than medicine in controlling the symptoms and effecting a recovery.   For the maintenance of life we must not only have the required amount of food but it must also consist of the properly balanced proportions of the food elements.   These food elements consist of proteins, carbohydrates, fats, water, mineral salts, and vitamins.

*b.* Diets are classified as regular, light, soft, liquid, and special.

(1) The *regular* diet is the one served in the general mess and to certain patients in the wards.

(2) The *light* diet consists of one in which certain heavy foods and certain kinds of meat are restricted.

(3) The *soft* diet consists of foods which are very easily digested, with fluids in addition.

(4) A *liquid* diet, as the name implies, consists only of fluids such as broths, strained soups, strained gruels, fruit juices, milk, milk drinks, ice cream, tea, and coffee.   The fluid intake of a patient might be forced or restricted.

(5) A few examples of *special* diets are the diabetic, Sippy, convalescent ulcer, salt-free, low residue, and high-vitamin high-caloric diet.

*c.* Silverware, cooking utensils, dishes, and glassware should be kept scrupulously clean. All dishes, including glasses and silverware, which come in contact with infectious or contagious cases should be sterilized by washing in boiling water. The silverware should be kept polished.

*d.* For the psychic effect upon the patient, the dishes served to patients should be as tempting and appetizing in appearance as possible. Painful emotions such as worry, anxiety, depression, fear, anger, and nervousness tend to inhibit the flow of digestive secretions and interfere with the proper digestion and assimilation of the food. Pleasurable sensations and emotions such as cheerful surroundings, the sight of appetizing and garnished dishes, and cheerful frame of mind tend to increase the flow of digestive secretions and aid in digestion. An important duty of the nurse or ward attendant in serving food to certain types of patients is to prevent, if possible, the painful emotions which inhibit digestion and to stimulate those pleasant emotions which aid digestion.

*e.* It is very important to serve hot food *hot*, preferably on warm dishes, and cold food *cold*, preferably on *cold* dishes. Meals should be served at regular intervals. This is extremely important in certain types of cases who require frequent feedings at regular intervals.

*f.* Ambulant patients in military hospitals are usually served cafeteria style in the general hospital mess. Bed patients, and semiambulant or convalescent patients are served on trays in the wards. In some of the larger Army hospitals dietitians aided by mess attendants serve the ward patients. In many of the military hospitals, the serving of trays to patients in the ward is taken care of by the nurse and ward attendants.

*g.* Bed patients should be prepared for their meals 15 to 20 minutes prior to mealtime. This might necessitate giving the patient a bedpan or urinal followed by giving him wash water and brushing or allowing the patient to brush his hair. Most patients in hospitals look forward to mealtime unless they are too ill. The serving of meals is one of the things which has a tendency to break the monotony of the day. Bed patients should be arranged comfortably with pillows or by raising the head of the bed. The condition of many patients is such that they should not be allowed to exert themselves unduly. This type of case will have to be fed by the nurse or ward attendant. Fluids can be given to a strictly bed patient by drinking tubes or a spoon. *A delirious patient should never be given fluids by a glass drinking tube.* Many semiconscious patients can be given fluids slowly by a spoon. The touch of the spoon on the lips and tongue stimulates the swallowing reflex. In these cases, food or fluids should be given very slowly and one must be positive that the food enters the esophagus and not the larynx.

*h.* The trays used in serving patients should be thoroughly clean. The various dishes served should be neatly arranged and all the necessary utensils should be present. If salt, pepper, sugar, and cream are allowed, they should also be present. The tray should be inspected before it leaves the diet kitchen for neatness, cleanliness, proper menu, and identification. Trays should immediately be removed from the ward after the patient has finished his meal.

*i.* Prescribed diets, particularly a diabetic diet, should be entirely consumed by the patient without any substitution. Medication should not be taken with the meals unless specifically ordered. A period of quiet and rest after a meal is desirable.

**196. General nursing care and comfort of patient.**—*a.* Nursing is the art or science of caring for the sick and wounded. Nursing objectives in general include the promotion of health, the prevention of disease, the cure of disease, the restoration to health, and the comfort of the patient. In nursing or treating patients in the hospital we are primarily interested in the care and comfort of the patient, the goal being the cure of the disease and the restoration to health.

*b.* The mental attitude of the patient has a marked influence on his condition. Every effort should be made to keep him contented and in a cheerful frame of mind. It is also necessary that he should have confidence in those attending him, including the medical officers, nurses, and ward attendants. His mind should be allayed so that he does not worry about his condition. To comfort is to strengthen, support, invigorate, refresh, gladden, cheer, and give relief from pain and trouble. The patient's recovery will depend to a great extent upon the patient's comfort, this in turn being dependent upon the general nursing care. Mental and physical relaxation, which are the results of comforting the patient, are therapeutic aids in restoring the patient to health. To make the patient comfortable, contented, and happy is one of the chief duties of the nurse or ward attendant and it is essential in successfully treating the patient.

*c.* Physical causes of discomfort in illness includes cramped and strained positions; weight and pressure on sensitive parts, such as the weight of the arms on the chest or the weight of the bed clothes; rubbing and chafing from such causes as restlessness, moisture, or temperature; interference with bodily function, including sleeplessness, thirst, indigestion, constipation, diarrhea, nausea, and vomiting; lack of cleanliness resulting in irritation of the skin and itching; pain and unskillful handling. The causes of mental discomfort are numerous, the main ones being homesickness, financial worries, apprehension, fear of pain, uncertainty, exposure, lack of privacy, confusion, and noise. It is one of the main duties of a nurse or ward attendant to be cognizant of the causes of discomfort, so that he or she might be more able and skilled in providing for the care and comfort of the patient.

*d.* The following procedures tend to add to the comfort of the patient and should be taken into consideration when caring for patients: bathing; attention to the mouth and teeth; proper care of the back and buttocks, so as to prevent bedsores; serving of meals at regular intervals; rest; attention to the morning and evening toilet; attention to elimination, furnishing bedpans and urinals when required; frequent changing of the position of the patient; avoidance of drafts; avoidance of bright lights; and prevention of noise. Undue noise is wearing and distressing to the sick. Medical officers, nurses, and ward attendants should endeavor to prevent unnecessary noise. Bedpans when placed under patients should be warm.

*e.* A nurse or ward attendant should always be assured that the patient is taken care of and should never wait for a signal from the patient. If signaled, this signal should be answered without delay. The routine work placed upon attendants in the wards, although very important, should never permit them to forget that their first duty is the care of the patient.

**197. Temperature.—***a.* The normal temperature of the body when taken by mouth is considered to be 98.6° F. (37° C.), but the normal temperature may vary slightly, depending upon the time of day that it is taken. The temperature might be a little lower in the early hours of the morning than during the day and it may be slightly higher after meals than before meals. The axillary temperature is approximately 1° lower and the rectal temperature approximately 1° higher than when taken by mouth. A variation of temperature below 97.5° F. or above 99° F. may be regarded as abnormal and an indication of disease. Abnormal temperature may be subnormal or elevated.

*b.* Subnormal temperature is often seen in cancer, nephritis, uncompensated heart disease, myxedema, shock, heat exhaustion, and wasting diseases. It is a rough measure of the degree of prostration. Subnormal temperatures occasionally are present in health.

*c.* Fever or an elevation of temperature above 99° F. is found in many diseases. After childhood the vast majority of fevers are found to be due to infectious diseases or inflammations of any type, toxemias without infection such as exophthalmic goiter, disturbances of the heat regulation such as in sunstroke, and occasionally after hemorrhage. A temperature of 100° to 101° F. is regarded as low fever; 101° to 103° F. as moderate fever; 103° to 105° F. as high fever and over 105° F. as hyperpyrexia.

*d.* Fevers are classified as continued, remittent, or intermittent. A continued fever is one in which the temperature is continually above normal, and there is a difference of not more than 1° between morning and evening. In remittent fever there is a decided drop some time during the 24 hours, but the temperature does not reach normal. In the intermittent fever (sometimes called hectic or septic) the temperature at certain intervals falls to or below normal.

*e.* The results of the temperature readings are recorded on W. D., M. D. Form No. 55h (Clinical Record Temperature, etc.). The temperatures of patients in the hospital are taken at the intervals ordered by the medical officer in charge. Unless otherwise stipulated it is taken and recorded in the morning and afternoon. The pulse and respiratory rates are taken and recorded at the same time. On very ill patients, the temperature, pulse rate, and respirations are taken four times daily. On ambulant convalescent patients one temperature recording each day is usually sufficient. If a graphic chart of the temperature curve is desired, it is recorded on W. D., M. D. Form No. 55i (Clinical Record Temperature, etc., Graphic).

*f.* Fevers may terminate in one of two ways. By crisis, when the fever drops suddenly to normal, never again to rise to any considerable degree unless a relapse or a complication sets in, or by lysis when the fever gradually declines until it reaches normal. Most fevers terminate by lysis. Examples of diseases which may terminate by crisis are pneumonia, influenza, and typhus fever.

*g.* The instrument for measuring the temperature of the body is called a clinical or self-registering thermometer. The thermometer consists of a glass bulb containing mercury, and a stem in which the column of mercury may rise. On the stem is a graduated scale representing degrees of temperature, the lowest degree registered being 95° F., the highest being 110° F. When the mercury column has risen above the normal line, which is usually indicated by an arrow, it must be shaken down by a sweeping motion of the arm before the thermometer is used again. The Fahrenheit scale is usually employed in this country, while the Centigrade scale is employed in European countries.

*h.* Temperatures are ordinarily taken in the mouth, the bulb being placed under the tongue, and the patient directed to close his lips but not his teeth, upon it. If the patient is very weak it may be necessary for the nurse to hold the thermometer in his mouth. With modern thermometers 3 minutes is ample for mouth temperatures. When the patient is delirious or unconscious, or is a child, it is not safe to take the temperature by mouth.

*i.* In infants and children the temperature is usually taken in the rectum. The bulb is well oiled and then introduced about 2 inches into the rectum and allowed to remain there for about 3 minutes. The rectal temperature is considered the most reliable and the most accurate estimation of the body temperature.

*j.* To take the temperature in the axilla, the arm pit is first wiped dry, the bulb put in place, and the arm carried across the chest as to bring the opposing skin surfaces in close contact with the thermometer. To obtain an accurate axillary temperature, the thermometer must remain in position 10 minutes.

*k.* Thermometers should be rendered scrupulously clean and free from infection after use. Clinical thermometers when not in use should be kept completely immersed in a two percent solution of phenol. Approximately 1 hour before they are required for use, they should be removed from the phenol solution thoroughly rinsed in cool water, and then completely immersed in 70 percent alcohol. Small thermometer trays are the containers usually used for this purpose. The thermometers are kept in the 70 percent alcohol until required for use, at which time they are removed and thoroughly wiped with cotton before placing in the patient's mouth. Upon removal of the thermometer from the patient's mouth, the temperature should be noted and recorded; the thermometer should be washed with soap and water and again placed in the phenol solution. This procedure should be repeated after each successive patient.

**198. Pulse.**—*a.* The pulse is the distention or pulsation of the arteries produced by a wave of blood forced through them by the contraction of the left ventricle of the heart. This expansion of the walls of the arteries happens at the same time as the heartbeat and is wave-like in character.

*b.* By pulse rate is meant the number of beats to the minute counted at any point of an artery's course where it may be seen or felt. The normal pulse rate in the adult male is 65 to 80, and in the adult female 70 to 80 beats per minute. The pulse is more frequent in the standing position than when lying down or sitting and is increased by exercise. In children it is much more rapid. Conditions which increase the heart action and pulse rate are fever, excitement, anger, injury, cold, and certain drugs. Conditions which depress the pulse rate include worry, shock, collapse, some toxins or poisons, and certain drugs, such as alcohol and ether. The condition of the pulse is very important, as it usually accurately indicates the condition of the heart and vital organs. A simple quickening of the pulse rate of 100 or over is known as *tachycardia*. It may be physiological, or may be caused by organic pathology. If the heart rate and pulse rate are slow, below 50 per minute, the condition is called *bradycardia*. This also may occur in normal individuals, or it may be due to conditions such as, exhaustion, toxemia, jaundice, certain heart conditions, certain mental conditions and cerebral hemorrhage.

*c.* The pulse may be taken by laying the fingers gently on any superficial artery, but the locations most frequently used are the radial artery, at the wrist; the temporal artery, in front of the ears; the cartoid arteries, in the sides of the neck; the facial arteries, where they pass over the lower jawbone just in front of the angle of the jaw; and the dorsalis pedis artery, on the dorsal surfaces of the feet.

*d.* The points to be noted when taking the pulse rate are the frequency, the rhythm, the condition of the wall of the artery, compressibility, and tension. The tension can be measured fairly accurately by the force with which the pulse strikes against the finger. The degree of pressure necessary to obliterate the pulse, that is, to prevent the pulse wave from going further along the artery gives us the compressibility of the artery. The blood pressure depends upon three factors—the elasticity and contraction or relaxation of the arteries, the volume of the blood, and the force of the heartbeat. The blood pressure is accurately measured by means of the sphygmomanometer or blood pressure apparatus. The blood pressure is taken by listening over the brachial artery just below the cuff of the blood pressure apparatus which is placed around the upper arm. This cuff is inflated and then the column of mercury allowed to fall slowly. The point where the tapping systolic sound first appears is known as the systolic pressure and the point where the sound suddenly changes from a sharp tap to a dull feeble thud is known as the diastolic pressure. The average readings in healthy adults vary between 110 and 135 millimeters of mercury for the systolic pressure, and between 60 and 90 millimeters of mercury for the diastolic pressure. The pulse pressure is the difference between the systolic and diastolic pressure readings.

*e.* The beats of the normal pulse are almost equal in force and are separated by intervals of almost equal length. In disease there might be an irregularity of the pulse in force or rhythm or both. Irregularity in force means that the beats are not all of equal strength. Irregularity in rhythm means that the intervals between the beats are not all of equal length and the beats do not follow in regular succession. An intermittent pulse is one in which a beat is missed at regular or irregular intervals.

**199. Respiration.**—*a.* The normal respirations occur at the rate of about 18 to the minute. In disease there occurs a marked variation in the frequency and character of the respirations; in narcotic poisonings the respirations are very slow, while in many diseases involving the lungs they are very rapid.

*b.* In taking respirations one should notice their frequency and regularity, whether difficult or easy, noisy or quiet, deep or shallow, and whether the same on the two sides of the chest.

*c.* Cheyne-Stokes respiration is that peculiar type of breathing which occurs in certain diseases of the heart, kidneys, or brain. The respirations gradually increase in frequency and intensity up to a certain point, then slowly decrease until they seem to cease entirely; after a short pause the same cycle is repeated. In stertorous breathing there is a loud snoring noise with inspiration. Dyspnea is difficult breathing usually accompanied by sound. Edematous breathing is characterized by loud, moist, rattling rales, caused by air's passing through the moisture in the air sacs of the lungs.

*d.* In recording respirations it must be remembered that they are in a measure under control of the will, therefore, they must be counted without the patient's knowledge. This is done by laying the arm across the chest while taking the pulse and then, without removing the fingers from the wrist, count the respiration. With a little practice an attendant should become so expert that he can take the pulse and respiration of a sleeping patient without arousing him.

*e.* In the normal individual the temperature, pulse, and respiration rates have a definite relationship, and the three factors should always be considered together in disease, since a disturbance may have a very important meaning. In health the pulse rate is about four times the respiratory rate. When the respiratory rate is increased to a third or a half of the pulse rate, it is usually an indication of disease of the lungs, such as pneumonia.

**200. Symptoms.**—*a.* One of the most important duties of a nurse or ward attendant is to cultivate the habit of observing symptoms accurately and reporting them clearly and intelligently.

*b.* The physician can be with the patient only a short time. He must depend upon the nurse or ward attendant to inform him of everything that takes place in his absence; they may obtain and impart information of the greatest value in diagnosis and treatment.

Symptoms may be divided into two classes—*Subjective* symptoms, those which are apparent to the patient himself, such as pain, and *objective* symptoms, those which are apparent to others, such as redness and swelling. Sometimes the symptoms are feigned; then the patient is said to be malingering. It is always safer to assume, however, that the symptoms are real until the contrary is proved.

*c.* Not only must the nurse or ward attendant cultivate the habit of observing symptoms, but they must learn to attach to them their relative importance. Emergencies continually arise when they must determine what is to be done as whether the symptoms are of sufficient gravity to cause them to send for the ward officer.

*d.* The observations should commence with the giving of the first bath or putting the patient to bed.

(1) Are there any scars, wounds, or eruptions upon the body? Is the patient emaciated or dropsical? Does he appear weak and ill? The attitude and expression are sometimes characteristic. In inflammation of one lung the patient lies on that side so as to give free play to the uninjured lung. In appendicitis or peritonitis he is apt to lie on his back with one or both legs drawn up.

(2) Slipping down toward the foot of the bed means weakness and therefore is an unfavorable sign.

(3) With colic, the patient often lies on the abdomen with a pillow pressed against it, but when the pain is inflammatory he cannot stand the pressure.

(4) When the patient cannot breathe while lying down, there is usually trouble with the heart or lungs.

(5) Great restlessness is often a bad sign.

(6) An anxious look is unfavorable, while a tranquil expression is of the opposite import.

(7) Rattling in the chest with shortness of breath and bluish tint of the lips is a sign of edema of the lungs and often indicates approaching death.

(8) The mental condition gives important indications—whether the patient is conscious or unconscious, rational or irrational, depressed, excited, or muttering. The speech may be thick, clear, or hoarse.

(9) Concerning the eyes, note whether the pupils are dilated, contracted, or unequal and whether there is any squinting or yellowness or congestion of the conjunctivae.

(10) The hearing may be acute or it may be defective; there may be a discharge from the ear.

(11) Bad taste may be a complaint.

(12) The skin, especially of the face, may give important indications; it may be pale, flushed, livid, or jaundiced; hot, cold, dry, or moist. A moist skin with high temperature is usually a bad omen. A peculiar red spot high up on either cheek may be indicative of pneumonia or tuberculosis; pallor about the lips is a sign of nausea. One may find the waxy hue of Bright's disease, and the rashes of the eruptive fevers, the sallow color of narcotic users, the pallor of anemia, the blue tint of cyanosis, the bronzing of Addison's disease. Bluish spots, about the size of a fingernail, distributed about the trunk are often indicative of vermin infestation.

(13) The tongue offers many valuable indications; note whether it is dry or moist, clean or coated, large or small, bitten, or indented on the edges by the teeth. In malarial fevers and digestive disorders the tongue is apt to be heavily coated, but soon becomes dry and cracked; when such a tongue becomes moist and begins to clean up from the edges, it is a very favorable sign. In scarlet fever the bright red papillae showing through the white fur produce the characteristic strawberry tongue. In yellow fever the tongue is small, red, and pointed.

(14) Note at the same time the condition of the mouth and teeth; white, slightly raised patches on the inside of the lips and cheeks, at the corners of the mouth, and in the throat are frequently mucous patches, a sign of syphilis. The dark accumulations which occur on the teeth in fevers are known as sordes; their presence indicates that the mouth has not been well cared for.

(15) The odor of the breath is often significant—sweet in diabetes, urinous in uremia, fetid in disorders of the stomach, gangrene of the lungs, bad teeth, etc.

(16) The state of the appetite is of importance; it is usually lost in acute diseases, but occasionally is excessive. Observe with care how much food the patient actually takes. Nausea is often present with or without vomiting. The frequency of the vomiting, whether it is painful, and the character of the matter vomited should be noted. Usually the vomitus consists of food at first, but this may be followed by bile, mucus, or blood. When the blood has been retained in the stomach some time it becomes brownish in color, like coffee grounds; vomitus of this character is seen in yellow fever. Vomiting of fecal matter is a sign of great importance, and indicates obstruction of the bowels. Marked thirst is usually an indication of fever or hemorrhage.

(17) The number and character of the stools should be noted; in jaundice they are generally clay-colored; bismuth and iron color them

black; they may be liquid or solid, and may contain mucus, pus blood, or worms.

(18) Tenesmus, a constant desire to evacuate the bowels, is present in dysentery.

(19) Belching of gas, rumblings in the bowels, and distention of the abdomen are signs to be noted.

(20) The urinary functions should be carefully measured. In both suppression and retention, no urine is passed, but in the former, which is much the more serious condition, no urine is secreted; it may be distinguished from retention, which is caused by some obstacle to the escape of urine from the bladder, by the fact that in suppression the bladder may be shown to be empty by tapping with the finger just above the pubis; a hollow sound is produced if the bladder is empty.

(21) Incontinence of urine, that is, the inability to hold it, may be associated with retention, so that constant dribbling does not preclude the possibility of the bladder's being distended.

(22) The quantity of urine should be measured and the frequency with which it is passed noted. Useful information may be also obtained from observation of its color and odor. Blood gives it a smoky or reddish hue, pus a milky appearance, and mucus a stringy appearance. Bile imparts a greenish tinge, as does carbolic acid, while santonin gives a bright yellow color. Many drugs and vegetables impart a characteristic odor to urine.

(23) Cough is an indication of some irritation of the air passages; the matters coughed up are called sputa. When there is no sputum, the cough is said to be dry. The cough may be tight, loose, or painful; there is the hoarse, crowing cough of croup or diphtheria, the spasmodic whoop of whooping cough, the wheezing cough of asthma, the painful cough of pleurisy and the peculiar rasping cough of aortic aneurism. The character of the sputum varies—in bronchitis it is white or yellow and mucous; in pneumonia it is reddish or prune juice in color; in tuberculosis it is at first mucous and frothy and later purulent with cheesy nodules, and sometimes stained with blood.

(24) In gangrene of the lung the sputum is unbearably offensive, while in lung abscess it may or may not be offensive.

(25) Hiccough, when it is persistent in the later stages of acute diseases, is often a very grave sign.

(26) When a patient complains of feeling cold, take his temperature; a chill is nearly always accompanied by fever. Chills frequently accompany the onset of acute diseases; when they occur in the course of inflammation they often indicate suppuration.

(27) Hemorrhage from any part of the body is always significant.

(28) Pain is one of the most valuable signs which we possess, as it often points toward the location of the disease. The kind of pain should be described and whether it is constant or intermittent, severe or slight. Exaggerated sensitiveness to touch is called hyperesthesia and diminished sensibility anesthesia, the latter being often associated with loss of muscular power or paralysis. Paralysis of the lower half of the body is called paraplegia, and of a lateral half, hemiplegia.

(29) Disorders of motion include picking at the bedclothes, always a bad sign, twitching of the tendons (subsultus), slight spasms, and local or general convulsions. In convulsions always note the parts affected and whether the attack is attended with loss of consciousness.

(30) Under disorders of consciousness are included delusions and hallucinations, delirium, stupor, and coma. The character of the delusions should be noted, whether occasional or habitual, quiet or noisy; in stupor note whether the patient can be aroused; if he cannot, it is coma, a very serious condition. Coma vigil is a combination of sleeplessness, with partial unconsciousness, and is always a symptom of bad omen.

(31) The amount and character of sleep should be recorded; patient's statements on this point must be accepted with caution.

*e.* The nurse's observations are recorded on W. D., M. D. Form No. 55j, which in turn becomes part of the permanent hospital record of the patient in question.

**201. Collection of specimens.**—*a.* Collection of specimens is one of the important duties of a ward attendant. They should be collected in the correct manner, and sent to the right place in the laboratory at the proper time. In most Army hospitals it is customary for the night ward attendants to collect the routine specimens, such as urine, feces, and sputum, the first thing in the morning and take them to the laboratory as they go off duty.

*b.* Specimens are examined by chemical, bacteriological, and microscopic methods and the results of these examinations give the medical officer very valuable information. This information is useful in arriving at a diagnosis and also valuable in following the progress of the disease. It is necessary to have the specimen well labeled and to have the proper laboratory slip attached.

*c.* There are several designations for urine specimens, such as routine specimen, 24-hour specimen, day specimen, night specimen, and sterile specimen. The routine or single specimen, is routinely obtained from every patient admitted to Army hospitals. It is obtained in the morning, passed directly into the proper container, and at least 4 ounces are sent to the laboratory. Occasionally it is desirable to save the entire amount of urine passed in 24 hours. At least a 4,000-cc. container should be used for this purpose. A definite hour in the morning for the first voiding should be fixed, the first urine being discarded. All urine passed during the next 24 hours including that which can be passed at the end of the period should be saved, properly mixed, and measured. At least 4 ounces of this should be sent to the laboratory after marking on the proper slip the amount and the notation "24-hour specimen." Occasionally the urine is divided into day and night specimen, the day specimen consisting of all urine voided in the 12-hour period from 7:00 AM to 7:00 PM and the night specimen being collected from 7:00 PM to 7:00 AM. A portion of these specimens are likewise sent to the laboratory after placing on laboratory slip the amount and the proper notations, "day urine" and "night urine."

*d*. Specimens of feces are usually obtained the first thing in the morning, the specimen being sent to the laboratory in special feces bottles and accompanied by the proper laboratory slip. Occasionally specimens are placed in sterile containers, such as a sterile test tube or a sterile Petri dish. If amoebiasis is suspected it is desirable to keep the stool at body temperature. In these cases the specimens should be sent to the laboratory without delay.

*e*. Sputum specimens are usually collected in the paper sputum cups. The sputum which is coughed up from the lungs the first thing in the morning is usually the most desirable specimen. In some hospitals small wide-mouthed bottles are used to collect sputum specimens. It is advisable to have the patient rinse out his mouth with warm water before obtaining a specimen. If sterile specimens are ordered, the patient should cough and expectorate into a sterile Petri dish. Care should be taken so that the sputum is not deposited on the outside of the container. Care should also be exercised so that the hands are not soiled and they should always be washed after handling specimens.

*f*. Other specimens which might be obtained are spinal fluid, fluid aspirated from the chest or peritoneal cavity, stomach contents, specimens of pus in cases of infection, and throat cultures. These specimens are obtained by either a trained technician or a medical officer.

**202. Beds.**—*a*. The hospital bed is higher and narrower than the average bed found in the home, and this fact contributes greatly to the efficiency of the care and treatment of the patient, as it makes it easier for the attendant to care for the patient. The regulation hospital bed is of white enameled iron with an iron spring. In addition there is the surgical bed which is adjustable so that the head or feet might be elevated or lowered.

*b.* There are two mattresses listed in the standard supply table, the inner spring mattress and the cotton mattress. Mattresses must be smooth, without lumps or hollows, and must be firm, not loose or sagging. The mattress should always be protected with a linen or cotton mattress cover made to fit the mattress as closely as possible, so as to prevent soiling. Mattress covers should be changed frequently. Two pillows are allotted to each bed, often one hard hair pillow and one soft feather pillow. The mattress and sheets of beds for strictly bed patients are protected by a rubber draw sheet which should extend from several inches under the lower edges of the pillows to several inches below the knees, and should be long enough to tuck under the mattress about 8 inches on either side. As rubber should never be allowed to come in contact with the patient, the rubber draw sheet is covered with a cotton draw sheet, which should extend about 2 inches above and below the rubber draw sheet.

**203. Bed-making.**—*a.* Making a bed properly for the sick is an art and one worthy of much practice in order to accomplish it. The manner in which it is made not only can make or mar the whole appearance of the ward, but also can make or mar the patient's comfort and therefore hasten or delay his recovery. As the patient spends most of his time in bed, his comfort is largely dependent upon it.

*b.* There are certain principles to remember in bed-making.

(1) Have all necessary articles on hand before making or unmaking a bed.

(2) Proceed systematically.

(3) Work quietly. Avoid jarring the bed, or walking around it more than necessary.

(4) Avoid stumbling against the legs of the bed.

(5) Do not place soiled linen on the floor.

(6) Avoid exposure of the patient. Place screens around the patient.

(7) Blankets should be of light weight.

(8) Use a bed-cradle to relieve the patient from weight of bedclothes when necessary.

(9) Beds must be made comfortable and free from wrinkles; it must be kept so.

(10) Cleanliness of linen is essential; coverings must be kept straight.

(11) The finished bed must not be spoiled by untidy surroundings.

*c.* The bed linen of an occupied bed may be changed easily by a single attendant unassisted, and without seriously disturbing the patient. To change the lower sheet, first loosen all the bedclothes at top, sides, and the bottom, remove all the upper coverings except a sheet and blanket and roll up the bottom sheet lengthwise, together with the draw sheet, into a tight roll close to the patient's body; then in a like manner make one side of the clean sheet and draw sheet into a roll and place it alongside the first roll, tucking the free edges under the mattress. Now stand on the other side of the bed and with both hands turn the patient on his side with his face toward you; tuck in the rolls under his back, turn him back on his other side onto the clean sheet then withdraw the soiled one and pull the clean sheet into place. To remove the upper bed clothing, the covers should first be loosened as before, then spread the clean sheet and blanket over them and tuck in at the sides, after which the soiled clothes may be drawn out at the foot.

*d.* Bed linen should be changed whenever it is soiled, when a patient is discharged, and at least twice a week, depending upon the nature of the case. In infectious cases it should be changed daily.

## Section II

## MEDICAL PROCEDURE

**204. Baths.**—Baths are of several types and given for several purposes.

*a. Cleansing bath.*—(1) A cleansing bath may be in form of shower, tub, or sponge bath, depending upon the condition of the patient and the nature of his illness. A cleansing tub or shower bath is usually given to patients who require little or no assistance in bathing, but may be given to other types of patients if so ordered. A sponge bath, or bed bath as it is sometimes called, is given to patients who are unable to help themselves and who are confined to bed.

(2) A cleansing bath is given to promote cleanliness by removing dirt and skin secretions. This aids elimination of waste products by keeping the pores of the skin open, helps prevent bedsores, and is generally refreshing to the patient. At least one bath a day is necessary for an ill patient and in many cases two or more cleansing sponge baths a day may be advisable. Convalescent patients should bathe at least three times a week.

(3) When a sponge or bed bath is given, the bed should be protected with a rubber sheet covered with a cotton sheet. Only one part of the body is exposed at a time. This part is washed and then well dried before the bathing of another part is begun. The work is done quickly but carefully and special care should be paid in washing and drying between the fingers and toes, between folds of flesh, around the umbilicus and about the pubic region. The washcloth should be well wrung out and an excessive amount of soap should not be used. If possible, when washing the hands and feet immerse them in the vessel containing the bath water. The temperature of the water should not be greater than 96° F.; to maintain this temperature it may be necessary to add hot water from time to time. The room should not be below 72° F. and should be free from draughts. All clean linen and clothing should be within easy reach before the bath is begun. If patient is seriously ill and hard to move, a heavy bath towel may be used under the part being bathed and the protecting cotton sheet may be omitted. In giving the bath, start with the face, neck, and ears and work down the body.

*b. Therapeutic bath.*—Baths other than for cleansing purposes are given only upon order of the ward officer. These therapeutic baths are either hot or cold and may be very important in the proper nursing of patients. The reason for these baths is to promote a change in blood distribution and amount present in different areas, and for a local or general change in body temperature. Heat causes the peripheral circulation to speed up and the area becomes flushed and warm, perspiration is increased, and the temperature is raised. When cold is applied the opposite happens, that is, the peripheral circulation slows, the skin becomes pale and cold, perspiration is stopped, and the temperature is decreased.

(1) *Hot bath or hot pack.*—(a) Hot baths and hot packs are usually used to relieve excitement and to produce sweating or relaxation. Care must be taken to avoid burning patients, to prevent fainting and collapse, to prevent chilling, and to avert headaches. Feeling of

dizziness or faintness, increase in pulse rate, and weakness of the pulse are signs of undesirable effect, and if the changes are pronounced the treatment should be discontinued and the ward officer notified.

(b) Hot baths and hot packs are given principally to induce perspiration and to relieve muscular tension.

(c) The articles necessary for giving hot packs are an ice cap, four blankets, one towel, a foot tub lined with a rubber sheet in which to carry blankets wrung out of very hot water, five hot-water bags, pitchers of hot and cold water, a water glass and drinking tube, and a large rubber sheet.

(d) Soak two blankets in water at 150° F., leaving one corner of the upper and lower edge of each blanket out of the water (these corners should be diagonally opposite each other, as the blanket will then, when stretched, be somewhat on the bias); wring each blanket separately (two attendants are required, each taking a dry corner and twisting in opposite directions until the blanket has been wrung dry). Place the blanket in the foot tub lined with a rubber sheet covering hot-water bags, and repeat the process with the second blanket; carry the blankets to the bedside while the rubber sheet is still folded over them; pass two dry blankets with rubber sheet between under the patient; remove the pajama suit; wrap the patient in the dry blanket upon which he is lying; and turn the upper bedclothes over the foot of the bed. Place one hot blanket under the patient and one over him; fold the rubber sheet over the wet blankets; pull up the bedclothes, placing a towel around the patient's neck; apply an ice cap to the head and hot-water bags to the hips, arms, and feet. Watch the patient's pulse and encourage him to drink freely, unless directed to the contrary. The usual duration of this pack is 20 minutes.

(e) During and after removing a hot pack take the pulse at the temporal artery frequently; give plenty of fluids while the patient is in the pack; watch for collapse, in which case discontinue the pack and apply external heat; remove the wet blankets under cover of a dry one, thus avoiding exposure; wrap the patient in a dry blanket and leave an ice cap applied to the head and a hot-water bag to the feet. Draw up the bedclothes and let the patient remain between blankets for 1 hour, at the expiration of which time dry the patient and give him an alcohol rub.

(2) *Sedative bath.*—(a) The sedative bath is for the purpose of quieting and inducing sleep; it may be continued for hours or even

days; the temperature of the water is usually just below that of the body—about 96° F.

(*b*) The arrangement is practically the same as for the Brand bath, described in (6) below. Hot water must be carefully added from time to time to maintain a uniform temperature.

(3) *Sweat bath.*—To produce sweating or relaxation, hot-water, hot-air, or steam baths are used.

(*a*) The hot-water bath is given in the tub in the ordinary way except that the head is kept cool by cold cloths or an ice cap. Care must be taken not to continue the bath too long, to the point of fainting; 15 to 20 minutes is sufficient, after which the patient is taken out and, without drying, placed on hot blankets and covered by three or four more which are wrapped closely about him, up to the neck. Hot weak tea or hot water is given freely to encourage sweating. After about an hour the blankets are gradually removed, and the patient sponged off, under the last one, with alcohol and water, this being followed by a brisk rub with dry towels.

(*b*) Hot-air and steam baths may be given to a patient who is in bed or sitting up.

    *1.* In the first method the bed is covered with a rubber sheet, upon which is placed a blanket on which the patient lies stripped. Over his body are placed two or three bed cradles or extemporized bed cradles. Bed cradles may be extemporized by tying together at right angles two half barrel hoops. Over the cradles and tucked in about the patient's neck is another rubber sheet and blanket. When electric light current is available, the simplest and safest method, and the one usually employed, is to suspend several light bulbs from the cradle frame and connect the bulbs with the lighting circuit by means of an extension cord. With the patient securely closed in, the air in the confined space about him quickly becomes heated the moment the current is turned on. In the absence of an electrical installation other methods may be resorted to. At the foot of the bed is placed an oil, gas, or alcohol heater with a section of stove pipe and an elbow to conduct the heat under the bedclothes, or, if steam is to be used, upon the heater is set a tea kettle with a hose attached to the spout for the same purpose. After the steam or hot air has passed in long enough to get perspiration well started, the upper rubber sheet and the cradles are removed and the blankets tucked in closely around the patient's body after which the case is managed in the same manner as the hot-water bath.

2. To give these baths to a patient sitting up, after all clothing is removed he is made to take his seat upon a chair with perforated bottom; under the chair is placed an oil or alcohol lamp, an electric heater, light bulbs, or a pail of water in which are dropped hot stones or bricks. The patient is then surrounded from the neck downward by a rubber sheet and blankets arranged in the manner of a tent; this is a convenient method in the field, and for reclining patients a litter may be rigged up in the same fashion.

3. The following precautions are to be used with hot-air or vapor baths:

   (a) Be careful not to burn or exhaust the patient, or to set fire to the bed.
   (b) Keep an ice cap on his head.
   (c) Watch the pulse.
   (d) Give hot drinks freely.
   (e) Wrap the patient in a hot, dry blanket for an hour after the bath, then rub the patient with alcohol.

(4) *Foot bath.*—(a) Foot baths may be given with the patient either in the sitting position or in bed. They are employed in sprains to control the hemorrhage about the joint, and in internal diseases to draw away the blood from the congested part. For the latter purpose mustard is usually added to the hot water.

(b) To give a mustard foot bath in bed turn up the covers from the foot end of the bed, place a rubber sheet across it, and on this a pail or foot tub full of water, the temperature of which should be between 108° to 112° F. Dissolve a couple of tablespoonfuls of mustard in a cupful of hot water until a uniform cream is formed, and stir it into the pail of hot water. If the dry mustard is added to the pail of water without previous solution, particles of mustard will float around, and may adhere to the legs and produce blisters.

(c) When all is ready the patient, lying on his back, should flex his legs and immerse them in the hot solution for 20 or 30 minutes. The legs are then withdrawn, dried quickly, and wrapped in a blanket.

(5) *Sitz bath.*—The Sitz bath is another form of local bathing; the temperature of the water is the same as for a foot bath. The thighs and trunk of the body are immersed to the waistline. The duration of the bath is 5 to 10 minutes.

**(6)** *Cold bath.*—(*a*) Cold baths are given for stimulation of the vital processes, namely respiration, circulation, relief of congestion, stimulating or quieting of the nervous system, and for reducing temperature.

(*b*) In giving cold baths the patient should be watched for evidence of intense shivering, cyanosis (blueing of the lips, ears, fingernail beds), and increasing pulse rate, as these signs are evidence of ill effect and the bath should be stopped immediately and the ward officer notified.

(*c*) Cold tub baths are known as the Brand system of bathing. A portable bath tub on wheels is generally employed. The tub is brought to the bedside half filled with water at a temperature of about 90° F.; the naked patient is lifted from the bed and lowered into the tub feet first, and gradually, so as not to produce too much shock. For the purpose of lifting the patient from the bed and supporting him in the tub, an open-work stretcher, a hammock, or a cotton blanket with loops sewed in the edges is usually employed. In the absence of these a binder 18 inches wide should be fastened across the head of the tub to support the patient's head and shoulders. His head rests upon a circular air cushion and is kept covered with cold compresses; pieces of ice are added to the water so as to reduce temperature gradually to about 70° F. To ascertain the temperature accurately, a bath thermometer is employed. All the time the patient is in the bath the attendants should keep up a vigorous rubbing of his body. The duration of the bath as ordinarily advised was about 20 minutes, but such lengthy exposures are no longer considered advisable. Cold baths should generally last no longer than 5 minutes.

(*d*) When it is time to take the patient out, the tub is covered with a dry sheet, which is wrapped about the patient as he is lifted out and placed on a dry blanket. If shivering persists, a hot-water bag may be applied to the feet and a hot drink may be given internally, but the patient should not be wrapped in blankets. The temperature is taken in the rectum immediately after leaving the bath, and again an hour later. Ordinarily the bath is repeated whenever the temperature registers 102.5° to 103° F.

**(7)** *Cold pack.*—When the patient does not stand the cold tub bath well, or is too weak to bear moving, the cold pack may be employed. In this method the bed is protected by a long rubber sheet, and two sheets folded one or more times and wrung out of water at 70° F. are used. One is placed under the patient and the other over him and tucked in closely about the body and neck; or a single sheet may be used, enveloping the entire body except the head. The packs are changed about every 15 minutes, and three or four of them generally produce the effects of a single tub bath.

(8) *Cold sponge bath.*—The procedure is the same as that described in *a* (3) above except that the water is between 70° and 80° F.

(9) *Cold spray bath.*—(*a*) To give a patient a bath in bed, pass under him a rubber sheet the size of the bed, a bed sheet, and over this a large rubber sheet about 3 feet wider and 2½ to 3 feet longer than the mattress. Attach a small rope or cord to the head and foot of the bed, on each side, about 6 inches above the mattress, and stretch it firmly. Over this cord pass the large rubber sheet and fasten with clothes pins, thus forming a trough to carry off the water. Direct the lower end of the rubber sheet into a pail at the foot of the bed and raise the head of the bed a few inches on blocks.

(*b*) Remove the top covers and place a towel over the patient. Water, of desired temperature, may be sprinkled on with a watering pot, or from a pitcher or a siphon connecting with a pail placed above the bed. If the bath is cold, the patient should be well rubbed during its administration. After the bath is finished, drain off the water, and with a towel wipe the rubber sheet dry, withdraw it from beneath, and dry the patient with the sheet on which he will then lie.

(*c*) In the field, substitutes for a tub may also be extemporized. An ordinary camp cot may be taken, the canvas bottom punched full of holes, and a piece of rubber sheeting tacked across the frame below the canvas in such a way that it will form a gutter draining toward a pail placed at the foot. On this cot the patient is to be placed and cold water sprinkled or poured over him; or an upright frame may be made, to the sides and ends of which rubber sheeting may be attached in such a way as to form an extemporized tub. With a small piece of rubber sheeting, and a tin cup, perforated at the bottom as a sprayer, a cleansing bath may be given even on a litter or a bath board.

(10) *Alcohol bath.*—Sometimes when one of the cold type baths are not advisable, an alcohol or sponge bath may be given. As alcohol evaporates more rapidly than water, it cools the skin more readily. For this reason, good effects can be obtained with the use of a smaller amount of alcohol. Fifty percent alcohol is used. The bed is prepared by protecting the lower sheet with towels or a rubber sheet. All of the bed covering is removed except the top sheet, which is kept over the patient. As in the sponge bath, only one part of the body is bathed at a time. The alcohol should be applied briskly and with long, downward, sweeping strokes, care being exercised to

avoid the face, the genitals, and the anus. If the patient's condition is good, the alcohol may be dried by fanning; otherwise it must be wiped with a towel.

**205. Care of mouth and teeth.**—In the case of patients who are convalescents or not seriously ill, the teeth and mouth are cared for the same as in health, that is, the teeth are brushed two to three times a day. When patients are seriously ill, or unable to care for their mouth and teeth, this must be done by the attendants. In cases where the fever is high, there is an insufficiency of the normal oral secretions, resulting in a drying and cracking of the membranes of the mouth and gums. The teeth become covered with residue of food, mucous, dried epithelium, and bacteria. This is known as sordes and requires removal after every meal. Any of the several type mouth washes may be used. Herpes, "fever blisters", or "cold sores", are inflammation of the membrane or skin and unless properly cared for may result in ulcers. It is also well to cover the lips with cold cream, lemon juice in glycerine, or boric acid ointment to prevent drying and cracking; this to be done after the mouth and teeth are well cleansed.

**206. Morning and evening toilet.**—*a.* The morning toilet is the routine care given patients before their breakfast. The purpose is to clean and refresh the patient after the night and to make him comfortable and ready for his morning meal. The patient should be given the opportunity to use a bedpan or urinal if desired. The face and hands should be washed, hair combed, and teeth brushed. The bed should be made comfortable and the bedside table or bed made ready for the breakfast tray.

*b.* The evening toilet is the routine given to all patients before "lights out" at 9 PM. After the evening nourishment, the same procedure as described in the morning toilet should be repeated. In addition, it is well in most cases to give an alcohol rub. This relaxes the patient and promotes sleeping. Extra bed covering should be placed within easy reach, adequate ventilation afforded, bed lights checked and adjusted, and fresh drinking water provided.

**207. Care of skin and back.**—In the case of bed patients it is of utmost importance that skin and back be carefully watched to prevent bedsores or pressure spots. Special attention should be paid to the skin over all bony prominences. In most instances pressure sores or bedsores may be prevented by carefully examining the patient during the morning bath and giving an alcohol rub over the back with 50 percent alcohol at least twice a day. This stimulates and toughens the skin, makes it less sensitive, and lessens the chance for a destructive process to start. If evidence of pressure presents itself, it is well to afford some means of protection to the involved area by pads or rubber rings. It is also well to powder the areas well with talcum powder or starch.

**208. Bedsores.**—*a*. These are localized ulcers resulting as a rule from pressure and are caused by the patient's lying too long in an unchanged position. A similar condition may also be caused from excessive moisture between two skin surfaces and by interference with circulation from a too tight bandage or appliance. Bedsores result from body discharges, irritants, soiled or damp linen, lowered vitality, breaks in the skin, excessive sweating, improper care of the skin, and infrequent bathing.

*b*. The prevention of bedsores is the best treatment. In cases where there is evidence that a bedsore is starting, frequent bathing, alcohol rubs, and powdering over the pressure areas should be used. In some cases a water or air mattress should be used. Sometimes bedsores develop in spite of the best nursing care and in these instances the area surrounding the sore should be rubbed well with alcohol several times a day. The sore itself should be kept well cleaned and protected. Dressings or such other treatment as may be necessary will be prescribed by the ward officer.

**209. Food and water.**—*a*. These items are of utmost importance, and special attention is required to see that the patient receives the proper kinds and amounts. To a person who is required to stay in bed most or all of the time, there is nothing that adds to his well-being more than his food and drink when properly prepared and served. Meals are of utmost importance to the convalescent patient, as his appetite is returning.

*b*. Patients who are chronically ill or seriously ill sometimes become problems, as they are fastidious and notional as to what they want to eat and drink. It is imperative that an ill patient receives a sufficient quantity of nourishment and of the quality and type indicated for his condition and his ability to assimilate.

*c*. Patients who are helpless or seriously ill will have to be served, and it is important that they expend little or no energy in attempting to help themselves. Sometimes a patient should continue to lie flat in bed and eat, and in such an instance feeding cups or drinking tubes will have to be used.

*d*. The prompt serving of sufficient quantities of a tempting variety of food on an attractive tray or table means much in keeping a patient happy. The patient's desires should be catered to if reasonable and not contraindicated by his disease, providing such catering is practicable and hospital regulations are not violated.

**210. Body discharges.**—The elimination of the waste products from the body is a normal physiological process. These waste products are eliminated mostly through the intestine, urinary tract, and the skin. Defecation or elimination through the intestine is of great importance in the cure of a sick patient. Establishing regular time for bowel movements will tend to prevent constipation which is so common in bedridden patients. Bedpans or urinals must, however, be furnished without delay upon a request from a bed patient.

*a. Bedpans.*—Patients should never be subjected to a cold bedpan; it should always be warmed. This can be done by allowing warm water to run over it and then drying it thoroughly. Then take it, a cover, and toilet paper to the patient. Put the pan on the bed near the patient. Put the hand which is nearest the head of the bed under the buttocks, raise the patient, and slip the pan into position, being sure it is well placed. If possible, have the patient flex the knees and place the feet firmly on the bed, before the pan is put under him. The covers are then placed over the patient. When the pan is ready to be removed, the bed covers are arranged so as to not interfere with the removal of the pan. Be sure that the patient is clean and if unable to use the toilet paper, do so for him. As when the pan was placed under the patient, the hand is placed under the buttocks the patient raised, and the pan removed. This should be done easily so that none of the contents are spilled. The pan is covered at once. the room or ward is then aired. Before emptying and cleaning the pan, examine its contents and anything abnormal should be reported or shown to the ward surgeon.

*b. Urinals.*—(1) A urinal is used to collect the waste material, where the patient is weak, ill, or otherwise bedridden.

(2) The urinal should be adjusted and properly placed so as not to spill. It should be promptly removed after being used, care being taken not to spill its contents on the bed, causing unnecessary discomfort to the patient and unnecessary work on the part of the attendant. If it is necessary to carry the urinal outside of a room to empty it, it should be covered.

(3) After removal of the urinal, its contents should be inspected and any abnormal condition reported.

*c. Cleansing receptacles.*—In cleaning both urinals and bedpans, after they have been emptied, they should be well rinsed with cold water, scrubbed if necessary, and then washed in hot water. At least once a day both bedpans and urinals should be boiled or sterilized with steam. In cases where the waste products are infectious this should be done each time they are used and urinal and bedpan kept isolated and used only for the same patient.

*d. Sweating.*—The elimination of waste products thru the skin is known as sweating or perspiring, and is taken care of by proper bathing.

**211. Rest, sleep, and exercise.**—These measures are necessary to some degree for all patients, as they promote convalescence and the general well-being.

*a.* Rest comprises both physical and mental relaxation and is accomplished by the support of the body by a bed or chair without any effort expended on behalf of the patient. To obtain such a relaxed state, the bed or chair must be comfortable and the pillows and bed coverings arranged so as to suit the patient. In the case of bed patients it may be necessary to support the body or limbs by means of pillows, sandbags, etc., so as to attain the desired position and to avoid effort on the part of the patient. An attempt should be made to remove any cause for worry or restlessness.

*b.* Sleep is that condition where the entire body and all of the organs relax and repair processes proceed. It is most beneficial when unbroken. Care must be taken to avoid disturbing and awakening patients. Noises from any cause should be eliminated as much as possible.

*c.* Exercise plays an important role in the treatment of patients, especially in those who are convalescing. Even in patients who are confined to bed, exercise is desirable and possible in many cases, especially if there is no contraindication from the standpoint of treatment. Exercise tends to tone up the circulation, promote elimination, and help maintain the patient's strength.

**212. Administering medicines.**—*a. General.*—This procedure is one of the most important parts of proper nursing and is accompanied by a certain element of danger. The person giving medicines must be trustworthy and realize his responsibility. In order to avert mistakes, always have an order book in the ward. Follow orders for the administration of medicines as prescribed by the ward officer in the order book. There are several points of importance which must be borne in mind concerning the care, measuring, and administration of medicines.

(1) Keep the medicine cabinets locked and do not leave the key where patients can get it.

(2) Never keep medicines in unmarked bottles and do not use a dose of medicine that has been left in an unmarked glass.

(3) The person in charge of the medicine cabinet should examine its contents daily and make sure that there is an adequate amount of all necessary drugs on hand. Medicines should not be ordered in large quantities for many kinds deteriorate with age. Drugs that have undergone any change in color, odor, or consistency should not be used without first consulting the ward officer.

(4) Keep oils in a cool place. Also many of the antitoxine, vaccines, and drugs derived from animal glands need to be kept cold.

(5) Give medicines on time.

(6) While measuring medicines, never think of anything but the work on hand and never speak to anyone or allow anyone to speak to you.

(7) Measure exactly; never give a patient a drop more or less than the amount ordered.

(8) While pouring a medicine, hold the glass with the mark of the quantity you require on a level with your eye; if the mark is above your eye, you will give too little, if below, too much.

(9) Read the label on the bottle three times before taking it from the shelf, and before and after pouring out the medicine.

(10) Shake the bottle before pouring out medicines that are not perfectly clear or that contain a sediment unless the label prescribes otherwise.

(11) To avoid defacing the label while pouring a medicine, hold the bottle so that the label will be on the upper side, but do not let your hand come in contact with it, and before replacing the bottle on the shelf, wipe the rim of the bottle with a piece of gauze kept for that purpose.

(12) Recork or recap a bottle immediately after pouring out the drug, for many medicines contain volatile substances and will thus become either stronger or weaker if left uncorked.

(13) Never mix or give at the same time different medicines.

(14) Do not dilute syrup cough medicines, because dilution will minimize the soothing effect of the syrup on the mucous membrane.

(15) Make doses of medicine as palatable as possible. Therefore, have the water used for dilution either very hot or very cold.

(16) Give acids and medicines containing iron through a tube, because acids may corrode the teeth and iron discolors them.

(17) Never give food, drink, or medicine by mouth to an unconscious patient. Medicine should not be administered to delirious patients except in presence of a medical officer who may judge whether the medicine has been properly swallowed.

(18) Never allow one patient to carry medicine to another.

(19) Do not leave a patient until the medicine is swallowed.

(20) Never record a medicine as given until the patient has taken it.

*b. Orally.*—Administration of medicines by mouth or orally is the most common of all methods used and in measuring the medicine to be given, if liquid, the following procedure should be strictly followed:

(1) Take a medicine glass in the left hand and, after reading the label (*a* (9) above), the bottle of medicine in the right.

(2) Shake the bottle if necessary.

(3) Read the label.

(4) Take the cork between the third and fourth fingers of the left hand and extract it. Hold it thus while you are pouring out the drug.

(5) Raise the glass until the mark representing the amount of drug that is to be given is on a level with your eyes.

(6) Pour in the drug until it is on a line with this mark.

(7) If more than one patient is getting the same medicine, pour out the number of doses required; if not, put the cork in or cap on the bottle, wipe the rim of the latter with a gauze compress, read the label on the bottle, and return it to the shelf.

*c. By inhalation.*—This may be either by dry or by moist inhalations.

(1) Dry inhalations are of the gaseous type, such as oxygen. There are several methods, the simplest being to run oxygen through water. The amount and rate of flow is controlled by a valve which is attached to the oxygen tank. Other dry or gaseous inhalations are ether and chloroform.

(2) Moist inhalations are given in the form of steam in cases where it is desired to relieve spasmodic contractions of the bronchial muscles, to increase expectoration, and to sooth inflamed membranes. Usually some type of drug is placed in the water which is carried by the steam into the air passages. There are several types of steam inhalators but the simplest is a vessel containing boiling water covered with a heavy paper cover or bag with a small opening at the top which allows the vapors to escape near the patient's mouth and nose.

*d. Hypodermically.*—(1) Hypodermic medication is the giving of drugs into the subcutaneous tissues of the body. Drugs are given in this manner when—

(*a*) Quick action is desired.

(*b*) The drug cannot be retained because of vomiting.

(*c*) The patient is unconscious or cannot swallow.

(*d*) The drug will be affected undesirably by gastric or intestinal secretions.

(*e*) The drug is not readily absorbed from the alimentary tract.

(*f*) The effects are desired at the area of injection, as in the case of a local anesthetic.

(2) For giving medication in this manner, the hypodermic syringe and needle are used. The solution used should be freshly prepared; the needles must be clean, sharp, and aseptic; the syringe freshly sterilized; the skin where the injection is made must be cleansed.

(3) To render the needle aseptic boil it in a spoonful of water. Disinfect the syringe by boiling or by immersion in 70 percent alcohol. Never attempt to use a needle the point of which is dulled or bent. In making the injection care must be taken to avoid blood vessels, nerves, and bones; for this reason a fleshy part should always be selected and the injection made obliquely; the outside or lateral surface of the arm or the front or anterior surface of the thigh is usually chosen.

(4) Draw the medicine into the syringe, put the needle on the syringe with sterile forceps, hold the syringe vertically, needle up, and gradually press the piston until all air has been forced out as indicated by the escape of a drop of fluid, wash the skin at the point of injection with a little 70 percent alcohol, paint with tincture of iodine, draw the skin tight, and thrust in the needle quickly. When the needle has penetrated about half an inch, force out the liquid slowly, withdraw the needle, and press a clean gauze sponge for a moment on the puncture. Before putting the syringe away cleanse and dry it thoroughly; remove the needle, force out the last drop of fluid, and at once insert the wire into the needle.

*e. Intramuscularly.*—Intramuscular injection is one in which the drug is injected into the muscle. Absorption takes place quicker when given by this method than hypodermically and is also used where the drug is irritating to the tissues immediately below the skin or when a large amount is to be given. The muscles of the deltoid, lumbar, or gluteal regions are usually used. The equipment necessary is the same as in the case of a subcutaneous injection. The skin over the area where the injection is to be made is well cleansed and tincture of iodine applied. This is cleaned off with alcohol before the injection is made. The needle is inserted almost at right angles quickly and steadily into the muscle. If large amounts of the drug are to be given, it is well to cover the point of insertion with collodion to prevent leaking after the needle has been withdrawn.

*f. By venoclysis.*—(1) Intravenous medication or injection is so called because the solution of the drug is introduced directly into the vein. Usually a vein near the bend of the elbow is used. This type of procedure must be given by or under the supervision of a medical officer with the help of trained assistants. As a rule when intravenous medication is to be given, no food will be given until after completion of the procedure.

(2) At times the veins are not available and it is then necessary to cut through the skin and dissect out a vein for use. This becomes a surgical procedure and must be done by the medical officer.

*g. By hypodermoclysis.*—Hypodermoclysis is the giving of large amounts of fluids into the subcutaneous tissues. It is used to replace fluid loss from the body and is given to patients who are unable to take fluids by mouth. The loose tissue under the breasts, or the abdomen are the usual sites for injection. The site for injection should be prepared with care and precaution. The fluid to be given must be sterile. Usually about 500 cc. to 1,000 cc. is given at one time. Rapid flow of the fluid into the tissues must be prevented by controlling the rate of flow. The part receiving the fluid should be massaged.

*h. By proctoclysis.*—Murphy drip or proctoclysis is the instillation of fluid by a slow drip method by way of the rectum for absorption through the intestinal wall. Lost fluids may be replenished by this procedure and it is also used where fluids cannot be retained by mouth, in surgical shock, profuse perspiration, etc. A special apparatus is used so that the rate of flow may be regulated by means of a clamp (on tubing) or by elevating or lowering the container of fluid. The fluid to be given should be about 110° F. and this temperature is maintained by attaching hot-water bottles around the container. The top of the container should be well covered with a sterile towel and the tubing frequently checked for leaks. The tubing should be of ample length to prevent its slipping out of the rectum. The amount of fluid given should be noted and rate of flow can be calculated by observing from time to time the amount remaining in the container.

*i. By enemata* —This involves the injection of fluid into the lower intestinal tract or bowel by way of the rectum for therapeutic or nutrient purposes and is usually called an evacuant or retention enema.

(1) *Evacuant enema.*—An evacuant enema is given so as to cleanse the lower bowel because of constipation, to relieve distention by gas, and to increase or decrease the body temperature.

(*a*) The following routine equipment is required for giving an evacuant enema: a bath blanket or sheet; an extra rubber sheet and covering; irrigator stand; irrigating can, fully equipped with tubing, connecting tubes, tip and rectal tube, and stopcock or regulator, all connected ready for use; pitcher of solution, properly prepared and of required temperature; bedpan and cover, lubricant and wooden tongue depressor; kidney basin; bath thermometer; gauze compresses; mixing spoon; basin with warm water for cleansing patient following enema; towel; bed screen. The following points should be remembered: Have all necessary articles assembled at the bedside; have patient properly screened; never expose patient; have mattress well protected with extra rubber sheet and a sheet.

(*b*) The simple soapsuds enema is probably the one most frequently given, but is irritating to the bowel wall and ordinarily less desirable than a simple enema of 1 to 2 quarts of plain warm water or water with 1 teaspoonful of sodium bicarbonate added to each pint. For a patient who can go to the toilet, 1 pint is often sufficient. For soapsuds there should be kept on hand a jar of liquid soap, prepared by boiling or dissolving some pure soap in sufficient water to form a soft jelly. To prepare the enema dissolve 2 or 3 ounces of this jelly in a pitcher of water at temperature of 108° F., mix well, and remove froth. If pieces of soap are used, after water becomes sufficiently soapy remove pieces to prevent clogging of the tubing. Carry solution, covered, to the bedside, where proper assembly of articles and preparation of bed and patient have been previously made.

(*c*) When giving an enema replace the upper bedclothes with a blanket or sheet; draw the patient to the right side of the bed, turn him on his left side, drawing up and flexing somewhat the right leg, and drawing the left leg down and back somewhat; have the correct amount of solution at proper temperature; lubricate the tube well to make insertion easy, and to prevent injury; expel all air from the tube by allowing the solution to flow through until of the right temperature; pinch the tube and insert it in the rectum. Use no force when introducing the tube or tip. If the sphincter muscles are tense, encourage and assist the patient to relax by reassuring him and explaining the necessity of so doing; remove pressure on the tube and allow the solution to enter slowly; if the patient complains of pain, and gas is heard rolling, shut the clamp on the tube for a moment and move it slightly back and forth, at all times urging patient to relax and prevent premature expulsion of the enema. Frequently where gas has accumulated behind the feces some will escape about the tube or, forcing back the fluid in the tube, escape through it in bubbles in the top of the can; following this relief from escape of gas, more fluid may be injected until a pint or more has been given.   Urge the patient to retain this for 5 minutes, or as long as he can without distress, when it should be freely and voluntarily expelled.   Occasionally a patient, because of weakness, constriction of muscles, or from temporary paralysis of peristalsis, is unable to expel the enema.   When this occurs hot stupes are sometimes used to stimulate muscles and relax rigidity, and if these are not effective the fluid is siphoned off by inserting the rectal tube and draining the fluid into the bedpan.   When this is necessary the object of the enema has been accomplished only partially, for peristalsis has not been stimulated and the abdominal muscles have not been relaxed as they should have been.   The resulting relief is much less; in fact, this is sometimes a dangerous symptom as, when following an operation, it may indicate peritonitis; or in typhoid it may indicate a perforation of the intestine.   Sometimes when too small a quantity has been taken or when the system, needing fluids, has absorbed much of the enema, a second enema will have to be given.   When this is necessary use the routine procedure, but watch carefully for any untoward symptoms.   Stop immediately and siphon off fluid if excessive discomfort, distention, or other unpleasant symptoms occur.

(*d*) When the enema has been expelled remove the bedpan, cover it, and take it from the ward immediately.   Thoroughly cleanse the patient, remove the extra rubber and draw the sheets, replace pajamas, straighten and tidy the draw sheet, and replace the bath blanket or sheet with the bed covers, leaving the patient comfortable and clean.   Remove all utensils and return them to their accustomed places in readiness for the next time needed.   Air the room thoroughly, and make a complete and correct record of results of the enema.   The rectal tube or tip should never be placed in the enema can, but removed from tubing and placed in a receptacle for that purpose.

(2) *Retention enemata.*—Retention enemata are given where it is desired to—

(*a*) Supply the patient with fluid or food because he is unable to retain anything by mouth, is unconscious, dehydrated, or unable to swallow.

(*b*) Administer medicines.

(*c*) Administer anesthetics.

(*d*) Apply local application to the rectum and lower bowel. The amount of fluid given in retention enemata varies, 6 to 8 ounces being the usual maximum amount when given within a short period, but may be considerably more if given drop by drop over an extended period of time. The temperature of the fluid should ordinarily be 100° F. Retention enemata should be given strictly according to specific directions as to quantity, rate of speed, and length of time to be retained. Before giving ascertain that the lower bowel has been emptied sufficiently long to allow peristalis to have subsided. For small amount of fluids a rubber catheter with funnel attachment may be used. Following the introduction of the fluid a hot compress applied with pressure to the anus for a few minutes will often assist greatly in preventing expulsion of the enema. Remove the catheter slowly, pinching the tube or applying the shut-off before and during the removal of the tube.

(3) *Nutritive enemata.*—Nutritive enemata consist of specially prepared foods in liquid form. They are prepared according to various formulae, depending upon the conditions for which given; and the preference of the medical officer prescribing.

(4) *Sedative enemata.*—Sedative enemata usually contain some drug or special preparation for quieting or soothing and are given according to specific directions. The patient should be made as comfortable as possible before the sedative enema is given so that he may be ready for sleep following it.

(5) *Astringent enemata.*—Astringent enemata consist of hot water (120° F.) or of some astringent preparation for drying up or lessening intestinal secretions or for stopping hemorrhage. They are given under definite instructions from the medical officer.

(6) *Carminative enemata.*—Carminative enemata are occasionally used. These are of many types but two are of sufficient importance to be mentioned here. These are the turpentine enema and the milk and molasses enema. These cause an increased expulsion of flatus.

(*a*) Turpentine enemata are made by mixing 1 dram (1 teaspoonful) of turpentine with 1 ounce of cottonseed or mineral oil. This mixture is then added to 1 pint of soap suds and is stirred constantly while it is being given.

(*b*) Milk and molasses enemata are made of equal parts of milk and molasses (usually 7 ounces of each). This mixture should be retained by the patient as long as possible and then followed by a simple cleansing enema.

**213. Counterirritants and other external applications.**—As the name implies, counterirritants are applied for the purpose of producing irritation over an affected area, which promotes relief from inflammation, from congestion, and from pain. This is accomplished by dilating the superficial blood vessels and at the same time by reflex action causing a contraction of the deeper ones, thus drawing the blood away from the affected part. Counterirritants are classified as rubefacients, those causing only redness of the skin; vesicants, those producing blisters; and the caustics, which cause a burn or slough.

*a.* Rubefacients usually employed are mustard, liniments, heat (both dry and moist), stupes, and cupping. Special care must be exercised in applying any of these to prevent blistering.

(1) Hot-water bottles and electric heating pads are forms of dry heat.

(*a*) In the case of the hot-water bottle, the water must be hot but not scalding; fill the bottle only about half full and force the air out of the bag before the cap is screwed on; the bottle should then be covered with a towel or cover provided for this purpose, so as not to burn the patient. The skin of the patient should be watched from time to time.

(*b*) Electric heating pads require special precautions. All wires should be well insulated, so as to prevent a short which might result in burning the patient or bedclothes. It must also be remembered that unless the pad is especially made, it can never be used with a wet dressing. A short circuit may result, which may cause severe burns. If an electric pad is to be used for any length of time, it should be checked frequently, as it may burn the patient.

(2) Hot wet dressings are applied by wringing out gauze compresses or towels in a hot solution. They are then applied to the part and covered with oiled silk or rubber sheeting so as to protect the bedclothes and mattress. A hot-water bottle should then be applied over the rubber sheeting or oiled silk so as to maintain the heat. The dressing should be kept wet and hot at all times.

(3) Mustard plasters are prepared by mixing a paste of flour and mustard (about 1 part of mustard to each 5 to 8 parts of flour) and adding water so as to make up a smooth paste, which is spread evenly on a piece of thick muslin. The edges of the muslin are turned in and the surface which is to be next to the skin is covered with a piece of gauze. The application should be watched carefully and should not remain on the patient over 15 to 20 minutes. After the mustard plaster is removed the skin should be dried and kept covered. If the skin is very red, a bland ointment may be applied. If

mustard leaves are used, they need only to be dipped in tepid water, allowed to drip onto a piece of muslin or directly on the skin, and allowed to remain on the patient for 5 to 10 minutes. Blistering is more likely and the skin must be watched closely. After removal, the skin must be carefully dried and covered.

(4) Poultices are made of various substances in the form of a soft, hot paste which holds heat and moisture. Flaxseed meal is generally used as it retains heat and moisture for a considerable period of time. To make a flaxseed poultice, add flaxseed to about 2 cups of boiling water until a paste consistency is obtained, stirring constantly while the flaxseed is being added so as to have the paste smooth and to prevent sticking. Apply the paste to a piece of muslin, spreading it to within 2 inches of the edges; turn the edges back over the paste and cover with another piece of muslin. Before applying the poultice, the patient's skin should be prepared by oiling well. Make sure the poultice is of the desired temperature and apply. Cover the poultice with a binder. The poultice should be renewed every 30 to 45 minutes, never using a previously used poultice. When flaxseed is not available, oatmeal or cornmeal may be used.

(5) Stupes or hot fomentations consist of a couple of layers of flannel wrung out of hot water and applied to the skin, which has been oiled to prevent blistering. The flannel is then covered with oiled silk or rubber sheeting. The flannel is wrung out by placing in a piece of canvas or a towel, so as to prevent burning the hands. Stupes are changed about every 30 minutes to 1 hour. If a turpentine stupe is desired, it is desirable to mix the turpentine with olive oil, mineral oil, or cottonseed oil in a proportion of 1 part of turpentine to 2 parts of oil. The mixture is heated and stirred so the two substances are well mixed. Apply the mixture to the skin with the fingers and then apply the heated flannels as already described.

(6) Iodine may be used as a counterirritant by "painting" the area with a swab or camel's-hair brush. This is allowed to dry. Before applying the tincture of iodine make sure that the patient is not sensitive to iodine, and that *it is never applied on a surface where bichloride of mercury, mercurial ointments, or mercurial preparations have been recently used.* Never cover the "painted" area, as blistering will result.

(7) Cupping is the application of glass cups to the skin. A vacuum is created in the cup when applied and is usually created by suction, although heat will also do it by heating the rim of the cup and applying to the skin, making sure that the edges are not too hot.

By cupping an actual extravasation of blood beneath the skin takes place. Never try to apply a cup over an irregular surface. To remove a cup, hold it in one hand and with the index finger of the other hand press the skin just beneath the edge of the cup so as to admit the air, when the cup will drop off.

*b.* Vesicants are used when a more marked effect is desired and are used to cause absorption or removal of inflammatory waste. The most common vesicant is cantharides in the form of a plaster or collodion. Before applying, the skin must be asceptically prepared. A thin coating of cantharidal collodion or plaster of the desired size should be applied. After the blister has formed, usually in 4 to 8 hours, the plaster is removed, taking care not to break the blister. If cantharidal collodion is used, it is removed with a sterile gauze sponge wet with ether. The blister is then covered with a dry sterile dressing and is opened only when ordered by the medical officer.

*c.* Caustics are used when prolonged action is desired.

(1) They are used when it is desired—

(*a*) To stimulate healing.

(*b*) To produce death and sloughing of the tissues.

(*c*) To remove warts, etc.

(2) Potassium hydroxide, copper sulfate, nitric acid, sulfuric acid, oxalic acid, arsenic, and the actual cautery are the ones usually used.

(3) A caustic must be used only by or under the supervision of a medical officer, and great care must be exercised. When the desired action is obtained, the caustic is usually neutralized so as to stop its action.

*d.* Cold is used to relieve pain and to reduce inflammation, and is usually used in the form of ice, ice water, ice caps, cold coil compresses, local baths, or irrigations.

(1) In using ice caps, the ice must be broken into small pieces. After filling the ice cap about half full, the air should be expressed and the cap screwed on securely. The bag should be covered with a towel or a cover provided for such purpose. To crush the ice, a mallet and canvas bag can be used if a mechanical devise is not available.

(2) Cold compresses consist of several layers of gauze or cotton which have been dipped into ice water, well wrung out, and then applied to the desired part. They must be changed frequently so as to maintain the cold temperature desired. Provided compresses are to be used over the same part, they may be used over and over.

## Section III

## SURGICAL PROCEDURE

**214. General.**—Surgical procedure in nursing and ward management deals with the performance of methods essential to the proper preoperative and postoperative care of patients undergoing surgical operation. It also deals with the performance of certain procedures which are in general use in the care of patients receiving surgical treatment.

**215. Preoperative preparation.**—An individual undergoing a surgical operation needs preparation both mentally and physically.

*a.* Patients in a proper state of mental condition withstand surgical procedures better than those who are not in a proper mental condition. Thus, it is necessary for all individuals engaged in the care of patients prior to operation to extend every effort to properly prepare the patient mentally for the procedure which he is to undergo. Ward attendants may be of great help in maintaining a cheerful attitude, in being considerate of the patient's desires, and explaining to him that he will receive the best possible care both before, during, and after the operation. In addition to these general reasons for mental preparation, there is a special reason—namely, that of anesthesia. All of the anesthetic agents produce their desired effect best and less of them is required, as a rule, if the patient takes them calmly and in the spirit of cooperation with their purpose. This is particularly true in the case of those anesthetic agents which are given by inhalation methods. Spinal anesthesia is also easier of performance and better in the production of anesthesia if the patient is calm and mentally desirous of having the procedure performed. An anesthesia which is not smooth and unobstructive is a handicap to everybody engaged in the operative procedures. The proper mental preparation of a patient undergoing surgery is one of the most important tasks of surgical nursing and ward management.

*b.* The physical preparation of a patient for operation demands exactness in the performance of required preoperative procedures. The site of operation is thoroughly cleansed with soap and water, carefully shaved, and the skin cleansed with ether. The area prepared should extend well beyond the specified point of incision to prevent danger of contamination from skin surfaces during the operation. Certain features of the preoperative preparation will vary depending upon the type of operation to be performed and upon the anesthetic to be used. In general, patients undergoing operation will be given a soapsuds enema the night prior to operation. If an anesthetic agent is to be used which is administered by rectum, it is important to cleanse thoroughly the lower bowel by repeated enemata, usually using only tap water, until the return flow from the enema is clear. Following the enema the patient usually retires and is given a sedative in order to promote relaxation and assure a restful sleep. On the day prior to operation a complete urinalysis and blood count should be performed. On the morning prior to operation a soapsuds enema is given 2 hours before operation and often another sedative is given. A hypodermic injection of morphine usually combined with atropine or scapolomine is given 1 hour prior to operation. The diet of a patient scheduled for operation should consist of a light supper and no food or liquids after midnight prior to the day of operation. In certain instances these procedures will be altered. The preoperative orders as written by the medical officer should be carefully followed. Before a patient is taken to the operating room any money or jewelry he may have should be removed and turned over to the proper authority for safekeeping. Artificial teeth should be removed and placed in boric acid solution in a labeled receptacle. Patient should be encouraged to urinate before going to the operating room and the time and quantity of urine voided should be recorded.

**216. Postoperative care.**—The postoperative care of a patient begins with the completion of the operation. Thus, the operating room personnel has a very important part in the immediate care of the patient following operation. The patient is transferred from the operating table to the ward for further postoperative treatment. The transferring of a patient from the operating table to a stretcher, or from the stretcher to a bed, must be performed with care. Three or more attendants are necessary to transfer the patient properly. The tallest and strongest attendant should stand in the center, having one arm under the hip and the other under the thigh of the patient. One attendant should place his arms under the patient's shoulder, one elbow supporting the head and the other extending well down on the back. The third attendant keeps the lower legs from dangling or striking the foot of the bed. At a given signal all three should take firm hold of the patient's body and lift, turn, and place him gently on the bed or stretcher. During the transfer the patient should be well covered. The bed on which a recently operated patient is placed is known as an "anesthetic bed" and is prepared as described in paragraph 218. On return to the ward the patient is placed in the bed in the position prescribed by the medical officer. This position will vary depending upon the type of operation performed and the patient's condition following operation.

217. **Recovery room.**—*a.* A designated room or ward in which attendants are especially trained in the postoperative care of patients provide the best manner of postoperative supervision. Such a room or ward is designated as a "recovery room" or "recovery ward." Visitors are not allowed unless the patient is seriously ill. The room must be quiet and properly ventilated but without draft. The attendants must be constantly alert to detect any unusual signs or symptoms during this postoperative period. After the patient has returned to the recovery room he should not be left alone until he fully regains consciousness. The pulse and respiration should be recorded every 15 minutes during the first 2 hours and longer if necessary. Blood pressure readings will, in certain instances, be required at 15- to 30-minute intervals.

*b.* If a general anesthesia has been used the patient's jaw should be held upward and forward until consciousness has been regained to prevent the tongue from falling back into the throat. If such procedure is not followed respiratory difficulty may be encountered due to the tongue's obstructing the air passages. The head should be turned slightly to one side to make it easier to care for the vomitus and remove mucous from the mouth and throat. When vomiting occurs raise the head slightly, tipping it forward and to the side with a basin placed beneath the angle of the jaw and supporting the patient's head with one arm and hand. With the other hand wipe the patient's mouth and face and remove the mucous from his mouth. Frequently dry the patient and replace the damp clothing and linen as soon as it is wise to disturb the patient, taking care to avoid exposure of any part of the body surface. If spinal anesthesia has been used the patient is usually conscious on return to the recovery room. It must be remembered that he is usually unable to move the lower portion of his body. Nothing is given by mouth until ordered by the proper medical officer.

*c.* Special complications to watch for and report promptly include hemorrhage, collapse, difficulty in breathing, blueness of skin (cyanosis), and undue excitability of the patient.

(1) Occasionally morphine excites rather than quiets the patient.

(2) Hemorrhage is denoted by the presence of bloody drainage on the patient's dressings, by a weak, rapid, and irregular pulse, by pallor, excessive restlessness, and an anxious expression. The patient often gasps for air, a condition called air hunger, and frequently complains of being unusually thirsty. Blood may also be present in the vomitus, stools, or in the urine.

(3) Collapse or shock is indicated by a weak and rapid pulse, marked general weakness, and a cold, clammy skin.

(4) Cyanosis is noted as a blue or blue-tinged color to the patient's lips, fingers, or face.

(5) The prevention of certain complications, chiefly those related to the pulmonary system, is of particular importance in the early postoperative care. All patients, if their condition permits, should be turned from side to side and encouraged to cough and expectorate any sputum or mucous which collects in the throat. Deep breathing should be encouraged and 10 deep breaths should be taken every 15 to 20 minutes. The only way to assure the proper performance of these details is by the close attention of the attendants.

*d.* Every recovery room should have readily available a mouth gag, fluid for intravenous medication, oxygen, and carbon dioxide. Patients operated upon under spinal anesthesia are placed in a bed which has been elevated at least 6 to 12 inches. The blocks used for elevating the bed are not removed until ordered by the medical officer. The diet of patients during the postoperative period will be prescribed by the medical officer. Usually liquids such as warm water or tea are permitted as soon as the patient has reacted from this anesthesia and nausea or vomiting have subsided. Often a proctoclysis will be prescribed immediately on the patient's return to the recovery room. Patients usually remain in the recovery room 48 to 72 hours.

**218. Anesthetic bed.**—An anesthetic bed, formerly called ether bed, is prepared especially for patients who are or who have recently been anesthetized. The object of an anesthetic bed is to provide accessibility, safety, warmth, and comfort for the patient. In preparing such a bed, the following equipment is required in addition to that usually required for bed making—namely, three blankets, one pajama coat, one hand towel, one paper bag and a safetypin, four hot-water bottles with covers, and two shock blocks. On the bedside table should be placed a swab can, a two-sponge basin, a quantity of gauze wipes, paper, pencils, and a watch with a second hand. Make the bottom of the bed in the usual manner of preparing the bed for any bed patient. Place across the middle portion of the bed a rubber sheet which is covered by a folded white sheet, this being known as a draw sheet. The top of the bed is prepared as follows. A blanket is placed on top of the draw sheet. This blanket is in turn covered with an ordinary sheet. Additional blankets may be added as needed, usually two being used, the final blanket being covered with a sheet. Hot-water bottles, three or four, distributed over the surface of the bed between its top and bottom portions. On arrival of the patient the top covers are folded along the opposite side of the bed, the hot-water bottles are removed, and the folded blankets are placed over the patient. The hot-water bottles are then placed between the blankets. In warm weather fewer blankets are needed.

**219. Shock blocks.**—Shock blocks are solid cubes of wood about 6 inches square, varying from 4 to 18 inches in height. In the center of the top a hole is bored large enough to receive the end of the bed leg and deep enough to hold the leg without danger of slipping. The purpose of the block is to elevate the head or the foot of the bed, as desired. When using bed blocks care should be taken not to jar or jolt the patient while raising or lowering the bed. Both blocks are of the same height in order to maintain uniform elevation. If the bed is elevated at the patient's feet, the head of the bed must be protected to prevent the patient's head slipping against the bed bars by securing a stiff pillow on the inner side of the bars, and when permissible, elevating the knees of the patient by raising the knee support of the bed.

**220. Administration of fluid.**—The administration of fluid by rectum (proctoclysis), subcutaneously (hypodermoclysis), intramuscularly, and by injection into the blood stream (venoclysis), has been described in section II. However, the administration of fluids is of such importance in many individuals undergoing surgical treatment that it will be described in somewhat more detail in this section. Fluids are given to replace fluids lost during or following operation and to provide an adequate fluid balance during the early postoperative days. In general, patients who have recently been operated upon should have an intake of 2,000 to 3,000 cc. of fluid during each 24-hour period. At least 1,000 cc. of fluid is lost in the urine if the proper fluid balance is maintained.

*a.* The simplest form of administering fluids is into the rectum. This is known as proctoclysis, and is commonly called "Murphy drip." The fluid given is usually normal saline solution to which has been added 5 percent of glucose. The fluid is usually permitted to drop at the rate of 30 drops per minute from the proctoclysis container into a tube which is connected with a catheter inserted into the rectum. Fluid is absorbed slowly by rectum. However, approximately 500 to 1,000 cc. of fluid may be given daily by this method. It is customary to permit the flow or drip to continue for 2 hours and then discontinue for 1 hour. Careful attention must be given to the position of the catheter to avoid its being expelled and the fluid's running onto the bed.

*b.* The next simplest form of administering fluid is what is known as the subcutaneous method or hypodermoclysis. Fluid, usually normal saline solution, is given by injecting the fluid beneath the skin into the subcutaneous tissues. Sterile precautions are necessary. The fluid is administered by inserting a needle, usually a 19-gage needle, into the subcutaneous tissues of the breast, the thigh, or buttocks. The fluid is permitted to flow from a container by gravity to the tissues. The container is usually placed about 20 inches above the level of the patient. Ordinarily 500 cc. is given into the tissues of the breast on either side or in the thigh.

*c.* Intramuscular injection of fluid is carried out in the same manner as subcutaneous, except the needle is put into the muscular tissues.

*d.* The administration of fluid through the blood stream is known as venoclysis. The equipment necessary for intravenous infusion in addition to the specially prepared sterile infusion apparatus includes a stand for elevating the gravity tube, a tourniquet, skin sterilizing and draping supplies, sponges, and dressings. For the administration of the infusion the gravity tube is hung on the elevating stand at a height of about 20 inches above the patient and filled with the solution; the patient's arm is sterilized and draped sterilely; the tourniquet is applied; the needle is inserted into the vein and as the blood flows backward through it the tourniquet is removed; the solution is allowed to flow through the delivery tube to free it of air; with blood flowing thus from the needle and solution from the tube the two are connected and the solution allowed to flow slowly into the vein. The fluid should be warmed and maintained at a temperature of approximately 100° F. The rate of administration should permit approximately 500 cc. of fluid to flow into the vein in 30 minutes. The infusion should be discontinued if the patient complains of any unusual symptoms such as a chill or dizziness. A patient receiving venoclysis should be constantly watched.

**221. Surgical dressings.—***a.* Surgical dressings prevent contamination of the area surrounding a wound and absorb secretions from the wound. Sterile gauze and cotton are the materials used in the preparation of surgical dressings. The edges of the gauze are folded so that no ravelings are free to get into the wound. Absorbent cotton made into pads of various sizes and covered with gauze is used for covering the dressings of discharging wounds. Hot wet dressings consist of gauze moistened with a solution and covered with some protective material, such as oil silk, to aid the dressing to retain its heat and moisture. The proper dressing of surgical wounds requires a knowledge of certain facts relative to the nature of the healing of wounds and the conditions which interfere with such healing. (See chapter 3 on minor surgery.) All the necessary equipment for a surgical dressing should be readily available on a dressing tray or dressing carriage. Ample light is essential and the patient should be in proper position for his comfort and convenience for the dressing of the wound. Always dress aseptic or clean wounds before beginning the dressing of septic or suppurative wounds. The maintenance of absolute aseptic technique in the dressing of all wounds is necessary. Avoidance of unnecessary conversation while performing the dressing is essential. When removing adhesive strips, pull them quickly toward the wound to prevent pulling or spreading of the incision or wound.

*b.* On opening a sterile dressing container do so quickly and without contaminating the contents. In removing a cover from a jar or a stopper from a bottle, the contents of which are sterile, be careful not to contaminate the inner surface of the container. Remove the sterile contents of the container with a sterile instrument and replace the cover immediately. When pouring a disinfectant solution from a bottle onto a surgical dressing, pour a small quantity of the liquid into a basin before pouring any onto the wound or dressing. When lifting or holding a sterile basin containing a solution, place the hand well under the basin and hold it steadily.

*c.* The equipment of a dressing tray or carriage varies according to the nature of the dressings, the responsible medical officer, and the general routine of the hospital. Certain facts are applicable in all conditions. Each article on the tray or carriage should be kept in its own particular place in order to avoid delay in finding such articles. The tray or carriage is covered with a sterile cloth, usually a sheet, on which the sterile articles are placed and is again covered by a sterile cloth which is turned back in a manner which prevents contamination of the inner surface of the cover. The instruments needed for a dressing carriage include hemostats, groove directors, scissors, syringes, and needles. Materials for a dressing include gauze, pads and sponges, applicators, safetypins, and gloves. All of these articles should be sterile. The dressing carriage should contain a shelf for unsterile articles on which should be neatly arranged such articles as bandage scissors, oil silk or paper, binders, safetypins, rubber operating pads or rubber sheets, and attached to this carriage there should be a bucket for discarded or contaminated dressings. The essential drugs include iodine, alcohol, sterile vaseline, and certain special preparations as required by the medical officer. A simple surgical dressing is performed by first arranging the bed linen and pajamas of the patient so as to expose the wound. The adhesive tape along with the outer dressing is removed and discarded. Using aseptic technique the remaining dressings are removed, the incision cleansed with an alcohol sponge, care being taken to cleanse away from the wound, never toward it. Never go over the same area twice with the same sponge. Dress the wound as directed, applying sterile dressing.

**222. Catheterization.**—Catheterization is the withdrawal of urine from the bladder by the introduction of a sterile rubber or metal tube along the urethra into the bladder. Its purpose is to relieve the patient's discomfort, to obtain a specimen of urine under sterile precautions, or to drain a paralyzed bladder.

*a. Ordinary.*—(1) All articles used in this procedure must be sterile. Those needed include saturated boric acid solution, sterile lubricant (oil or jelly), catheters (sizes 16 to 18 French), 2 towels, sterile gloves, and a hemostat. The foreskin is retracted and the penis thoroughly washed with soap and water. The operator thoroughly cleanses his own hands and puts on sterile gloves. A sterile catheter is lubricated and with one hand holding the penis the catheter is introduced into the urethra without force until it enters the bladder from which urine flows through the catheter. The urine is collected in a urinal or sterile container and the quantity removed together with the time of its removal is recorded on the patient's treatment record. If the bladder is greatly distended, not more than 600 cc. should be removed at one time. Withdrawal of the catheter completes the procedure of catheterization.

(2) Recently operated patients should not ordinarily be catheterized less than 18 hours after operation. Methods should be tried to cause voluntary urination before resorting to catheterization. These include applying a hot-water bottle to the bladder area, allowing water to run from a nearby faucet, and fluids by mouth, if permitted. Allowing the patient to sit in bed, stand on the floor, or placing the patient in a hot bath often produces voluntary urination, but are resorted to only at the direction of the medical officer.

*b. Retention.*—Catheterization as described in *a* above is performed and the catheter anchored to the penis by adhesive tape. The end of the catheter outside of the penis may be closed by a rubber band or metal clamp and opened every few hours for drainage of urine, or the end of the catheter may be left open and connected to a large bottle at the side of the bed or to a urinal if the patient is up and about. The catheter should be irrigated with a mild antiseptic solution such as a 10 percent aqueous solution of argyrol once daily. The catheter should be changed once each week and permanently removed as soon as the condition of the patient permits.

**223. Bladder irrigation.**—*a.* Bladder irrigation is the washing of the bladder. The equipment for this procedure is the articles needed for catheterization, a Y-shaped connecting tube, a 1,000-cc. irrigating can, a sterile solution of saturated boric acid, and rubber tubing. If the irrigation is carried out with the patient in bed, it is desirable to have a rubber operating pad or other protection for the bed and a bucket available to receive the return flow from the bladder. The irrigating container is placed about 12 inches above the patient's hips and the solution is allowed to flow through the tubing of the container until the air is expelled. The tubing is then attached to the inflow of the Y-tube, the stopcock is opened, and fluid allowed to flow into the bladder. Allow 250 cc. of the solution to flow into the bladder. Open the stopcock on the outflow of the Y-tube and allow the solution to run out of the bladder. Continue until a total of 1,000 cc. of solution has been used. Because of the restriction of the outflow at the beginning there is at all times in the bladder sufficient solution to bathe its walls thoroughly. Sterile technique is carried out during this procedure.

*b.* The bladder may also be irrigated by the syringe method; that is, the patient is catheterized and the irrigating solution is introduced into the bladder through the catheter by means of a syringe. A 30-cc. syringe is used and filled with irrigating solution. Usually 5 or 6 syringefuls are run into the bladder. Then the solution is permitted to drain out of the catheter.

**224. Abdominal paracentesis.**—Abdominal paracentesis is the withdrawal of fluid from the abdominal cavity through the abdominal wall. Sterile technique is required in this procedure. The procedure is usually performed under local anesthesia and the fluid removed is placed in a sterile container. A 2-cc. syringe and a small needle with 2 percent novocaine solution are used for producing anesthesia of the skin, superficial tissues, and muscles. The fluid removed is measured and generally forwarded to the laboratory for microscopic and cultural studies.

**225. Ear irrigation.**—Never use a sharp instrument, as it may puncture the drum of the ear or cause other injuries and abrasions with the introduction of infection which may be serious. When applicators are used for cleansing the auditory canal, the ends of the applicators should be tightly padded with absorbent cotton. Never use force in introducing the instrument or fluid. The patient may be in the sitting position or, if necessary, irrigation of the ear may be carried out with the patient lying in bed with his head turned somewhat to the side and slightly forward. Cleanse the outer ear of the auditory canal of its discharges or secretions with an absorbent cotton swab applicator. Place the irrigator can, containing usually boric acid solution, about 12 inches above the patient's head. Permit the fluid to run through the rubber tubing of the irrigator can to expel the air. Grasp the lobe of the ear and draw it gently downward and backward in order to straighten the canal. Direct the stream of the irrigation against the upper surface of the ear without force. The outflow from the canal should be continuous in order to remove foreign matter. Following the irrigation, the auditory canal should be dried with cotton swab and the external ear cleansed and dried. Sometimes a small piece of cotton is placed in the outer opening to retain medication which may be applied or to absorb remaining portions of the solution. All instruments used should be resterilized.

**226. Gastric lavage.**—Gastric lavage has been described in section II. The use of continuous or intermittent suction applied to the stomach or small Levine tube which has been introduced into the stomach is a frequently used surgical procedure. The tube is introduced either through the mouth or nose and is attached to a suction apparatus which permits the immediate and continuous removal of gastric secretions. It also permits the washing of the stomach by allowing the patient to drink water and then withdrawing it by the suction apparatus. The tube is kept in place by fastening it to the nose or face with small strips of adhesive tape. The fluid intake by mouth and the drainage into the bottle of the suction apparatus must be carefully recorded. Frequent examination of the apparatus is necessary to insure its proper functioning. Gastric lavage should be performed only under the supervision of a medical officer except in certain cases of emergency such as ingestion of poison. The Wangensteen apparatus is a suitable suction apparatus and may be easily constructed or purchased from commercial hospital supply companies.

**227. Conclusion.**—The importance of the proper preparation of a patient undergoing a surgical operation and his care following operation has been emphasized. The careful attention to details and accuracy in the performance of all surgical procedures is mandatory. The medical department soldier will be capable of rendering valuable assistance in this field only after he has become thoroughly familiar with the basic information detailed in this and related sections.

### Section IV

## COMMUNICABLE DISEASES

**228. General.**—Communicable diseases are those which may be transmitted from one person to another. These diseases are caused by living organisms or germs which invade some part of the body. Communicable diseases include those which are often referred to as contagious, infectious, or epidemic diseases.

**229. Definitions.**—Certain words and terms as they apply to communicable diseases must be understood in order to care for and control these diseases. Some of the more common and important of these are listed below.

*a. Isolation.*—The separation of an infected person from direct or indirect contact with other persons.

*b. Carrier.*—One who harbors and transmits a disease without having the symptoms of the disease.

*c. Excreta.*—Respiratory secretions, feces, urine, vomitus, and sweat.

*d. Discharges.*—Includes excreta and any abnormal matter (pus, etc.) eliminated from the body.

*e. Contaminated.*—Soiled by the infectious agent or by discharges containing the infectious agent.

*f. Disinfection.*—The destruction or great weakening of the infectious agent by physical or chemical means.

*g. Concurrent disinfection.*—The application of disinfection *during* the contagious period.

*h. Terminal disinfection.*—The application of disinfection at the *end* of the contagious period.

**230. Classification.**—Communicable diseases may be classified according to the principal method of transmission.

*a. Respiratory diseases.*—The infectious agents are found in the discharges from the nose, throat, or lungs and are usually spread by coughing, sneezing, and spitting. Transmission may result directly by contact or indirectly by contaminated food, eating utensils, drinking cups, fingers, etc. Some examples of this group are the common cold, diphtheria, influenza, measles, mumps, pneumonia, pulmonary tuberculosis, and smallpox.

*b. Intestinal diseases.*—The infectious agent is eliminated from the body in the feces (also vomitus or urine in some cases) and is transmitted to others by means of contaminated water, milk, food, utensils, fingers, etc. Generally speaking, the infectious agent must be swallowed for infection to occur. Examples of this group include typhoid fever, amebiasis, bacillary dysentery, cholera, and common diarrhea.

*c. Insect-borne diseases.*—The infectious agent is transmitted from person to person or from animal to person by means of blood-sucking insects. Malaria, dengue, typhus fever, yellow fever, and Rocky Mountain spotted fever are examples.

*d. Venereal diseases.*—The infection is practically always transmitted by direct contact during sexual intercourse. Syphilis, gonorrhea, chancroid, lymphogranuloma inguidale, and granuloma inguinale are the venereal diseases.

*e. Miscellaneous diseases.*—This group includes—

(1) Diseases which are not transmitted by the methods outlined above, for example, trichophytosis, known also as "dhobie itch" or "athlete's foot", which is usually transmitted by indirect contact.

(2) Diseases which are not ordinarily transmitted from person to person, such as rabies, which is usually transmitted from animal to man by the bite of the animal, and tetanus, which is a disease caused by a wound infection.

**231. Importance of nursing.**—It can readily be seen that careful and expert nursing and ward management are important for the following three reasons:

*a.* Since most of these patients are acutely or even seriously ill, they require more attention and nursing care than ordinary patients.

*b.* The nurse or attendant must know how to minimize the chances of becoming infected with the disease himself.

*c.* Marked care must be exercised to prevent the transmission of the disease to other patients or persons.

**232. Isolation technique.**—By *isolation technique* is meant the method of applying and enforcing isolation.

*a.* Segregation may be accomplished by placing the patient in a—

(1) *Room* alone.

(2) *Ward* with similar cases.

(3) *Cubicle* prepared by hanging sheets or curtains around the bed.

*b.* The patient must not leave his room, ward, or cubicle.

*c.* Visitors are not allowed.

*d.* In most cases wear a cap and gown while in the patient's room. In some cases it is advisable to wear a mask, and sometimes rubber gloves. None of these articles are worn outside the room or ward. Gowns should be folded with the contaminated side (the outside) out if they are left in the room, whereas they are turned inside out if they are left just outside the room.

*e.* After any contact with the patient attendants should wash their hands and faces well. In any case, before leaving the room or ward, the hands should first be washed in soap and water (a pan of warm green or soft soap solution is ideal), then rinsed in water, and then immersed in a disinfecting solution, such as 70 percent ethyl or denatured alcohol, 3 percent cresol solution, or 1–2,000 solution of bichloride of mercury. The hands and face should always be washed again just before eating.

*f.* Avoid unnecessary close contact with the patient. Be particularly careful to avoid unnecessary contact with any discharge, and in handling any object contaminated by discharges.

*g.* The bed, room, and ward must be kept scrupulously clean. If the furniture, walls, or floor become contaminated by discharges they should be carefully washed with a disinfecting solution such as 3 percent cresol.

*h.* Disinfect dishes, utensils, food, and linen as follows:

(1) Dishes must be sterilized before being returned to the kitchen. They should be boiled if facilities permit. In small hospitals they

may be sterilized by soaking in 3 percent cresol solution for 30 minutes. In some cases it is advisable to keep the patient's dishes separated from those of other patients.

(2) Utensils may be handled in the same manner as the dishes

(3) Unused food is burned.

(4) Bedding and linen are collected separately and must be sterilized before being added to the other linen. Steam sterilization is preferable but, if this is not possible, sterilization may be accomplished by boiling or by soaking in 3 percent cresol solution for 30 minutes.

*i.* Disposal of excreta, dressings, and rags is accomplished as follows:

(1) Sputum and other discharges from the respiratory tract should be collected in paper cups.

(2) Soiled surgical dressings and cleaning rags are burned.

(3) Feces and urine are best sterilized, when necessary, by adding at least twice the amount of 3 percent cresol solution and allowing them to stand for at least 1 hour.

*j.* It is advisable for each patient to have an individual thermometer. Thermometers should always be kept sterilized.

*k.* The patient's room should be well screened. Insects should be searched for and destroyed. This applies even to those diseases which are not classified under insect-borne diseases, since any insect may become contaminated and thus act as a purely mechanical carrier and contaminate other objects.

*l.* Efficient vaccines or other immunizing substances are available for the prevention of many of the communicable diseases. Potential or actual attendants of cases of cholera, typhoid fever, yellow fever, and smallpox are always vaccinated or revaccinated.

*m.* Although venereal diseases are transmitted primarily by direct contact during sexual intercourse, it is occasionally possible for an "innocent infection" to occur. Separate latrines, or at least separate toilet bowls, should be reserved for venereal cases. Moreover, venereal cases should be further separated into groups of the same venereal disease. The hands of patients and attendants must be kept scrupulously clean, particularly after contact with venereal discharges. Gonorrhea may produce a very severe infection of the eyes, leading to blindness in some cases. Syphilis may be transmitted in certain stages by discharge from any ulcer or mucous membrane, including the mouth.

*n.* Immediately after the patient is undressed his clothing and equipment should be disinfected. Steam sterilization is the most effective procedure for this, but it causes injury to woolen cloth, leather, and metal. Fortunately, in most of the communicable diseases, it is sufficient to thoroughly sun and air clothing and equipment. Before they are returned to the patient, woolens should be dry-cleaned, washable clothes laundered and, if advisable, certain items of clothing and equipment wiped with a disinfecting solution, such as 3 percent cresol. In each case, therefore, the method of disinfection will depend upon the orders of the medical officer.

*o.* When the patient is no longer a source of infection the following procedures are carried out:

(1) Bathe patient and give him clean clothing.

(2) Disinfect dishes, utensils, linen, and articles which may have become contaminated.

(3) Thoroughly clean room, bed, and furniture by washing with soap and water or a disinfecting solution as required. When possible, the room and bedding should be sunned and aired for 24 to 48 hours.

**233. Special procedures and precautions in certain diseases.**—Isolation technique, as usually practiced in the nursing and treatment of patients with communicable diseases, has been given in detail in the above paragraphs. The isolation technique for many of the diseases discussed hereafter should be practiced exactly as given above, although there are some variations that should be mentioned and certain points must be stressed. For this reason "concurrent disinfection" and "terminal disinfection" will be mentioned separately, although they are necessarily important parts of isolation technique as a whole. For the sake of brevity and simplicity as well as to avoid needless repetition of detailed technique, an outline form will be followed where possible. The same policy will be adopted in the presentation of "nursing care", since the general phases of this subject have been covered in preceding sections.

*a. Respiratory diseases.*—(1) *Common respiratory diseases.*—These include the common cold, pharyngitis, trench mouth, tonsillitis, and bronchitis.

(*a*) *Isolation technique.*—Desirable. The cubicle system of isolation is usually employed.

    *1. Concurrent disinfection.*—Of respiratory discharges and articles contaminated by them.

    *2. Terminal disinfection.*—General cleaning and airing.

(*b*) *Nursing care.*—General.

(2) *Influenza.*—(*a*) *Isolation technique.*—As for the common respiratory diseases.

> *1. Concurrent disinfection.*—Of respiratory discharges and all
> articles contaminated by them.
>
> *2. Terminal disinfection.*—General cleaning and airing.

(*b*) *Nursing care.*—During the acute illness allow latrine privileges only. In some cases weakness is very severe, and convalescence may be prolonged.

(3) *Diphtheria.*—(*a*) *Isolation technique.*—Strict and mandatory until ordered discontinued by the medical officer.

> *1. Concurrent disinfection.*—Disinfection of all discharges and
> contaminated articles.
>
> *2. Terminal disinfection.*—Thorough cleaning and airing.

(*b*) *Nursing care.*—Absolute bed rest is necessary for at least 2 weeks because of the danger of involvement of the heart. Gargles and throat irrigations are usually employed. Fluids are given in abundance. Be alert for evidence of difficult or noisy respiration, as this may indicate that the infection is spreading into the larynx or trachea. *Notify the medical officer at once* if there is the slightest sign of respiratory distress.

(4) *Measles.*—(*a*) *Isolation technique.*—As for the common respiratory diseases and until all abnormal discharges from the respiratory tract have ceased; a minimum of 5 days after the appearance of the rash.

> *1. Concurrent disinfection.*—Of respiratory discharges and articles contaminated by them.
>
> *2. Terminal disinfection.*—General cleaning and airing.

(*b*) *Nursing care.*—General. Darkening the room is not necessary unless the eyes are acutely inflamed, or unless patient complains of the light's hurting his eyes.

(5) *German measles.*—(*a*) *Isolation technique.*—As for the common respiratory diseases and for 1 week after the onset of respiratory symptoms.

> *1. Concurrent disinfection.*—Of respiratory discharges and
> articles contaminated by them.
>
> *2. Terminal disinfection.*—General cleaning and airing.

(*b*) *Nursing care.*—General.

(6) *Meningococcic meningitis (epidemic meningitis, cerebrospinal fever).*—(*a*) *Isolation technique.*—Rigidly applied until ordered discontinued by the medical officer. Caps and masks are worn.

> *1. Concurrent disinfection.*—Vigorous disinfection of respiratory discharges and contaminations.

*2. Terminal disinfection.*—Thorough cleaning and airing.

(b) *Nursing care.*—Maintain absolute bed rest and quiet. Many cases are restless and delirious and constant attendance is necessary. Apply bed rails if they are available. Bed rails may be improvised.

(7) *Mumps (epidemic parotitis).*—(a) *Isolation technique.*—As for common respiratory diseases and until the inflammation of the salivary glands subsides.

 *1. Concurrent disinfection.*—Of respiratory discharges and contaminations.

 *2. Terminal disinfection.*—General cleaning and airing.

(b) *Nursing care.*

 *1.* Mouth wash (such as normal saline, Dobell's solution, or liquor antisepticus) every 3 hours.

 *2.* Liquid or soft bland diet.

 *3.* Orchitis (inflammation of the testicles) is thought to be minimized by absolute bed rest and by avoiding even slight blows or rough handling of the testicles. If orchitis develops, support the testicles on a soft pad placed on adhesive tape fastened high across the thighs. Cold compresses or ice bags may be used.

(8) *Pneumonia, acute, lobar.*—Certain cases of primary bronchopneumonia are quite similar to acute lobar pneumonia, while others are secondary to many other diseases.

(a) *Isolation technique.*—As for common respiratory diseases. Single rooms are preferred.

 *1. Concurrent disinfection.*—Of respiratory discharges and articles contaminated by them.

 *2. Terminal disinfection.*—Thorough cleaning and airing.

(b) *Nursing care.*

 *1. Absolute bed rest* is mandatory.

 *2.* Do not let the patient talk, feed himself, or brush his own teeth.

 *3.* Do not let patient sit up or turn in bed unassisted.

 *4.* Gently wipe the secretions and discharges from his nose and mouth with a paper or gauze handkerchief. Do not let patient sit up or lean over to spit or cough.

 *5.* Do not let him out of bed for any reason until the medical officer permits it.

(9) *Scarlet fever.*—(a) *Isolation technique.*—Employed until all abnormal discharges have ceased and, in any case, for a minimum of 3 weeks.

      *1. Concurrent disinfection.*—Of all discharges and articles contaminated by them.

      *2. Terminal disinfection.*—Thorough cleaning and airing.

  (*b*) *Nursing care.*—Absolute bed rest is required. Give gargles or throat irrigations every 3 hours. Because of the fairly frequent complication of acute nephritis, the amount and appearance of the urine should be carefully observed and recorded.

  (10) *Pulmonary tuberculosis.*—(*a*) *Isolation technique.*—Required even though certain cases may appear healthy and may have latrine privileges. A perfectly well feeling and appearing patient may disseminate countless numbers of tubercle bacilli every time he coughs, spits, or sneezes. He should be taught to use paper handkerchiefs every time he coughs or sneezes, to use his sputum cup and to keep it covered, and not to stand near anyone while talking.

      *1. Concurrent disinfection.*—Of all respiratory discharges, particularly the sputum, and of all contaminated articles. Collect handkerchiefs and paper sputum cups in paper bags and burn them promptly. Disinfection of eating utensils is very important. Individual dishes are preferable.

      *2. Terminal disinfection.*—Thorough cleaning and airing. Sun the room and furniture if possible.

  (*b*) *Nursing care.*—Always be on the alert for possible hemorrhage from the lungs. Even blood streaking of the sputum calls for placing an ambulatory patient in bed until the medical officer has seen him. In frank hemorrhage—

      *1.* Put the patient to bed and keep him there.

      *2.* Place an ice bag on his chest.

      *3.* Keep him still; reassure him; maintain quiet.

      *4.* Notify the medical officer at once.

      *5.* Keep all of the blood and sputum for measurement and inspection.

  (11) *Smallpox.*—Smallpox is characteristically transmitted by intimate contact with the patient but, since the infectious agent is found in all discharges, it may be transmitted by indirect contact and is frequently classified as a respiratory disease.

  (*a*) *Isolation technique.*—Very strict and rigid until all crusts and scabs have disappeared. Caps are always worn.

      *1. Concurrent disinfection.*—Vigorous and prompt disinfection of all discharges and contaminated articles.

      *2. Terminal disinfection.*—Thorough cleaning, washing with a disinfecting solution, and airing for 48 hours.

(*b*) *Nursing care.*

1. Apply olive oil or mineral oil to skin.
2. Wash the eyes frequently with boric acid solution.
3. Bandage the hands or apply cotton gloves.
4. Force fluids.
5. Cleanse the mouth frequently and gently.

(12) *Chickenpox.*—Chickenpox, like smallpox, is transmitted directly by contact with the patient, and indirectly by all discharges and contaminated articles. Chickenpox may be confused with smallpox, but they are entirely different diseases, and chickenpox is usually a much less serious disease.

(*a*) *Isolation technique.*—Applied for 10 days after the appearance of the rash.

1. *Concurrent disinfection.*—Of all discharges and contaminated articles.

2. *Terminal disinfection.*—Thorough cleaning and airing.

(*b*) *Nursing care.*—Only general care for mild cases; as for smallpox for severe ones.

*b. Intestinal diseases.*—In these diseases the infectious agent is eliminated primarily in the feces, but is also found in the vomitus and, in some diseases, in the urine. It should also be stressed that, for infection to occur, the infectious agent must usually be swallowed after being carried to the mouth by contaminated food, water, milk, fingers, dishes, or other objects.

(1) *Cholera* (Asiatic cholera).—(*a*) *Isolation technique.*—Rigidly enforced. Attendants must exercise strict personal precautions. Keep hands clean. Except for necessary food and drink, do not put anything in the mouth. Stay out of the kitchen.

1. *Concurrent disinfection.*—Vigorous and prompt disinfection of feces, vomitus, and all articles contaminated by them. Burn uneaten food. Linen is particularly liable to become grossly contaminated as vomiting may be frequent and diarrhea nearly continuous. Soiled linen is promptly sterilized by boiling or soaking in disinfectants.

2. *Terminal disinfection.*—Thorough cleaning, washing with a disinfecting solution, and airing for 48 hours.

(*b*) *Nursing care.*—Maintain intake of large quantities of fluids. Intravenous and subcutaneous salt solutions are required but, if it can be retained, a mixture of three parts of normal saline to two parts of water is very helpful by mouth.

(2) *Amebic dysentery—amebiasis.*—The term amebiasis,is being employed more and more in this condition, since many patients do not have and have not had "dysentery"—an aggravated form of diarrhea.

(*a*) *Isolation technique.*—Always applied in acute cases. Applied in the cases of carriers and chronic cases until they have been instructed as to the nature of the disease and how to avoid transmitting it to others. They must be taught how to disinfect feces if sanitary sewage disposal is not available to them. They must wash their hands thoroughly immediately after using the toilet. They must not act as food handlers.

> 1. *Concurrent disinfection.*—Of feces and vomitus and objects contaminated by them.
>
> 2. *Terminal disinfection.*—Thorough cleaning.

(*b*) *Nursing care.*—Chart the number and character of the stools. Save one or more stools for daily inspection by the medical officer.

(3) *Bacillary dysentery.*—(*a*) *Isolation technique.*—As for cholera and until ordered discontinued by the medical officer.

> 1. *Concurrent disinfection.*—Of feces and vomitus and objects contaminated by them.
>
> 2. *Terminal disinfection.*—Thorough cleaning and airing.

(*b*) *Nursing care.*—Same as for amebiasis.

(4) *Typhoid fever.*—(*a*) *Isolation technique.*—Rigidly applied until ordered discontinued by the medical officer. In typhoid fever the typhoid bacilli (the germs which cause the disease) are also found in the urine.

> 1. *Concurrent disinfection.*—Of all feces, vomitus, and urine and of all objects contaminated by them.
>
> 2. *Terminal disinfection.*—Thorough cleaning and airing.

(*b*) *Nursing care.*—Excellent general nursing care is required since the typical case has fever and is very sick for at least 3 weeks. Some are delirious and require constant attendance and bed rails if available. Absolute rest and quiet are indicated. The diet is soft, with no roughage, but the caloric value is high. Adequate fluids are given. No cathartics are given. Change the position of the patient frequently, using pillows for support. Give special attention to bathing and care of the skin to prevent bedsores.

*c. Insect-borne diseases.*—(1) *Malaria.*—(*a*) *Isolation technique.*—Consists only of protecting the patient from the bites of mosquitoes, either by placing him in an adequately screened room or by the use of mosquito netting. The *Anopheles* mosquito transmits malaria.

> 1. *Concurrent disinfection.*—None. Destroy all mosquitoes in the sick room.

    *2. Terminal disinfection.*—None.  Make a final careful search for mosquitoes.

 (*b*) *Nursing care.*

    *1.* Chart the temperature and record the chills.

    *2.* Apply blankets and external heat by hot-water bottles or heating pads during the chill.

    *3.* There is profuse sweating and headache after the chill. Change pajamas and bed linen as they become wet.  Apply an ice cap to the head.  Force fluids.

 (2) *Dengue.*—(*a*) *Isolation technique.*—Protection from the bites of mosquitoes for 5 days after the onset of symptoms.  Dengue is transmitted by the *Aedes aegypti* mosquito.

    *1. Concurrent disinfection.*—None.  Destroy all mosquitoes in the sick room.

    *2. Terminal disinfection.*—None.  Make a final search for mosquitoes.

 (*b*) *Nursing care.*—General.

 (3) *Typhus fever.*—There are two forms of typhus fever, the more dreaded *epidemic typhus*, transmitted by body lice (cooties), and *endemic typhus*, transmitted by rat fleas.  There is also some question as to whether other species of blood-sucking insects may transmit typhus fever in some cases.

 (*a*) *Isolation technique.*—Keep the patient in an insect-free room.

    *1. Concurrent disinfection.*—None.  However, destroy all insects on the patient and in his environment.

        (a) Destroy the vermin in his clothes and bedclothes by steam sterilization or by boiling.

        (b) "Delouse" him—rid him of all insects and their eggs.  Place him in a bathtub or, if he is too sick or a tub is not available, on a bed protected by a bedsheet over a rubber sheet.  Then wash him thoroughly, applying soapsuds literally from head to foot.  The most effective measure is then to shave the hair from his body.  If universal shaving is not desired by the medical officer, apply vinegar thoroughly to loosen the eggs, and then wash with a solution of three parts of warm soapy water to one part of kerosene.  Make a careful search for adult lice or eggs which may have escaped.  The eggs (nits) may be attached to the hairs, and can be removed with a fine-toothed comb.  (Characteristically, however, the eggs and adults of the *body* lice are found in the seams of the clothing.)

(c) The attendant should use, a "louse repellant" such as four parts of naphthalene to one part of soft soap, on his clothing, cap, and gown; wear rubber gloves which extend over the lower ends of the sleeves of the gown; and wear "boots", preferably made of an impervious material such as oiled silk.

(d) Use an insect spray on the bed, furniture, and room.

    *2. Terminal disinfection.*—None. Make a final careful search for insects.

(*b*) *Nursing care.*—General.

(4) *Yellow fever.*—The *Aedes aegypti* mosquito is the main insect concerned in the transmission of yellow fever, though recent evidence indicates that some other insect may transmit it in certain cases.

(*a*) *Isolation technique.*—Keep the patient in an insect-free room. Protect him primarily from the bites of the *Aedes aegypti* mosquito. Since this mosquito stays in and around human habitation by choice, it is safer to have each bed covered by mosquito netting, even though the bed is in a well screened room or ward. It is also well to know that the *Aedes aegypti* characteristically bites during the daytime. The patient cannot infect the mosquito after the first 4 days of the fever.

    *1. Concurrent disinfection.*—None. Destroy all insects in the sickroom.

    *2. Terminal disinfection.*—None. Make a final careful search for insects.

(*b*) *Nursing care.*—General. Observe and record the number and character of stools, and amount and character of the vomitus and urine.

*d. Tetanus (lockjaw).*—Strictly speaking, tetanus is not a communicable disease. It is an acute infectious disease caused by the toxin of the tetanus bacillus which has infected a wound. Puncture wounds, contused and lacerated wounds, and gunshot or high-explosive wounds are especially prone to be infected by the germs of tetanus. Tetanus can be prevented by the administration of *tetanus toxoid before* the incurrence of a wound or by the administration of *tetanus antitoxin* (ATS) *after* a wound is incurred.

(1) *Isolation technique.*—Not required, though "isolation" is necessary to insure absolute quiet.

(*a*) *Concurrent disinfection.*—None. However, soiled dressings from any remaining wound should be promptly disposed of by burning.

(*b*) *Terminal disinfection.*—None.

(2) *Nursing care.*—(*a*) *Maintain absolute quiet and be extremely gentle.* Even very slight noises or the slightest jarring of the bed may cause a convulsion.

(*b*) Intravenous, subcutaneous, or rectal fluids and rectal or nasal feedings are required.

(*c*) Intravenous, hypodermic, or rectal sedatives are required to keep the patient comfortable and to prevent and control convulsions.

## Section V

### DENTAL PROCEDURE

**234. General.**—Specific instructions for the care and treatment of dental patients are given by the dental surgeon when hospitalization is required. These will vary according to the nature and character of the dental disability. However, there are a few routine measures with which the ward attendant should be familiar.

**235. Preoperative cases.**—The most frequent dental causes for admission to the hospital during the absence of a dental officer are jaw fracture, root abscess, toothache, and trench mouth. These cases should be referred to the dental surgeon or, in his absence, to the ward surgeon at the earliest possible convenience for necessary emergency treatment.

*a. Jaw fracture.*—Fracture of the jaws is usually accompanied by pain, the amount depending upon the nature, location, and severity of injury. As in the care of any sick patient, the first requisite of good hospital care is to relieve the pain and make the patient as comfortable as possible. The usual measures to follow in these cases are as follows:

(1) For the relief of pain, codeine sulfate ½ gr., and aspirin 10 gr. In severe injuries, with intense pain, morphine may be indicated.

(2) The patient should be put to bed in a semi-inclined position, with the head slightly raised.

(3) Do not apply a head bandage unless specifically indicated to stabilize and support loose bone fragments or extensive soft tissue

injury. If a bandage is used, it should not be applied too tightly, as this will tend to displace the parts backward, increasing the patient's pain and interfering with breathing.

(4) Give the patient a warm saline mouth wash and instruct him to use it frequently. (Avoid the use of hydrogen peroxide or sodium perborate mouth washes.)

(5) Place on a liquid diet.

b. *Root abscess* (*alveolar abscess*).—A patient with an alveolar abscess should be given a sedative, if feeling marked pain. An ice cap should be applied to the affected side of the face; avoid the use of hot applications externally.

c. *Toothache* (*pulpitis*).—The patient is instructed to brush the teeth thoroughly and free the offending tooth as much as possible of food particles or other debris. Paint the surrounding gums with 3½ percent iodine in glycerine and carefully insert into the cavity a pledget of cotton moistened in eugenol. If this procedure fails to give relief after a reasonable length of time (10 to 20 minutes), a sedative may be given and applications of cold applied to the aching tooth. Cold water or ice will often afford temporary relief should the tooth be in a stage of abscess formation.

d. *Trench mouth* (*Vincent's infection*).—Trench mouth is a communicable disease and all reasonable precautions must be observed to prevent the spread of the infection. The following orders must be observed in the treatment of these cases:

(1) Caution the patient as to the infectious nature of the disease and instruct him to use his own towel, toilet articles, and drinking utensils.

(2) Have the patient rinse his mouth thoroughly every few hours with one of the following mouthwashes:

(a) Sodium perborate—1 teaspoonful to ½ glass of warm water.

(b) Equal parts of hydrogen peroxide and water.

(c) Potassium permanganate 1-2,000 dilution.

(3) Direct patient to brush the teeth carefully with a soft brush and tooth paste after each meal.

(4) Place the patient on a soft diet, including orange and tomato juice.

**236.—Postoperative care in the ward.**—a. *Following removal of impacted teeth, multiple extractions and alveolectomy, and other intraoral surgical operations.*—Specific treatment must be administered in the ward to alleviate the pain, to reduce the liability of infection about the field of operation, and to keep to a minimum the amount of tissue swelling. Ward instructions are usually as follows:

(1) An ice cap to affected parts immediately following return to ward for a period of 4 hours (intermittent application—on 30 minutes, off 30 minutes).

(2) The patient is not permitted to rinse his mouth for 4 hours to prevent a disturbance in the formation of a normal blood clot. The patient may have water to quench his thirst.

(3) After 4 hours discontinue the use of the ice cap and have the patient rinse his mouth with a warm salt solution. The patient should be cautioned to use the mouthwash mildly, and not forcefully to agitate between the jaws, in order to prevent the entrance of air into the tissues.

(4) Following operations, for the relief of pain administer codeine sulfate ½ gr. (0.032 gm.) and aspirin 5 gr. (0.324 gm.) and repeat every 4 hours if needed, for the first night only.

(5) The patient is placed on a soft or liquid diet. For cases without teeth, soft diet to be continued until dentures are provided. These instructions, complete or in part, as checked by the dental officer, should be carried out in the ward by the ward attendants.

*b. Following fractures of jaw.*—When fractures of the jaw have been reduced and immobilized by the dental surgeon, it is the duty of the ward attendant to acquaint himself with the necessary procedures in the specific care and treatment of that patient. Ward orders are as follows:

(1) Place the patient on a liquid diet, unless otherwise prescribed, with feedings from 7:00 AM to 9:00 PM, at 2-hour intervals.

(2) Direct patient to rinse the mouth with warm salt solution after each feeding.

(3) Direct patient to clean the teeth with a tooth brush as well as possible a minimum of three times daily.

(4) If the patient should strangle due to nausea, an acute asthmatic attack, or some other cause, cut the vertical wires holding the jaws together or remove the intermaxillary elastics which are commonly used for intermaxillary traction and fixation. Each patient with intermaxillary wires is provided with a small pair of scissors for this purpose, which should be suspended by a cord around the neck of the patient at all times.

(5) Record the patient's weight weekly.

*c. Postoperative hemorrhage.*—(1) Examine the patient carefully to determine the point of origin of the hemorrhage. Extensive bleeding from the soft tissues may usually be checked by having the patient remain quiet and holding sterile gauze over the affected area with digital pressure. The application of cold directly to the bleeding area or, where this is not practical, to some related area is also helpful.

(2) In the case of a bleeding tooth socket following the extraction of a tooth, if any large blood clots have formed in the patient's mouth, these should be removed. A piece of sterile gauze folded about the size of a walnut is placed over the socket and the patient instructed to close firmly on the pack. If this is held for 10 to 15 minutes with constant pressure and then carefully removed, the hemorrhage is usually arrested. As a supplement to the pressure, the patient should be placed in bed, keeping the head higher than the body, and sedatives should be administered to lower the blood pressure; avoid all stimulants.

## Section VI

## VETERINARY PROCEDURE

**237. General.**—The proper care of animals aims at keeping them at their highest degree of military efficiency by the prevention of disease and injury. Most diseases and injuries are preventable if all concerned are vigilant, intelligent, and untiring in the application of simple preventive measures. Frequently the development of serious diseases or injury can be prevented by prompt first-aid measures and early treatment. The treatment of disease and injury among animals, as well as prevention of disease, is one of the functions of the Veterinary Corps, and present organization provides that the services of a veterinary officer or trained enlisted man of the veterinary service will be available under practically all situations.

**238. The horse in health.**—Health is the condition of the body in which all the functions thereof are performed in a normal manner. It is particularly essential that the normal functions of the body of the animal be thoroughly understood, or else one cannot hope to recognize quickly any departure therefrom. Even the most elementary study of diseased conditions must be founded upon a very thorough knowledge of the normal body.

*a. Posture.*—The standing posture is the most common posture of the horse. Normally the front feet will both be on the same transverse line and bear weight equally. Any other posture of a forefoot is spoken of as "pointing" and is an indication of trouble. The hind legs are rested alternately; rarely does the horse stand with both hind feet squarely together on the ground; in fact it is difficult to make him take or maintain this position. Due to certain peculiarities of structure the horse can maintain the standing position without tiring and can sleep standing. Some horses never lie down, but no doubt they would rest better and their legs would last longer if they took their rest lying down. The horse lies down either obliquely on the chest with the legs somewhat folded under the body and head extended with the chin or teeth on the floor, or flat on his side with the legs and head extended. The horse is a very light sleeper, sleeping with his eyes partly open, but gets his deepest sleep and greatest rest when lying down.

*b. Expression.*—The expression should be alert but without evidence of fear or excitement. The normal horse notices what is going on about him; his eyes are bright and his ears are frequently moved toward the direction of sound.

*c. Mucous membranes.*—The visible membranes of the eyes and nostrils are a bright pink and there should be no discharge from either of these organs. The nostrils may be moist with tears flowing from the opening of the tear duct but they are relatively clean.

*d. Appetite.*—The appetite will be good, and unless overfed the horse will show an eagerness for his forage rations. He should readily consume an average (3 to 4 pounds) feed of grain.

*e. Skin.*—The skin is loose, supple, and easily moved about over the structures underneath. One should be able to pick up a handful of skin with ease. The coat is smooth, sleek, and glossy. During cold weather the hair may stand up and the coat becomes coarse and heavy. The old coat should be shed quickly and easily in the spring.

*f. Pulse.*—The normal pulse rate varies from 36 to 40 per minute, depending upon the age, sex, temperament, and breeding of the horse. The pulse rate increases with exercise or excitement. The rate after a 5-minute gallop will be 60 or 70 per minute. After very strenuous work the rate may be as high as 80 to 90. In a horse that is well conditioned the rate should return to approximately normal in a few minutes after exercise. The pulse rate will not return to the normal rate at rest as rapidly as the respiratory rate will subside. The pulse should feel strong, full, and regular. It is determined by placing the tips of the fingers on an artery and counting the pulsations for 15 to 30 seconds at least twice, averaging the counts and multiplying the average by four or two, according to how many seconds were counted. The artery most commonly used is the maxillary, and the count is made where it rounds the lower jawbone in front of the large cheek muscle.

  *g. Respiration.*—The breathing should be free, soft, and noiseless. After fast work the breathing is heard as a rushing sound of air but there should be no harsh, fluttering, whistling, or roaring sound. The breathing rate per minute is approximately as follows:

| | |
|---|---:|
| At rest | 9–12 |
| After walking 200 yards | 28 |
| After trotting 5 minutes | 52 |
| After galloping 5 minutes | 52–70 |

The above rates are for horses in good condition. After cessation of exercise the breathing rate should subside quickly to normal. The quickness with which the breathing rate subsides is an excellent indication of the fitness or condition of the horse. The breathing rate increases with exercise more rapidly than the pulse rate and after work subsides more quickly than the pulse rate. The breathing rate is counted by watching the rise and fall of the flanks, the movements of the nostrils, or on a cold day the steamy expiration of breath.

  *h. Temperature.*—The normal body temperature of the horse at rest is about 100° F., but may vary 1° in either direction; however, a temperature of 101° F. is uncommon. The temperature varies with exercise and excitement and air temperature. One hour's work at walk and trot may raise the temperature one or two degrees. Hard, fast, or prolonged work, especially under a hot sun may build the body heat up to 103° to 105° F. When the temperature reaches this reading the horse is approaching "overheating." The temperature is taken with a clinical thermometer in the rectum. The thermometer is moistened or oiled, the mercury is shaken down to 96° or below, and the bulb of the thermometer is inserted in the anus and allowed to remain 3 minutes, when it is withdrawn and the temperature noted.

  *i. Urine.*—Urine is passed several times daily in quantities of a quart or more. During the act of urination, the animal straddles, grunts, and assumes a very awkward position that might be mistaken for pain. Lack of water and profuse sweating decreases the amount of urine voided. Some horses hesitate to urinate on a hard floor, but habitually wait until placed on bedding. The urine of the horse is a thick, yellowish fluid and at times cloudy.

  *j. Defecation.*—(1) Defecation occurs 8 to 10 times in 24 hours. Normal droppings should be fairly well formed but soft enough to flatten when dropped; free from offensive odor or mucous slime; vary in color from yellow to green, according to the nature of the food; and not filled with grains that are either wholly or partially unmasticated. The amount of droppings passed in 24 hours varies from 36 to 40 pounds, depending upon the size of the animal and the amount of food given.

(2) Because the droppings are a good indication of the condition of the teeth and the digestive tract, an examination of the fresh droppings should be made frequently. An examination may reveal the following irregularities:

(*a*) Hard droppings may indicate a lack of water, a lack of exercise, too dry and indigestible food, or a combination of all of these. This can be corrected by giving a few bran mashes, by watching the watering, by grazing, and by an hour of exercise daily.

(*b*) Very soft or watery droppings may indicate too hard work, fatigue, too much grazing, excessive use of bran, or a slight irritation of the intestines. Reduce the work; omit bran and grazing. If it persists, withhold all food for 24 hours.

(*c*) Slimy or mucous covered droppings or those having an offensive odor indicate too highly concentrated food or an irritation of the intestines. Reduce the food; give bran mashes and plenty of water.

(*d*) Unmasticated grains indicate that the teeth are sharp or diseased, or that the animal eats too rapidly. Have the teeth examined; feed chop and dry bran with the grain.

**239. Indications of disease.**—Every disease has different indications, and the symptoms vary so greatly that only exhaustive study can acquaint one with these many indications.

*a.* The most common preliminary indications of disease are partial or complete loss of appetite, elevation of temperature (101° F. or more), accelerated breathing, increased pulse rate, listlessness, dejected countenance, profuse sweating, stiffness, nasal discharge, cough, diarrhea, constipation, pawing, rolling, lameness, inflamed mucous membranes, unhealthy coat of hair, itching, or unnatural heat or swelling in any part of the body.

*b.* The best time to inspect animals for evidence of sickness or injury is while they are being fed and at time of grooming. One of the first and most important symptoms of sickness is impairment of appetite. Take the temperature of animals that refuse their feed. Sick animals in a corral are inclined to stand by themselves.

**240. Nursing.**—Good nursing is indispensable in the treatment of sick and injured animals. It implies the attention to every detail which conduces to the comfort or benefit of the patient. The chief points to consider in nursing are:

*a. Ventilation.*—Allow plenty of fresh air but protect from draughts. Avoid extremes of temperature, and in the field provide shelter from wind and rain.

*b. Clothing.*—The amount of clothing must be regulated by the climate. In winter woolen bandages on the legs are useful, and as many as three or four covers may be used. In summer fly sheets are extremely comforting.

*c. Bedding.*—A good clean bed induces an animal to rest and produces a soft springing surface for foot cases. It should be shaken up several times daily and be kept free of urine-soaked straw. Animals which are weak from illness will occasionally lie down for days at a time and require considerable attention to prevent the occurrence of decubitus (bedsores). These are pressure galls on those regions where the weight of the animal is greatest when lying, and occur on the outside of the shoulder and point of the hip and stifle. To prevent these cases the patient should be turned over from time to time and the bedding leveled and kept thick and soft.

*d. Stalls.*—A roomy box stall, well bedded, should be used whenever possible. Keep a bucket of water in the stall and change the water frequently. Patients suffering from severe abdominal pain and those exhibiting certain central nervous disturbances may throw themselves so violently they become seriously injured. For these cases a large stall should be provided which is tight, free from mangers or other projections, and preferably equipped with a "knee board." A knee board is a heavy false partition about 4 feet high with its lower edge set in the stall 2 feet to reduce the right angle of the floor and stall sides. A thick bed of sawdust affords good protection for violent cases.

*e. Shoes.*—The shoes may be removed and the feet leveled if the animal is to remain in a stall for more than a few days.

*f. Exercise.*—Convalescent patients should receive just as much exercise as each individual case permits. It must be borne in mind, however, that absolute rest is frequently the best treatment.

*g. Grooming.*—Animals that are weak and depressed should not be worried with unnecessary grooming. Such animals should be carefully hand rubbed at least once a day, and their eyes, nostrils, and docks should be wiped out with a sponge or soft cloth. The feet should also be cleaned. Animals that are only slightly indisposed should be groomed in the usual way.

*h. Food.*—Some sick animals retain a good appetite. The principal things to observe in their cases are that they are not overfed, that droppings are kept soft, and that they have plenty of water. Sick animals with impaired appetites require special attention. They often relish a change of diet, a bran mash, steamed oats, chopped alfalfa, grass, roots, and apples. Feed small amounts often; do not allow uneaten portions to remain in front of them; keep mangers and feed boxes clean; induce eating by hand feeding; sprinkle a little sweetened water over the hay and grain. The forced feeding of liquid foods by means of the stomach tube or enema may be used as a last resort.

**241. Medication.**—Frequent medication for the average sick animal is unnecessary and may even be harmful. Medicines are administered to animals through the same agencies as to man. They are introduced into the mouth by means of capsules placed on the back of the tongue with a "balling gun"; liquids are injected into the pharynx with a dose syringe or gravitated directly into the stomach through a stomach tube. Any of these methods require a technique which can be learned only by personal instruction and practice, and all of them are more or less dangerous to the patient when attempted by a novice. Until the animal nurse has learned by supervised practice to administer medicine he should not attempt it, as more harm than good may result. In some cases medicines are administered by placing them in the food or water.

**242. Records.**—Ward records include a list of property pertaining to the ward, individual feeding and watering instructions (usually indicated on a card on heel post or stall door), any special instructions as to care and treatment, and such clinical records as may be necessary. (See sec. VI, ch. 6.)

# Chemical Warfare

## SECTION I

## CHEMICAL AGENTS

**348. Use in war.**—The United States is a party to the Geneva Gas Protocol of 1925. The terms of this international agreement forbid the use of poisonous gases in warfare. However, in the event of war with a country not party to the Geneva Gas Protocol or which disregards that agreement, it is necessary for all soldiers, but more particularly medical soldiers, to understand certain fundamentals. These fundamentals pertain partly to the soldier's self-protection and partly to knowing how to care for a patient who has been injured or disabled by one or more chemical agents.

**349. Definition.**—A chemical agent is a substance which, by its ordinary chemical action, produces—

*a.* A toxic effect on the body.

*b.* An irritant effect on the body.

*c.* A screening smoke.

*d.* An incendiary action (fire).

**350. Kinds.**—The following types of chemical agents may be used in warfare. Each group includes several substances of widely different chemical composition, but which act on the human body in the same general manner, and are therefore placed in the same group.

*a.* Tear gas.

*b.* Nose irritant gases.

*c.* Lung irritant gases.

*d.* Blister gases.

*e.* Gases which paralyze.

*f.* Incendiary agents (those which set fire to flammable objects).

**351. Physical state.**—A chemical agent is not always a gas. The term "gas" is used because it is convenient and has become sanctioned by long use. Some chemical agents are gases, some are liquids, and some are solids.

**352. Concentration.**—The amount of chemical agent in air (that is, the concentration) influences the effect produced by an exposure to such agent. The higher the concentration, the greater is the effect upon exposure to any chemical agent for any period of time.

**353. Recognition in field.**—Chemical agents in the field may be recognized by their odor and other immediate effects on the body. See table II, page 439. See section II for description of effects of chemical agents.

**354. Basic rules for identification by odor:**

*a. No. 1.*—Do not inhale deeply. Sniff.

*b. No. 2.*—Sniff only once. Repeated sniffing dulls the sense of smell.

*c. No. 3.*—First sniff, then think. The memory of odors can be trained by practice.

*d. No. 4.*—Every perception of odor must be named. Learn odors by memory of the thing sniffed, rather than by the name of something else. A thing is odorless only when no perception of odor is obtained.

*e. No. 5.*—After each test, breathe out strongly through the nose several times. Do not sniff a new sample until the old perception has vanished.

*f. No. 6.*—Do not smoke while sniffing. Smoking dulls the sense of smell.

**355. Importance of ability to recognize.**—Every soldier should, for his own protection, be able to recognize the odors of chemical agents. The medical soldier, in addition, must recognize them so that he may the better protect a disabled or other wounded man in his care.

**356. Distinguishing between mustard and lewisite.**—The two chief blister gases are mustard and lewisite. Both of them possess the general characteristics of the group as a whole, but differ in the following important details:

| Mustard | Lewisite |
|---|---|
| 1. Entirely insidious; presence hard to detect. | Presence easily detected. |
| 2. Has a feeble and not very definite smell. | Has a strong and definite smell of geraniums. |
| 3. Produces no immediately detectable effect on the body (unless a drop gets into the eye, when a mild irritation may be felt). | The vapor, if breathed for a few minutes produces a severe sensation of burning and irritation of the nose; the liquid produces a sharp tingling in contact with the skin, and immediately severe pain if a drop falls into the eye. |
| 4. Cold or warm water has practically no effect except after long periods of time, such as days or weeks, but boiling water destroys fairly rapidly. | Contact with water at any temperature rapidly destroys. |
| 5. Immediate application of the paste made of bleaching powder and water is effective in preventing burns. Bleach ointment is also effective. | Immediate application of the paste made of bleaching powder and water is effective in preventing skin burns, but bleach ointment is not effective. |
| 6. Extremely persistent_____ | Not so persistent, largely because of the action of water. |
| 7. Effects are local and no general poisoning is caused. | When the skin has been heavily contaminated, symptoms of arsenical poisoning may accompany those caused by the burning. |
| 8. Blisters should not be broken_____ | Blisters should be opened because they contain arsenic. |

## Section II

## INDIVIDUAL PROTECTION

**357. Gas mask.**—The Army gas mask is the best individual protection against chemical agents and is entirely satisfactory for this purpose. *The Army service gas mask will not protect* against carbon monoxide or ammonia gas and is not suitable for use in fighting fires or in industrial accidents where ammonia fumes are present. It is important to learn by practice how to put on and take off the mask quickly.

**358. Solutions.**—In the absence of a gas mask breathe through a handkerchief saturated with a solution of cooking soda (sodium bicarbonate) or soap suds. Use urine to wet the cloth if no soda or soap suds are available. Tear off a piece of shirt for this use if no handkerchief is at hand.

**359. Other articles.**—Obviously the gas mask cannot protect the individual's body against chemical agents. Since gas passes through the ordinary uniform, only a complete gasproof suit can protect the whole body. It is ordinarily impracticable to use such suits. Protection, therefore, depends on destroying chemical agents, protective covers for material, use of gasproof shelters, etc.

**360. Tear gas.**—Tear gas, or lachrymator gas, may be any one or more of chemical compounds which act upon the eyes. They produce acute pain, profuse outpouring of tears, and spasm of the eyelids.

*a. Effect on eyes.*—Tear gases do not usually do permanent damage to the eyes, for the effect is generally of comparatively short duration. But they cause an almost complete inability to see for the time being.

*b. Effect on sympathetic nerves.*—Tear gases sometimes cause vomiting.

*c. First-aid treatment.*—Since the damage is usually only of short duration, first-aid treatment is not so necessary as in other chemical injuries. The eyes should be protected from the gas and when the gas is no longer present, the eyes should be exposed to fresh air. The patient should be warned not to rub his eyes, as this increases the irritation. The eyes should be bathed with warm water, normal saline solution (1 teaspoonful of salt dissolved in a pint of water), or a weak solution of bicarbonate of soda (cooking soda). It is not necessary to evacuate patients whose only injury is from tear gas.

*d. Mental effects.*—Tear gas, like all other warfare chemicals, has another effect on human beings. It produces fear if its actual nature is not understood.

**361. Nose irritants.**—Nose irritants (sternutators) cause irritation of the nose and throat and a watery discharge from the nose. There is also coughing, pain at the base of the nose, severe headache, and nausea. Mental depression is a characteristic effect of this group of chemicals.

*a. Damage.*—Usually little or no permanent damage is caused, though there is at the time very real distress. The effect of nose irritants may be either immediate or delayed for as much as 30 minutes or longer.

*b. First-aid treatment.*—The patient should be put at rest and his clothing loosened. The nose and throat should be bathed with warm, weak solutions of sodium bicarbonate (cooking soda), 10 grains to 1 pint of water. Keep the patient away from heat. If vomiting has resulted from this gas, copious drafts of the weak sodium bicarbonate solution will help to relieve him. It is usually not necessary to evacuate patients whose only injury is from a nose irritant gas. However, the more serious cases of this kind may have to be evacuated.

*c. Mental effects.*—Besides the mental depression caused by nose irritant gases, the effect on morale must be considered. If the patient does not understand that his condition is not serious his fear may be very great. Medical soldiers should understand the condition and therefore be able to reassure patients.

**362. Lung irritants.**—Lung irritant gases are very dangerous chemical agents which may cause death if the patient is exposed to them for a long period. However, slight or brief exposures are not likely to cause such serious results. Lung irritants affect the patient's ability to breathe.

*a. Symptoms produced.*—These vary considerably with the particular gas encountered and with its concentration. They are usually irritation of the nose and throat with coughing, difficulty in breathing, pains in the chest, vomiting, and a blue pallor of the lips and ear lobes. The face takes on a grayish pallor.

*b. Appearance of symptoms.*—The symptoms of damage to the lung do not as a rule come at once. Usually about 2 hours elapse before such symptoms appear. There is sometimes what is called "delayed action"—that is, the effect of the gas seems to be absent at first, only appearing after some time has elapsed. It is important to remember that even though the symptoms seem slight, more serious effects may come on later.

*c. Treatment of casualties.*—Patients suspected of being injured by lung irritant gases should not be allowed to walk. All casualties known or even suspected to have been seriously exposed to one of these gases should be treated as litter cases from the start.

*d. First-aid treatment.*—Remove the patient from the gas atmosphere if possible. The gas mask must not be removed until the patient has been removed to a place where the air is free from gas. Loosen the clothing and keep the patient at absolute rest. Do not allow him to walk. Keep him warm with blankets, hot water bottles, etc. Give such nonalcoholic stimulants as hot coffee or tea. The administration of oxygen is required in extreme cases. Such patients should be evacuated to aid stations as soon as possible.

*e. Danger period.*—The most dangerous period for the patient who has been exposed to lung irritant gas is the first 48 hours. Most deaths occur within this time. Therefore, exercise great care when patients are first seen.

*f. Precaution against artificial respiration.*—Artificial respiration is not to be performed on lung irritant gas casualties. The lungs are seriously damaged and likely in a waterlogged condition. Artificial respiration would probably do more harm than good and might even cause sudden death.

**363. Blister gases.**—This group of gases produces special and peculiar characteristics which are so important individually and which cause so many different problems that their five principal effects are considered separately below:

*a. Persistence and power.*—(1) *Persistence.*—Members of this group are normally liquids of a somewhat oily consistency. Under normal weather conditions in temperate climates they persist up to 3 weeks if the original contamination was heavy and if the area affected is sheltered from direct action of wind and sunlight.

(2) *Power.*—The power of these chemicals is so great that a drop the size of the head of a small pin can produce a blister the size of a quarter. The exposure to a vapor of one part per million parts of air for an hour is capable of producing a casualty. The action on the eyes is particularly marked.

*b. Penetration of materials and of the human body.*—The ability of blister gases to penetrate is one of their characteristics. They "soak in" just as ink soaks into a blotter. This is not the same as "eating in" as when an acid acts on a metal. In other words the "soaking in" takes place without any damage to the material (clothing, etc.). These chemicals also "soak into" the body. About the only substances which withstand this power of penetration are metal, glass, and highly glazed resistant materials such as tiles or porcelain.

*c. Insidious character.*—By this is meant that the presence of such a gas (for example, mustard gas) may not be very obvious, either by smell or by producing any particular sensation such as burning. On the other hand, lewisite, another of the chemicals of this group, has a characteristic smell (like geraniums).

*d. Delayed action.*—One of the important peculiarities of this group, and one which makes them very dangerous, is that while the actual damage takes place rapidly the recognizable signs of such damage do not appear for a considerable time. Thus a patient may be contaminated without knowing it (insidious character) and yet may show no signs of damage for 24 hours. However, the average time of the development of clinical signs or symptoms is about 4 to 8 hours for mustard gas, and even sooner for lewisite.

*e. Universal action.*—Unlike the agents of the other groups, the effects of this group are not confined to any one area of the body. The blister gases have the power to burn and blister *any area* with which they come in contact, either as a liquid or as a vapor. This is equally true of areas *within the body*.

**364. Effects of blister gases.**—The damage caused by this group of chemicals varies somewhat with the area affected. The various parts of the body affected by the blister gases are considered below:

*a. Eyes.*—The eyes are very liable to injury, whether from liquid or vapor. Though there may be some delay in appearance of signs, such delay is less than in other areas of the body. A few hours after exposure, inflammation (conjunctivitis) sets in, with smarting, watering, and finally closure from swelling of the eyelids. Conditions rapidly get worse and there is much pain, especially on exposure to light (photophobia), with discharge coming from between the swollen lids. Actual destruction of the eye and consequent blindness is rare, but there may be some impairment of vision due to scars.

*b. Respiratory system.*—Inflammation of the throat and windpipe (trachea) as a result of breathing air contaminated by the vapor of these liquids is fairly common. It produces dry and burning mouth and throat, with harsh, ringing cough. This cough is very characteristic and very distressing. Partial loss of the voice due to inflammation of the throat (laryngitis) is common. In most severe cases burning of the lungs may produce pneumonia.

*c. Digestive system.*—Inflammation of the stomach, with pain and vomiting may occur. This is the result of swallowing contaminated saliva, or the swallowing of contaminated food or drink. It is not serious as a rule.

*d. Skin.*—Injury to the skin develops in three stages: Reddening (erythema) with a fine rash not unlike "hives", blistering, and finally ulceration. How far the casualty progresses toward the final stage depends on the original concentration of the chemical agent and the length of the patient's exposure to the poison. In case of contamination by liquid, blistering always occurs if steps are not taken at once to counteract the effects. The areas of skin most likely to suffer from exposures to vapor are those which are normally moist, such as the bend of the elbows and knees, the armpit (axilla), the crotch, and the inner side of the thighs. The genitals are particularly liable to attack.

**365. Death rate from blister gases.**—It is encouraging to remember that while the number of casualties due to these agents is high, chiefly due to their persistence and insidiousness, the death rate is *low*. It was only about 2 percent in the World War.

**366. First-aid treatment of patients injured by blister gases.**—It must be remembered that *preventive treatment* is very important. First-aid must take into consideration the "insidiousness" and the "delayed action" of this group.

*a. Eyes.*—The only first-aid for blister gas in the eyes is free washing either with plain, warm water, normal saline solution (1 teaspoonful of salt in a pint of water), or sodium bicarbonate (cooking soda) solution of about 10 grains to a pint of water. This washing should be carried out as soon as possible after exposure. The solution should be run directly to the eyes by means of a rubber tube from an enema can or similar container. A little vaseline on the edges of the eyelids will prevent their sticking together.

*b. Breathing passages.*—Cases in which signs of damage to the breathing passages have developed, including the mouth and throat, have evidently been exposed to relatively high concentrations of vapor for a considerable period of time. Such cases are likely to be serious. Most of the deaths caused by blister gases are due to this. The hard, dry, "brassy" cough is very characteristic of this condition. One of the earlier symptoms is loss of voice from inflammation of the throat (laryngitis). First-aid cannot cope with this condition. The patient must be hospitalized as soon as possible.

*c. Digestive system.*—The pain in the stomach and vomiting can be temporarily relieved by draughts of warm sodium bicarbonate (cooking soda), 10 grains to 1 pint of water. Such cases should be hospitalized as soon as possible.

*d. Skin.*—It is important to remember that there is a delay of some hours between the time that the chemical agent comes into actual contact with the individual and the time at which he develops recognizable signs or symptoms of damage. Yet, as a matter of fact, the damage has already begun almost immediately, and the delay is only in the development or the signs that we recognize.

There are two measures which may be taken in first-aid treatment. The chemical agent may be removed by washing or wiping, and it may be neutralized. If the actual liquid has reached the skin, treatment must be begun in less than 5 minutes to be satisfactory. If only the vapor has reached the individual, the time is longer. The only efficient agent to neutralize blister gases is chloride of lime (bleaching powder). This neutralizing agent is itself irritating and must be removed by subsequent washing. If bleaching powder is not available, immediate soap and water baths may remove some of the poisonous agent. If the liquid chemical agent, such as mustard, has reached the skin, much of it may be removed by wiping with a clean cloth moistened with kerosene (coal oil) or straight gasoline (but not gasoline containing lead). When bleaching powder is used, the most effective method of its application is to make a paste of a small quantity of the bleaching powder with water, the mixture being carefully stirred while being prepared. Usually equal volumes of water and of bleaching powder are used. The contaminated area of skin is covered as well as the immediately surrounding area. The paste is rubbed in well for about 1 minute and then removed by wiping with a dry rag or by flushing off with a large quantity of water, if available. A subsequent bath with soap and water is desirable. Care must be taken not to get the bleaching powder paste into the eyes. If the skin has already begun to show definite redness or blisters, the bleaching powder should not be used, as it is irritating.

**367. Paralyzing gases.**—*a. General.*—Gases which cause paralysis have been used in warfare, but without much success. There are three gases which may be used for their paralyzing effect:

(1) Hydrocyanic (prussic) acid.

(2) Sulfureted hydrogen (hydrogen sulfide).

(3) Carbon monoxide (called fire damp by miners).

Such gases are very dangerous and some of them may result from the explosion of projectiles. Hydrocyanic acid has the faint odor of bitter almonds (peach kernels). Hydrogen sulfide has definitely the smell of rotten eggs. Carbon monoxide has no odor. It is the gas that results from incomplete combustion, such as from charcoal flames or automobile exhausts.

*b. Symptoms.*—These begin with uneasiness, dizziness, and rapid heart beat and breathing. Unconsciousness and convulsions follow rapidly, and death occurs through paralysis of the part of the nervous system which controls the breathing (respiratory center).

*c. First-aid treatment.*—Treatment must be immediate. Prompt removal from the poisonous atmosphere, artificial respiration, and administration of oxygen. A valuable addition to the oxygen is 5 to 7 percent of carbon dioxide. This last stimulates and increases respiration and helps flood the lungs with oxygen and wash out the poison in the blood. The patient must be kept warm.

**368. Incendiary agents.**—*a. General.*—Incendiary agents are chemical agents which cause fires. The more common forms are white phosphorus and thermite.

*b. First-aid treatment.*—The treatment is essentially that of ordinary burns. Particles of white phosphorus may be adhering to the skin and hence have to be picked off. The chief use of white phosphorus in warfare is as a smoke-producing material.

### Section III

### COLLECTIVE PROTECTION·

**369. Small areas.**—It is possible to remove contaminating chemical agents from the areas involved, provided the area is not too extensive. Extensive areas cannot be decontaminated because such a large amount of the neutralizing agent is required. Chloride of lime (bleaching powder), standard article of issue for this purpose, can be used under field conditions to neutralize a small mustardized area.

**370. Large areas.**—When large areas in the field cannot be decontaminated such areas are evacuated if possible. Warning signs should be posted on all avenues of approach. Remember that high vapor concentrations will be found in the areas immediately downwind from mustardized areas. They should be treated the same way as the mustardized areas themselves.

**371. Food.**—*a. Protection.*—All food supplies at the front should be kept in airtight containers until required for use. Ration carts and kitchens should be covered by paulins for protection against chemical spray.

*b. Contaminated foods.*—Food having a peculiar odor or taste, and suspected or known to have been exposed to a chemical agent should be discarded.

*c. Susceptibility to contamination.*—Some foodstuffs absorb chemical vapors more quickly than others. Fatty and oily substances, such as meat and butter, and meal and flour, are quickly contaminated by vapors. Green vegetables are less readily affected by vapors.

**372. Water.**—Water contaminated by mustard gas should be avoided. If necessary, however, such water may be rendered safe for use by settling or chlorination. When such water stands, the liquid mustard sinks to the bottom. Allow the water to settle for not less than 4 hours. Siphon off the top portion, leaving a layer 10 or 12 inches in a container of the dimensions of a barrel. This lower layer should be thrown away. Chloride of lime (bleaching powder) in the proportion of one-fifth of a pound to the gallon of water, should then be added and the water should be boiled for at least 1 hour. Contaminated water in shell holes should be avoided. Water contaminated by lewisite, irritant smokes, or white phosphorus cannot be purified by this method.

**373. Clothing.**—*a. Removal.*—Only rarely does the actual liquid chemical agent pass through the clothing. That only takes place when the clothing is soaked with it. On the other hand the vapor readily passes through clothing. Therefore, remove all of the patient's clothing and treat his whole body by washing with soap and water. Remember that the clothing after removal from the patient's body is still contaminated. Men have been seriously burned by picking up contaminated clothing.

*b. Decontamination.*—Contaminated clothing should be collected into receptacles, preferably metal ones with close-fitting lids (such as G. I. cans). These cans should be turned over to the details whose duty it is to do this work. Men of the Chemical Warfare Service when available are assigned these duties.

**374. Precautions against enemy's chemical agents.**—*a. In the field.*—All chemical agents are heavier than air and settle in shell holes, depressions in the earth, dugouts, trenches, etc. Therefore, seek high ground and open spaces which are free from gases insofar as the military situation permits.

*b. Precautions in presence of gas cloud.*—Move out of the gas cloud as quickly as possible. Proceed cross-wind, if possible. If a gas cloud envelops a building, close all doors and windows tightly, put out all fires, plug all chimneys, and go to the upper floors of the building.

*c. Procedure during gas attack.*—As soon as it has been established that a gas attack is in progress, the alarm should be given by all means available. Masks are adjusted, doors of gasproof shelters are lowered, fires are put out in such shelters, matériel is protected, and, in general, all routine measures of individual and collective protection are carried out. Casualties are removed from the gassed area as soon as possible and first-aid treatment given.

**375. Evacuation of gas casualties.**—In the evacuation of a patient who has been injured by chemical agents, the following measures should be employed:

*a. At aid stations.*—Examine gas mask and if gas is still present in the surrounding air, leave it on the patient. Remove the equipment and loosen the clothing. Remove the clothing if it is contaminated with blister gas (mustard or lewisite) and wrap the patient in a clean blanket. If affected by mustard gas, wash the patient's eyes with 2 percent sodium bicarbonate (cooking soda) solution. Apply dressings to wounds caused by other war weapons. See that the patient avoids unnecessary movement if suffering from a lung irritant. Keep him quiet. Produce vomiting by giving the patient tepid salt water, if safe to remove the mask. Inspect the emergency medical tag and make the proper notation thereon. Expedite evacuation to the collecting station.

*b. At collecting stations.*—Change the patient's clothing and thoroughly bathe all individuals who have been affected by blister gases. Completely demustardize all clothing and matériel where time and facilities permit. Adjust dressings. Give special treatment as indicated, including administration of oxygen if available in cases of lung damage. Prepare the patient for evacuation.

*c. At special degassing stations.*—Administer neutralizing chemicals and degas clothing by the group method.

*d. At clearing stations.*—Sort and classify the patients, separating them according to the nature of the chemical agent that injured them. Bathe. Retain critical cases for observation. Demustardize if this has not been previously and thoroughly done. Administer oxygen if available when indicated. When patient is fit for transportation, evacuate to the rear.

# MEDICAL CARE OF CHEMICAL CASUALTIES

**376. Cases requiring hospital care.**—Any patient suffering from disability due to the action of a chemical agent should be treated in hospital whenever and as soon as possible. This is particularly true if the patient is also suffering from a wound.

**377. General nursing care.**—Patients suffering from injury from chemical agents are usually both physically and mentally depressed. They must be handled with both gentleness and firmness. All ordinary nursing cares must be intensified. All precautions must be taken to prevent infection and pressure sores (bed sores, etc.). The eyes must receive earliest possible attention. Pure air and rest are essentials. All strain on the heart and lungs must be avoided or relieved. In general, the treatment must be carried out in accordance with the patient's condition. It is impossible to give specific directions covering all cases. Common sense is needed.

**378. Treatment of shock.**—As all patients of this kind are suffering from some degree of shock, the first essentials are warmth, complete rest, and fresh air. They should be reassured as soon as possible that their troubles, however trying, are temporary; above all, they must be encouraged to be hopeful.

**379. Clothing.**—Both the clothing worn by the patient and the bed clothing should be light, loose, and warm. Pillows should be arranged according to the degree of shock and the comfort of the patient.

**380. Position of patient.**—See paragraph 379. In order to allow the escape of fluid from the mouth, the patient's head and shoulders should be supported and turned to one side. There should be hot-water bottles, back rests, rubber sheeting, etc., according to the needs of the individual.

**381. Observation.**—Each case requires constant observation because of the necessity of reporting immediately any alarming or new symptoms.

**382. Diet.**—The diet should be liquid, warm, and nourishing. If the patient vomits, there should be copious draughts of warm water and sodium bicarbonate (cooking soda) (a level teaspoonful to 1 pint of water). Thirst is not an outstanding feature. Patients must therefore be encouraged to take sufficient fluid.

**383. Nursing of cases.**—*a. Tear gas.*—These cases are unlikely to be admitted to hospital, and even if admitted the effects of the tear gas are so transient that usually no nursing problem arises. The patient can usually bathe his own eyes with plain warm water. Where time permits, a drop of olive oil, mineral oil, or castor oil may be dropped into the eyes.

*b. Nose irritant.*—(1) Such cases are usually so slightly severe that they do not reach the hospital. However, if the exposure to the gas has been abnormally long or severe, there may be such complications as mental depression, occasionally leading to suicidal tendencies.

(2) The initial coughing and sneezing may be followed by dizziness, occasionally merging into unconsciousness. Patients are often mentally dulled, indifferent, and disinclined to exert themselves.

(3) A possible early complication is a temporary paralysis of the limbs. This soon passes off. The weight of the bed clothes should be supported by bed cradles.

(4) Later, sometimes after about 4 days, there may be numbness or shooting pains in the arms and legs. Such symptoms may cause alarm because one may think that they arise from injuries other than poisoning by nose irritants.

(5) In addition to ordinary nursing care, some patients are relieved by nasal douching with a weak solution of sodium bicarbonate (cooking soda), a level teaspoonful to a pint of water. The same solution may be used as a gargle or may be administered internally.

(6) Symptoms of arsenic poisoning may be suspected. They include restlessness, irritation of the skin or mucous membrane, pain in the throat and abdomen, nausea, etc.

*c. Lung irritant.*—(1) All such cases must be admitted as litter cases, and require complete rest, with sparing of all exertion, extreme gentleness in handling, and constant attention. The condition of the patient on admission depends on the degree of lung damage already developed. This damage, as it develops, causes difficulty in breathing and heart strain.

(2) The clinical picture depends upon the degree of the edema of the lungs that has been produced. In an advanced case the face and neck are flushed and blue (cyanosed) and the respiration appears forced and difficult. Patients with such symptoms are sometimes called the

"blue type." Unless this condition is checked, heart failure results. This is indicated by an increased pallor. This stage is sometimes described as the "grey type."

(3) The administration of *oxygen* is always indicated.

(4) *Venesection* (blood letting) followed by intravenous administration of saline solution may be indicated.

(5) *Sedatives* may be ordered, but morphine is contra-indicated since it may tend to depress the respiratory center (the area of the brain that controls breathing).

(6) *Heart stimulants*, such as hypodermic injections of camphor or pituitrin, may be ordered.

(7) Raising the foot of the bed, a few minutes at a time, sometimes relieves the "waterlogging" of the lungs by assisting the patient to get rid of the exudate.

*d. Blister gas.*—(1) *First-aid measures.*—See paragraph 366.

(2) *Objects.*—The nursing of such cases has three main objects:

(a) The prevention of secondary infection.

(b) The healing of actual injury.

(c) Suggestion and tactful firmness to combat the patient's tendency to mental depression.

(3) *Delayed action.*—Remember that the effects of blister gases are delayed for periods varying from 2 to 48 hours.

(4) *Eyes.*—(a) The patient must be reassured that his sight will not be lost. Severe inflammation results from contamination, either by the vapor or the liquid chemical agent, the latter being more serious. The conjunctivae may be so swollen as to protrude between the swollen and edematous eyelids. The discharge soon becomes pussy.

(b) Treatment should be immediate. It consists of frequent and copious irrigation with a warm solution of sodium bicarbonate (cooking soda), a level teaspoonful to a pint of water. This is followed by the instillation of a few drops of olive oil, mineral oil, or castor oil. The eyes should *not* be bandaged, but an eyeshade may help. Drops of a 2 percent solution of argyrol or protargol may be ordered. Frequent bathing or hot applications *outside* the lids may help to relieve the pain.

(5) *Nose and throat.*—(a) Sneezing, coughing, and hoarseness may be eased by gargling and douching with any bland solution, spraying with any suitable antiseptic solution, or by inhaling steam from a pint of boiling water containing a teaspoonful of a mixture of menthol (10 grains) in compound tincture of benzoin (1 ounce). Patients should breathe through a perforated mask (pad of gauze

moistened with an antiseptic and pain-deadening mixture prescribed by a medical officer).

(*b*) Secondary bronchitis or broncho-pneumonia may occur in cases showing damage to the respiratory tract. Therefore, when practicable, treat such cases in a separate ward.

TABLE II.—*Identification of chemical agents*

| Chemical agent | Symbol | Odor | Other immediate effect |
|---|---|---|---|
| Chlorine | CL | Disagreeable; pungent. | Choking; coughing; discomfort in chest; smarting of eyes. |
| Mustard gas | HS | Garlic; horseradish | None. |
| Ethyldichlorarsine | ED | Biting; irritating | Nasal irritation. |
| Phosgene | CG | Silage; fresh cut hay | Coughing; tightness in chest; eye irritation. |
| Chlorpicrin | PS | Sweetish; flypaper | Flow of tears; nose and throat irritation; vomiting. |
| Adamsite | DM | No pronounced odor | Headache; vomiting. |
| Diphenylchlorarsine | DA | No pronounced odor | Sneezing; vomiting; headache. |
| Chloracetophenone | CN | Locust or apple blossoms; ripe fruit. | Flow of tears; irritation of skin in hot weather. |
| CN solution | CNS | Sweetish; flypaper | Flow of tears; irritation of skin. |
| Brombenzylcyanide | CA | Sour fruit | Flow of tears; nasal irritation. |
| White phosphorus | WP | Matches | Glow from burning particles; incendiary effect. |
| HC mixture | HC | Acrid | Slight suffocating feeling. |
| Sulfur trioxide in chlorsulfonic acid. | FS | Acrid (strong) | Prickly sensation on skin; eye irritation. |
| Titanium tetrachloride. | FM | Acrid (mild) | Very slight irritation of eyes. |

(6) *Skin.*—(*a*) Skin should be cleansed *gently* with soap and warm water, and the hair on the affected areas clipped. Erythema (redness) is frequently followed by blisters which may result in ulceration. Every effort must be made to prevent secondary infection of these raw surfaces.

(*b*) The itching of the early inflammation may be relieved by the application of calamine or other alkaline lotions, dusting powders, or ointments, as prescribed by a medical officer. Blisters must be opened under antiseptic precautions, and the blister fluid carefully removed. Dressings of old sterile linen are better than those of gauze, since the latter tends to stick. The use of oiled silk or other material that retains discharges must be avoided. The resulting scars are weak and must be protected even after healing.

(7) *Lewisite injuries.*—Lewisite has greater rapidity of action than mustard. Penetration of the skin is much quicker, and irritation is intense. The serum from the blisters must be evacuated aseptically, the epithelium (top layer of the skin) removed, and the raw surfaces irrigated. This is done to lessen the absorption of arsenic compounds (lewisite contains arsenic). The patient's eyes must be irrigated and the same general measures taken as described above.